P9-DBI-113

Published in the USA 1997 by JG Press
Distributed by World Publications, Inc.

The JG Press Imprint is a trademark of
JG Press, Inc.
455 Somerset Avenue
North Dighton, MA 02764

First published in Great Britain in 1991 by
Collins & Brown Limited
London House
Great Eastern Wharf
Parkgate Road
London SW11 4NQ

Copyright © Collins & Brown Limited 1991
Text copyright © John Buckland 1991

All rights reserved. No part of this publication may be reproduced, stored in a
retrieval system, or transmitted in any form or by any means, electronic,
mechanical, photocopying, recording or otherwise, without the prior written
permission of the copyright owner.

Art Editor   Frances de Rees
Editor   Richard Dawes
Art Director   Dave Allen
Design Assistant   Victoria Furbisher
Editorial Director Pippa Rubinstein

9 8 7 6 5 4 3 2 1

ISBN 1 57215 242 7

Printed in Slovenia

CONTENTS

FOREWORD

We at *The Royal Coachman*, a journal of fly fishing around the world, get a little forgetful. After many years of fly fishing it's easy to lose sight of how much underlying architecture there is in knowing and loving this sport. More books have been written about fishing than about Shakespeare.

The Game Fishing Bible starts where much that has been written about trout and salmon fishing of late does not, at the very beginning. It shakes you by the hand, says it's glad to hear you want to know about the basics, pulls you off to the side of the party, sits you down and tells you straight as your Uncle Joe.

This is not a 'just do it' sport. It is also not difficult, requiring no special athletic talent at all. At day's end you've had a lovely walk in the woods along a babbling brook. But you've had an eight foot long *pole* in your hand. And what did you do with it?

John Buckland doesn't miss much on the subject. He tells you what it means if you're walking upstream or downstream, where you should look and where you should stop. What you should wear and what should be in your pockets. He may even send you back to the car to get a 6 ft rod, if that's what fits the situation.

A good fly fisher isn't grim about success, but as Mr Buckland is saying here, he goes about his pleasant task with enough knowledge to understand a fish in hand is only a good scene in a fine movie. Of course he likes just knowing lots about the colorful quarry, wonderfully graceful creatures. Real fishers also love their equipment, they love choosing and living years of little adventures with it, and it sits in the closet all winter biding a friendship. When they use it, they look around at the slice of the world they are visiting and enjoy knowing just which of their rods, which of their lines, which of their leaders, which of their flies (of dozens and dozens of charmers) to use that particular hour. They love the art of gently flickering out line 50 ft and more to just where they want to try luck. That's all what this book is about.

There you are, a fisher yourself now, out in the water up to your knees (not cold, he told you about insulated waders). Having read this primer you can read the river before you, it must be said, like a book. In fact like a mystery story. You know enough to see clues. Perhaps the little ring on the surface a feeding fish leaves behind. Perhaps a set of boulders channeling the current and thus the food it carries so a good fish really is likely to be holding just *there*. And *there* too. And you know which of the two to try first, so you don't spook the other. You know where to stand to try and where to aim your fly (not at the fish). You sure can do all this. But you cannot just do it.

We are glad to see *The Game Fishing Bible* and commend it to beginners. We confess to having learned or relearned more than a few points ourselves.

One subject beyond this book we would add, as your Uncle Al at the same family party. Use fly fishing to see the world. And not just, as it serves so well, a microcosm of nature in better balance than certain hominids are capable of. Use it to travel the broad world. We do, and filling six issues a year with fishing adventure stories has shown us that rivers do indeed run through the best of every country on every continent.

The Royal Coachman
LOS OLIVOS, CALIFORNIA

INTRODUCTION

There is a golden thread in fishing when all comes right – the river or lake is the wild and unspoiled landscape of your dreams, there is that kindness of sun and cloud that is a blessing on the human race, and the fish are there, cautious but brave, susceptible to skill. The challenge, the mystery, the satisfaction are all present. Fishing is the ultimate leisure pursuit: solitary or companionable; competitive or lazy. An obsession it may be, but it provides both mental and physical therapy, and the greater the skill applied and the more interesting the method used, the greater the stimulus and enjoyment.

It is a great mistake to elevate fishing to the status of an art, which gives it an undeserved mystique, for it is an easily acquired skill which even in its early stages of proficiency produces results. Although fishing is, world-wide, one of the most popular of outdoor sports, the idea that the fisher must be an 'expert' frightens him into leapfrogging some of the simple homework which would make him even more successful. He needs to know the lifestyle of the fish – how they live, feed, breed and protect themselves – the waters they live in; the food forms; and what stimulates them to take. If he knows nothing of his quarry's senses, which both protect it and lead to its downfall, his fishing will be haphazard and his catches less.

It is not necessary for the fisher to know by heart the Latin names of the first forty insects likely to be in a trout's diet in May; practical field observation – his own and that of others – will tell him what food forms are in abundance. If he can recognize a swimming nymph from a crawling nymph, he can choose a more accurate imitation and fish it in a way that is as close to nature as possible. He is already an entomologist, storing the information for future use; and it was as simple as inspecting the surface of the water and the bankside vegetation. If he chose to cut open a fish rather than release it, an examination of its stomach contents would confirm (or confound) his observation.

He had found his fish just *there*, where a cold spring welled up through the river bed: he is now in addition both ecologist and ichthyologist, for he knows that in rivers certain fish thrive best at certain temperatures. In the heat of early summer it is his knowledge of the river bed and fish behavior that has given him his catch. There is no art to this; nor to casting. The latter is an ability, a proficiency which, when well executed, admittedly looks 'artistic.' But, though it is best learned through person-to-person coaching, this skill can be gained from videos or books. Without reasonable proficiency, however, both enjoyment and success are much reduced.

Some techniques must be learned; for example, to be able to choose when to fish on the surface, in the surface or below the surface needs a combination of dexterity, observation and experience. Even so, as soon as he can cast adequately, the game fisher is in with some chance. The angler who learns to curb his impatience catches more and better fish, for he knows the old adage 'It only takes one cast to catch a trout.' He also knows that a trout (or other game fish) is too valuable to be caught only once, and is fully aware of the enormous pressures placed on rivers and lakes both by large-scale pollution and thoughtless individuals. His concern for the environment and his love of fishing will make him do his best to ensure the survival of both for later generations.

Dawn and dusk are magical periods, and the bigger,
warier fish are often taken at these times.

Chapter 1

THE FISH

AND

THE HABITAT

An understanding of the biology of game fish is incomplete without a basic knowledge of what makes a suitable habitat for them. While the trouts, salmons and other members of the salmon family – the salmonids – are hardy in the face of climatic pressure, they require water of a certain quality if they are to survive. Broadly speaking, the water which is most suitable for us to drink is generally near to ideal as a habitat for game fish. However, in some areas the water that suits us lacks enough oxygen to be breathed by the fish species in which we are interested. There must be enough free oxygen in addition to that combined with hydrogen, otherwise the eggs do not hatch, the young fish do not thrive, and the mature fish do not achieve viable spawning.

The stillest of waters can harbor trout, often of good size. The variety of food items differs from water to water, but chironomids (midges) thrive in ponds such as this one.

THE HOME OF GAME FISH

If the habitat does not contain at least 3.5 parts of oxygen per million, game fish will not survive, however much water passes through their gills. Their oxygen requirements are least at low water temperatures, and vastly higher near their maximum temperature tolerance, so the free oxygen in the water must also remain within an optimal range for each species. If it is regularly at the top end of the game fishes' tolerance, other fish attempt to fill the available ecological niche, competing with them for food and sanctuary. If it is regularly at the bottom end of their acceptance, food forms will probably be rare and the habitat inhospitable to all fish.

The food pyramid

Fish share the water with myriad other organisms, most of which are more lowly forms and part of the food pyramid (also described as a chain). Game fish are near the top of the pyramid, preying on many forms below them, but may also be subject to predation by even more predatory fish such as pike, or by aquatic animals or birds – bears, otters and cormorants, for

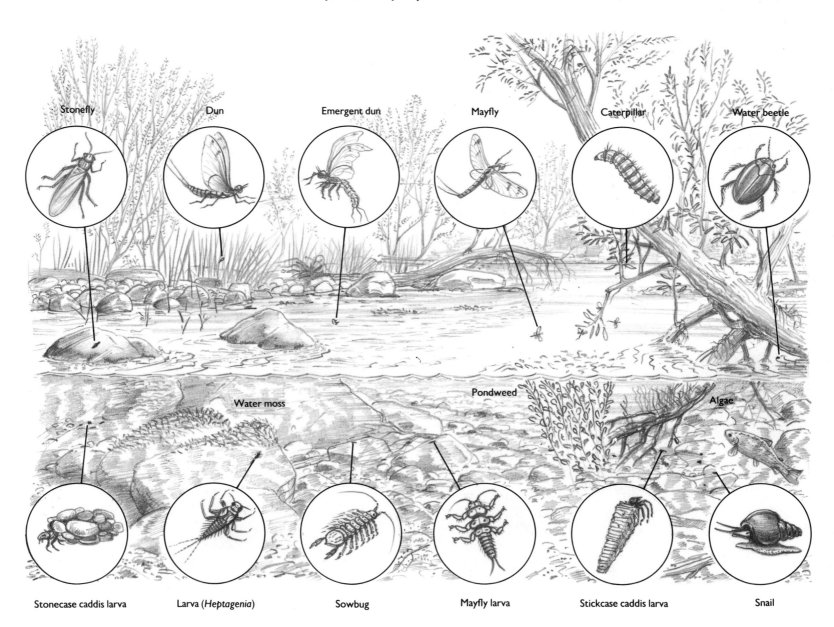

Stonefly   Dun   Emergent dun   Mayfly   Caterpillar   Water beetle

Water moss   Pondweed   Algae

Stonecase caddis larva   Larva (*Heptagenia*)   Sowbug   Mayfly larva   Stickcase caddis larva   Snail

example – while further up the chain there may be man, the ultimate predator and despoiler.

Free oxygen is introduced to water via its surface or by aquatic plants. One of the greatest delights of game-fishing rivers, along with the scenery, the hills, and the steep valleys, is the sound of running water. Water as it bubbles and falls gathers oxygen, the fast flows at the heads of pools being more oxygen-rich than the slow, calm flats at the tails. In lakes, rain and wind provide the surface with oxygen which then supplies the lower layers.

Pure distilled water does not sustain life; the water needs minerals and trace elements, plus the extra oxygen, to sustain living creatures, of which the algae are some of the lowest forms. Algae are edible, so another link in the food chain crops the algae, to be cropped in turn by creatures higher up the chain. Game fish are carnivores, but are sometimes meat to other species, even to their own kind.

Nature adds to the joys of fishing by providing spectacles such as the perfect form of this lily.

A pattern of predation

Biologists suggest that there is a factor of ten at each stage in the food chain – ten times more plant material than there are grazing creatures; ten times more grazing creatures than the types of animal life feeding on them; and so on. The higher predators may reach down the chain to a lower layer – for example, rainbow trout specializing in zooplankton – and so for a water to support a large population of fast-maturing, large fish, it must be rich, which means alkaline, with a make-up which includes calcium. Aquatic plants respond vigorously to alkaline waters, and even if the water flow becomes less speedy and apparently less well oxygenated, the plants in their cycle of transpiration help to oxygenate it sufficiently. The plants are food in themselves and host to plant foods; they are the breeding grounds, home and forage areas to the creatures in the food chain. They temper fast flows and trap silt, enlarging the scope of the habitat and increasing the potential for a variety of insects and other organisms. To flourish they need sunlight, which can only reach them if the water is clear. Permanently turbid waters harbor fewer plants than clear waters and the release of oxygen is inhibited in darkness, particularly under snow or ice onto which snow has fallen.

Regardless of whether they are rivers or lakes, waters differ widely in their make-up, and some are unable to support an extended food chain. Although clean and well oxygenated, they may be too cold for much of the year, yet support a large population at specific times. The rivers of Alaska in late summer may look ideal for a large resident population, but they are usually frozen up in winter and when the ice breaks up it scours and gouges the river bed dislodging higher plant life and its animal content. Such rivers may prove ideal spawning habitats, and when the young fish have outgrown the limited amount of small food items available, they head downstream to richer waters and richer feeding. Some make for freshwater lakes, others for the sea, but in neither case will they venture up the river again until they are mature and feel the urge to spawn. Those which go down to the sea to feed are described as anadromous, or migratory fish. This author uses the term 'resident' for those fish which stay in fresh water, whether they are trout, grayling, char or landlocked salmon (and the differentiation is made if they have sea-going strains).

Rivers and lakes which support wider ranges of organisms have resident fish, and the different species have preferences as to habitat and food. The food should be nutritious and as easily available as possible and the habitat should combine 'comfort' (oxygen availability), 'safety' (sanctuary from predators higher in the food chain) and access to spawning grounds.

FEEDING

Game fish do not eat vegetable matter, but seek live prey, and daphnia and similar organisms are the right size for the young fish as they start to find food for themselves. As they grow they seek larger organisms, not necessarily always neglecting the smallest, and yet not trying to swallow anything much larger than can pass whole through the throat into the stomach. A major part of their diet is aquatic, formed of insects and creatures of the water. Some of these may appear at or on the surface, but most will be subsurface.

There will also be a terrestrial food supply consisting of creatures not necessarily dependent on an aquatic environment but which have fallen on or into the water, and are recognized by the fish as food. There may be an element of what seems like personal preference in the fishes' selection of food – for example, they may choose to take tiny *Caenis* flies rather than larger mayflies when both are present. Usually they seek maximum food value with the minimum expenditure of energy. A stream sampled by a biologist may produce higher densities of caddis than of mayflies, yet in fish autopsies the stomach contents may show the opposite bias. The conclusion we may come to is that one food form is easier than the other for those fish to gather.

You do not have to be much of an entomologist: just check cobwebs on bushes and branches to see which insects have been hatching.

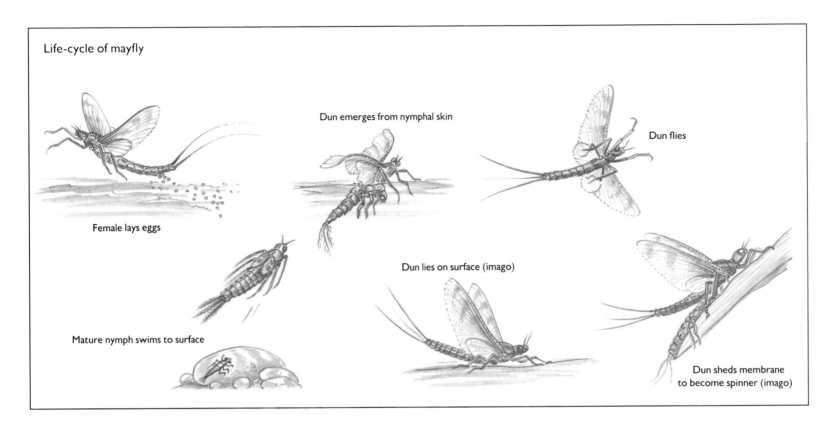

Life-cycle of mayfly

Dun emerges from nymphal skin

Dun flies

Female lays eggs

Dun lies on surface (imago)

Mature nymph swims to surface

Dun sheds membrane
to become spinner (imago)

There is no need to be an expert entomologist to fish successfully. But it is worth while to use the Latin names of the insects since they prevent confusion and misidentification. For example, the name 'sulphur dun' means different insects in different regions, whereas 'Dorothea' means just that insect.

Insects of the freshwater forms are not found in the estuaries or bays: the food forms are larger – crustacea and small fish – and there is nowadays a great deal of sport with Pacific salmon. Fly-fishers and bait-casters present to the salmon, at their various depths, suitable imitations or 'illusions'. The colors of these bait-fish from the sea tend toward silvery, with whitish bellies and bluish or greenish backs, and bright patterns which simulate their iridescence are widely used.

When the migratory fish reach fresh water, their need to feed vanishes but we try to stir in them perhaps a feeding memory, a wish to kill a runt or cripple, or curiosity strong enough to make them seize the fly or bait. As they progress further into fresh water, it becomes more difficult to know what will stimulate them to take: much depends on temperature and water levels, water clarity, and how large, how deep and how fast the fly or bait is fished. However, for all the fish caught on 'illusions,' only a few will take natural baits such as earthworms, and periods of intense insect activity might trigger them to take a direct insect imitation.

On the spawning beds, for reasons of territory or mere aggression, the fish may take, and at this time the fly or bait must be presented at a very precise depth. (Note that not all fishing regulations permit fishing for the spawning fish on their spawning beds.)

Aquatic insects

The mayflies are the most graceful of the aquatic insects and can produce regular rises, the fish showing as much selectivity when feeding on natural insects as when offered imitations. The life-cycle is *egg* to *small nymph*, to *nymph* which has fully grown to *dun* (subimago) to *spinner* (imago).

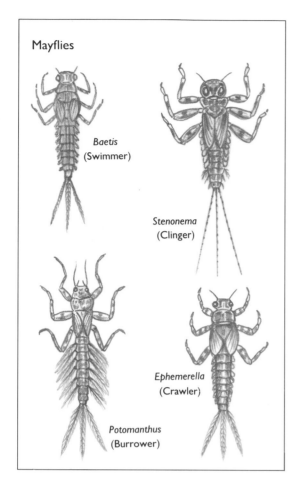

Mayflies

Baetis
(Swimmer)

Stenonema
(Clinger)

Ephemerella
(Crawler)

Potomanthus
(Burrower)

Mayflies can be grouped according to the behavior of the nymph. Some of them crawl, some cling to rocks or stones, some burrow in silt, and some are swimmers. The families of mayflies within each group may therefore be classified as follows:

Crawlers: *Ephemerella*
Leptophlebia
Paraleptophlebia
Caenis, Brachycercus, Tricorythodes

Clingers: *Stenonema*
Epeorus
Heptagenia
Rhithrogenia

In fast, broken streams like this, trout shelter in the deep pools behind the boulders. From here they have to move rapidly to catch food items as they are swept past at speed. The roll cast will prevent the fly tangling with the bankside vegetation.

Burrowers: *Ephemera*
Hexagenia
Potomanthus

Swimmers: *Baetis*
Pseudocloëon
Callibaetis
Centroptilum
Isonychia
Siphlonurus

Stoneflies are important food items, particularly in streams in the western states. The usual family names are: *Petronarcys*, *Acroneuria*, *Perla*, and *Isoperla*, and the appearance of all these is similar to that of those in the generalized diagram on the right.

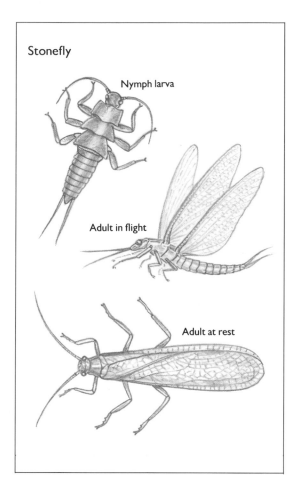

Stonefly

Nymph larva

Adult in flight

Adult at rest

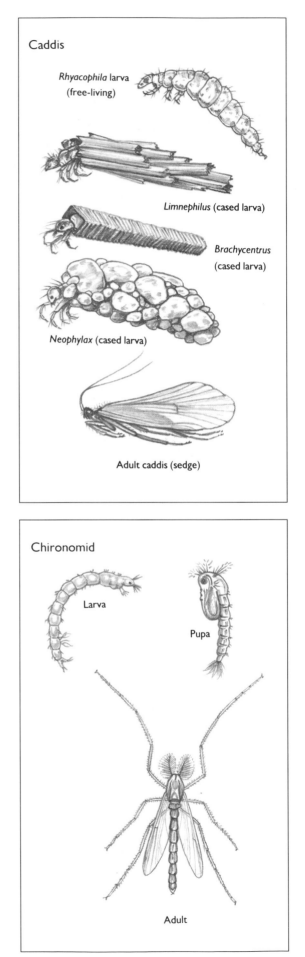

Caddis

Rhyacophila larva
(free-living)

Limnephilus (cased larva)

Brachycentrus
(cased larva)

Neophylax (cased larva)

Adult caddis (sedge)

Caddis or sedge are more important in some waters than both mayflies and stoneflies. Common examples are *Limnephilus* species, *Brachycentrus* and *Rhyacophila*. The illustrations on the left show the different styles of case the larvae build.

Damselflies and dragonflies are at times nearly irresistible to fish.

The chironomids or midges occur in a vast number of sizes and colors. These are inhabitants of the slower waters, particularly reservoirs and the larvae can tolerate very low oxygen levels. If a watercourse shows a notable

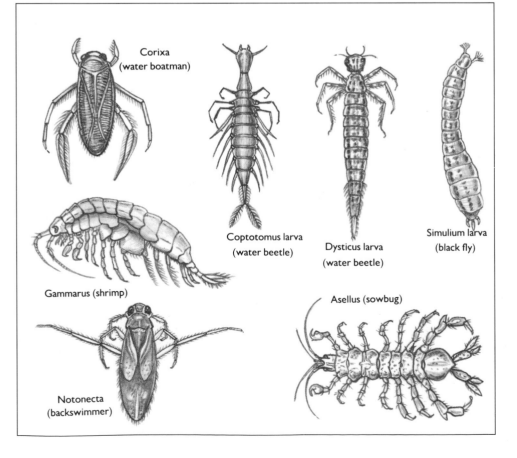

Chironomid

Larva

Pupa

Adult

Corixa
(water boatman)

Coptotomus larva
(water beetle)

Dysticus larva
(water beetle)

Simulium larva
(black fly)

Gammarus (shrimp)

Asellus (sowbug)

Notonecta
(backswimmer)

increase in numbers of chironomids and a decrease in other fly life, it is often an indication that water quality is deteriorating.

Other aquatics, incidental rather than the main subsistence, are shown below left and below.

Leeches, salamanders, crayfish and shiners and minnows are taken if available and the predator/prey size relationship is appropriate. Sculpins are particularly favored on some streams. Nor are young game fish safe from their elders.

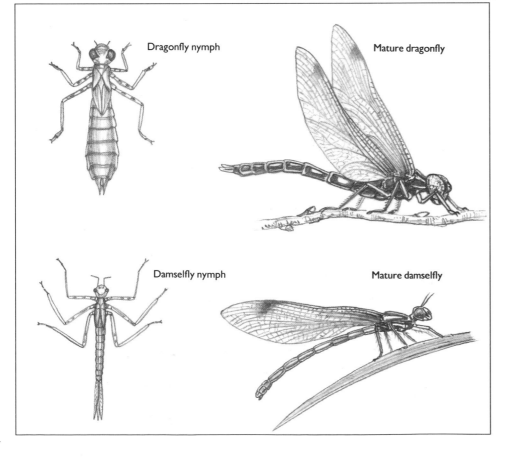

OPPOSITE   *A caddis larva emerging from its case.*

ABOVE LEFT   *Damselfly.*

ABOVE RIGHT   *Dragonfly.*

Dragonfly nymph

Mature dragonfly

Damselfly nymph

Mature damselfly

RIGHT *A cutthroat, the native wild trout of the western USA, is returned to a small West Coast stream.*

Terrestrials

The term 'terrestrials' describes a wide variety of land-based insects which might come the fish's way. It is always advisable to carry ant imitations, for while rises to them may come only a few times in a lifetime, they will be outstanding. Lee Wulff checks out lies near bridges by flicking the odd coin into the water – its free-fall flicker often entices a fish out to look or to strike. Charles Brooks always recommended a mouse imitation for the times when the big fish were on the serious hunt.

Success with terrestrials depends to a large extent on what lies at the water's edge. Beside rich waters, trees, grasses and rushes flourish, harboring insects and other life-forms, some of which may fall or be blown onto the water. Such vegetation may also shelter aquatic insects from the weather, and offer them a resting place as they shuck their last skin and turn into imagos. Aquatic vegetation which emerges above the surface is a landing spot for some fliers or a pathway for creepers or crawlers to come up to the air. A further benefit of aquatic and bankside vegetation is that it provides extra oxygen for the water and can affect its temperature.

The range of food forms is so wide that it is surprising that game fish are not easier to catch. Sometimes they are, and provided the presentation (see pages 154-5) is good, the nature of the imitation is often of little importance. And yet at other times the fish are very selective.

Waters can be divided into the following very rough categories: 1: hungry and headstrong – any well-presented imitation of a likely food has a fair chance of being taken; 2: not too greedy and with a sense of caution – this water is rich enough to have regular but not very intense insect hatches, so the fish cannot afford to pass everything by; 3: extremely selective – such waters are usually rich and slow. Insect hatches are profuse and regular and the water is so clear and the fish has so long to examine the fly that success is not as assured as the feeding activity might suggest. This third category is particularly fascinating and challenging, and is responsible for the affection felt by so many anglers for the mayfly in its many families and species, and stages of development. Real happiness for so many of us is fishing a dry mayfly imitation.

We have yet to meet our quarry. There are characteristics common to all fish and some specific to the game species. Let us look first at these shared characteristics and then in more detail at the different species.

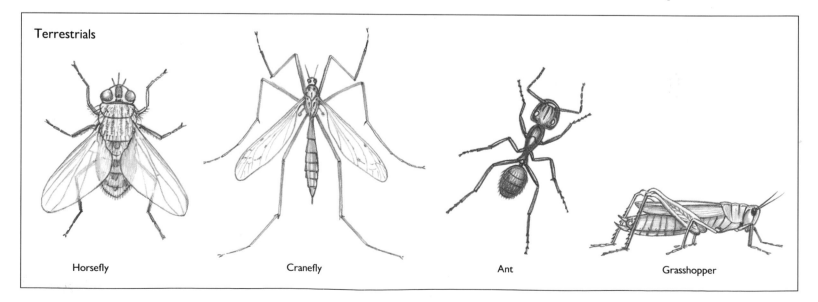

Terrestrials

Horsefly   Cranefly   Ant   Grasshopper

FISH SENSES

Normally we list the senses of fish as sight, taste, hearing, touch and smell. We may choose to add to these a number of less conventional but nevertheless extremely important senses. These are hunger, fear, love, home, balance, temperature, pain, play and humor, though the last two may seem somewhat anthropomorphic. Some senses overlap, others embrace what we might call 'well-being': a fish certainly behaves as if it has a sense of well-being when it is in good-quality water, supplied with plenty of food and under no stress from fear or the demands of spawning.

In all the species in the salmon family the prime sense is sight, for acuity of vision finds the fish its food and distinguishes the edible from the inedible: vegetable and not animal matter caught by the stream, or a clumsy imitation fished at an unnatural pace. Unless the food item was exactly in the water flow its scent would not have been carried to the fish, so smell has little place in food finding (although it enables migratory fish to locate their natal streams). Taste likewise is not of the greatest importance as the dentition of the salmonids is designed to take a firm grasp of the food item, which then is swallowed without chewing or biting. The feel of the food will be detected, and innovative fly and bait manufacturers spend much research-and-development time on trying to produce natural textures.

Hearing

Hearing in fish is complex: it may be a defensive mechanism, or detect an advantage – struggling food, for example. However, it is not the most highly developed of the major senses. A fish's hearing apparatus has some similarities to the human ear, but there is no outer ear which collects the sound waves, nor an ear drum or middle ear, although the fish's inner ear performs the same aural duties. This is composed of three fluid-filled semicircular canals lying in a capsule of fluid. In the lower part there is a stone – the otolith – which rests on the sensory cells which pass the nervous message to the brain. Sound travels through water about five times as fast as it travels through air, and the stone vibrates to water-borne sound waves.

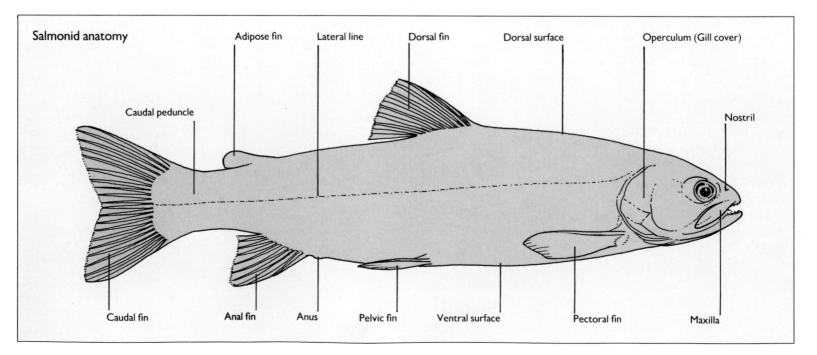

Salmonid anatomy

Adipose fin · Lateral line · Dorsal fin · Dorsal surface · Operculum (Gill cover)

Caudal peduncle · Nostril

Caudal fin · Anal fin · Anus · Pelvic fin · Ventral surface · Pectoral fin · Maxilla

The swim bladder

A more efficient system is the swim bladder, a chamber filled with gas which more readily compresses in response to sound waves than does fluid. The swim bladder assists hearing in some species, but in the salmonids it is not connected. It is, however, important to the sense of balance. The semicircular canals in the ear detect changes of level so that the fish can correct its posture by adjusting its fins – either by propelling or flapping movements, or merely by change of angle – and the swim bladder, being set lower than the fish's center of gravity, would lead to instability if it was not permanently being corrected by the fish. The value of this arrangement lies in a far quicker response time in maneuvering: either to feed or to escape enemies. If the swim bladder made the fish stable, the response time would be slower as the fish's inputs to change direction would first have to overcome the stability. Nature long ago provided a system used nowadays in modern attack aircraft (some of which are so unstable that they have to have a computer to enable them to fly at all).

The fish has a further device for detecting sound waves of the lowest frequencies – its lateral lines, which run from the gill covers down to the tail and show as a regular, but very faint interruption in the usual smooth gloss of the scales. Beneath the surface are cells lined with small hairs; the latter are connected to the nervous system and record the pressures on the fluid in which they are surrounded. The cells also provide the fish with a sense of temperature. Normally the fish's temperature is regulated by the water which surrounds it, but when the fish crosses the cold upwelling of a spring in the river bed, the lateral line detects the change, and in rivers like the Firehole, where volcanic activity heats some parts of the water to an excessive degree, the lateral line warns the fish that it should head for safer temperatures.

Stalking a fish is a stimulating prelude to catching it. Spotting fish in the water calls for polarizing glasses and considerable experience.

Smell

In the salmonids smell seems to have little importance for feeding: the brain section which controls it is small and it is clear that most feeding is triggered by sight. But there is enough evidence of fish detecting their enemies by smell to make further experiments unnecessary. Bear, otter and other 'enemy' scents, including human, in the water have deterred fish from running falls or using fish-passes until the water is free of taint again. Without actually applying 'beneficial' scents to flies or baits, sensible anglers choose not to taint their lures with the smell of tobacco from the fingers, or the chemicals in fly repellants.

The sensory chambers are above the mouth and have separate nostrils. The chambers do not connect with the throat, as do the nasal passages in the human. They are lined with the organs of smell, and water is brought into them and expelled by the movement of tiny hairs known as cilia. Some fish species can detect one molecule in an entire swimming pool of water, but the sensitivity of the salmonids is less than this. Even so, the sense of smell is strong enough in migratory salmonids for them to locate the chemical content of their natal stream – for they will return to it with almost 100 percent accuracy. Plugged-nostril experiments have proved this, but there remains some mystery about whether fish have stellar or magnetic-field navigation to help them in the sea.

Sight

The eyes of the salmonids are set fairly high in the skull and cover an area above and in front of the fish. Downward and backward vision is limited by the mouth and jaw and the swell of the body, which is close to its maximum breadth at the gill covers. Each eye gives monocular vision, but there is an overlap in front of the fish's nose. The benefit of this partial binocularity is that distance is more easily judged as two eyes are focusing. The binocular zone is where the fisher presents his fly or bait, although he is aware that this is the area of maximum sensitivity. Lateral monocular vision is valuable to the fish for detecting general activity, particularly danger or the reaction of other water inhabitants, rather than for directly seeking food.

Water poses the same problems of refraction to the fish looking out of the water as it does to the human looking into it. Practically every diagram of the phenomenon suggests that the water above a fish is flat calm and therefore every degree of every angle along which light passes can be minutely calculated. If this is indeed true then we should use every possible means to conceal ourselves from the fish's vision.

The fish's eye is assumed to be the pinpoint from which the cone above it is drawn. Within the cone is what the fish can see through the surface, while beyond the sides of the cone the surface is an opaque mirror and the fish can only see things in the water and their reflection in this mirror. The angle of the bottom of the cone is 97°; above the cone is approximately a circle: the bulk of the body lying behind its eyes may interrupt the fish's rearward vision so the top of the cone may be a distorted circle, more kidney-shaped than truly circular. If this were not so we would never manage to approach a fish from behind, while such proximity would alarm it if we approached from in front.

Since refraction bends light passing through a liquid, it allows the fish to see things outside what would appear to be a direct line of sight. The nearer vertical the object in view, the less pronounced the distortion, so anything on the surface is viewed by the fish in its exact location. Thus a large, tall insect such as a mayfly might just be observed by the fish because the top of

Field of vision of salmonid

Binocular vision (30°)

Monocular vision (180°)   Monocular vision (180°)

Blind area

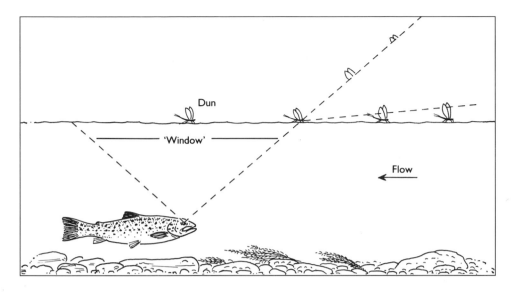

the wings would show. Then, as the insect continues to drift closer, more of it becomes visible. As soon as the mayfly is in the flat top of the cone there is no visual displacement – it is exactly where the fish sees it. However, since the water surface is affected by current swell and surge, waves and wind, the top of the cone is unstable, with light refraction occurring at all angles. This loss of sharpness helps to obscure the fisher's image and movements, and leaders, whether thick or thin, become indistinct because they are competing with other surface irregularities.

Some aspects of the mechanism of sight in a fish are similar to ours. The fisher's aim to imitate as closely as possible what we see seems to strike the 'accepting' chord in the fish. In any case we have no evidence that what they see is entirely different from what we see. They have muscles for altering the angle of the eye and they can focus; they can also see tone and color. What they cannot do is close their eyes – there is no eyelid – and this means that in the brightest of conditions there is no protective covering. There is also little means of adjusting how much light enters the eye – which is what our iris does – so the fish has two sorts of light-receiving mechanisms – rods and cones. The cones are used by day when light levels are high, the rods at night when they are low. Daytime vision perceives color, while night vision detects tonal variation between black and white.

At rest the human eye has a long-distance focus, which produces the least strain on its motor muscles. Our focusing arrangement is to have the lens and the retina a pre-determined distance apart but to change the shape of the lens – flattening it for distance and making it more curved for closer work. The fish cannot do this – it moves a far more spherical lens (which copes with refraction under water) nearer or further from the retina. Its most relaxed position is for short-range vision.

Armed with this information, the fisher will understand his salmonid quarry better. He will see that while the fish may concentrate with focused binocular vision on food in front of it at a relatively short distance, and does this with great discrimination, it also has a wider-ranged, less acutely focused field-of-view capable of picking up danger movements. This allows the instinct for immediate self-preservation to override hunger.

Hunger versus survival

A fish has no maximum size: it does not stop growing when it is mature, but as it gets larger it grows more slowly. Hunger is a strong spur when it is young, and it eats proportionately more for its weight than when it is older.

There is often as much satisfaction to be gained from admiring a fine fish as from catching it.

It also uses the food more efficiently and converts it better. Often nature proves herself very wise in dictating that there should be large quantities of young so that enough mature fish survive and perpetuate the species. What wading angler has not seen salmon parr feeding voraciously under the very rod tip inches from the top of his boots and willing to attack large salmon flies, wasps or other flotsam with total disregard for safety? Larger, more mature fish will have found a compromise between satisfying their hunger and exposing themselves to danger while doing so. Larger fish may be a strain genetically more wary than their compatriots in a stream. Or they may belong to a species which is warier than another – for example, the brown trout is far more cautious than the brook trout and larger fish come to the surface less than do the smaller, possibly because they can see less of the outside world the closer to the surface they are.

Sight alone is not a key or stimulus to the sense of fear in fish. By sound they can detect threats; by scent they can detect the emanation of fear from other fish in a state of panic; by their pressure-sensitive lateral line they can detect water movement which has an alarming frequency.

While the fisher seeks his fish as a recreational activity, for the fish survival is a serious business and it gains some reassurance from its sense of home. Most members of the salmon family, certainly the resident species in small stillwaters and rivers, have a very strong sense of territory and the strongest fish take the best places. These allow them to gather food with the least effort and to enjoy the benefits of a water flow that creates enough oxygen, and offer adequate depths and overhangs and a gentle current, all of which provide security in off-duty moments or when the fish are under threat. While a hooked salmon may dash up and down the length of a pool, a wily old brown trout will know every sharp rock and projecting underwater limb. He will know the thick weedbeds and the snags, know them and not swim into them in panic.

But one activity might take him from home: procreation. While they reproduce, fish have to take up residence in the environment which is best suited to the eggs and the newly hatched young; then the mature fish will hasten back to their own environment and home which is suitable for their age and status.

Spawning is a time when the fishes' sense of well-being is low. They barely feed and are vulnerable because they are out of the environment to which they are accustomed, and their bodies take the strain of producing eggs and milt. If the body weight falls by 40 percent or more they may not recover, and if they are Pacific salmon this stage of life is the final one before they die.

Pain

Fish probably do not feel pain as they die, although they show the effort of spawning – the shuddering spasm and the gaping mouth. Indeed there seems to be little scope in the fish's brain for suffering, which calls for imagination and memory. Furthermore, some of its diet can hardly be comfortable – a crayfish, for example, is a sharp, hard object to mouth and swallow, and a hook can scarcely cause greater discomfort. There may be a panic reflex when faced by restraints, rather than a spurt of speed indicative of pain. Whether fish learn to feel pain is debatable. What they may be able to learn is that our imitation fly or lure is badly presented. A fish which has learned to discriminate in this way may even lead us to believe that it has a sense of play or humor of which we are the butt.

Brown trout in lie

The brown trout, introduced into North America in the 1880s, has established itself widely, particularly in waters which were deserted by brook trout and other native trouts, and in rivers lacking natural stocks of game fish.

Spawning in game fish

Female digs redd

Female lays eggs. Male adds milt

Young rival males move in and are usually turned away

Female moves upstream and covers eggs when digging new redd

SPAWNING

The reproductive cycle in North American game fish is seasonal: most spawn in the late autumn or early winter. Fertilization takes place outside the body of the fish, the female (hen) depositing her eggs at the same time as the male (cock) releases his sperm. There is no postnatal care of the eggs. The hen will have dug a bed in the gravel by flexing her body to create hydraulic pressure. She sheds her eggs at intervals, moving upstream each time so that the displaced gravel will cover the previous batch of eggs. The fertilized eggs will be safe provided there is an adequate flow of clean, oxygenated water through the gravel. Depending on the water temperature, the eggs develop steadily until they hatch: the colder the water, the longer it takes. The hatchling – the alevin – relies on the egg yolk for its sustenance until it is time for it to emerge from the gravel and start to find food for itself. If it can establish a territory it is more likely to survive than supernumerary or displaced fry.

Migration

Within each game-fish species there is wide variation in how much migration takes place – either to the sea or to another part of the river. In those with the call of the sea in their make-up, the pattern of the parr marking is overlaid with a silvery deposit (guanine) before they start their migration. The residents continue to establish their territories according to their size and maturity. In time the migratory fish reach spawning maturity and return with a very strong impulsion to their natal areas. For the most part the fish of lakes migrate to the feeder streams or the outflow stream, to find suitable spawning areas. Some are obliged to lay their eggs in shallow depressions in the gravel bed of the lakes themselves, where the action of wind and waves ensures adequate oxygenation for the eggs and fry. The lake trout can spawn satisfactorily in lakes, finding reefs or outcrops at the right depth, and the brook trout also can reproduce in lakes, searching out lake-bed springs. The hen fish then uses her fins to scoop gravel backward over the eggs since there is no current to sweep covering gravel from further upstream.

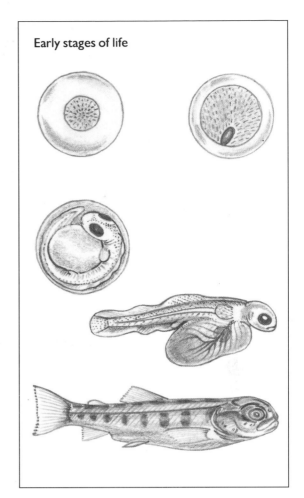

Early stages of life

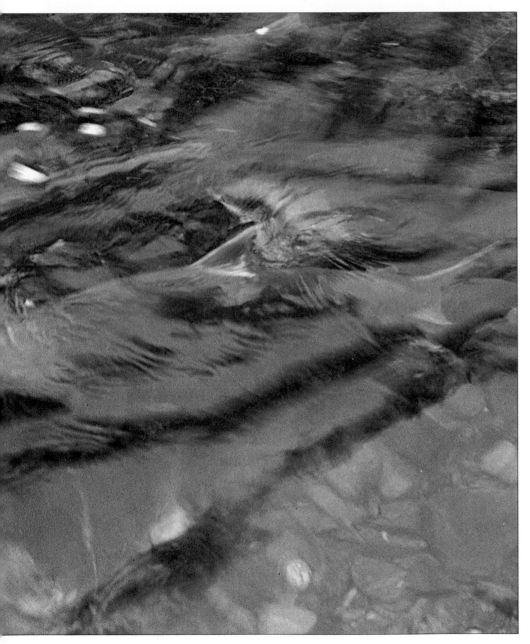

Field mouse raiding spawning redds
in low water

*The rivers of the North-West are
seasonally colored by the abundant runs
of Pacific salmon, which form a carmine
ribbon as they head upriver.*

As they mature, Pacific salmon lose their silvery sheen, their jaws and teeth enlarge, and they display dull, irregular stripes and blotches.

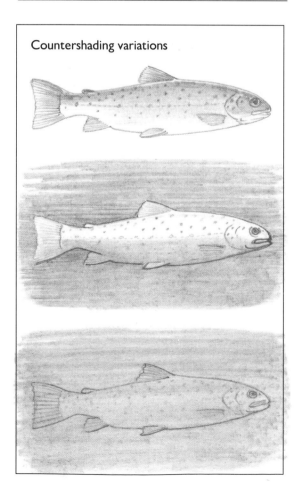

Countershading variations

Identifying features

Some features of fish are constant – for example, the design and growth pattern of the scales are established and unalterable from the time when the alevin, which is covered in skin, starts to grow them. But fish brought up in extremely low temperatures have greater scale counts than those of warmer waters (and usually lower altitudes). The chars, however, are smaller-scaled than the trouts. The genetic make-up of a game fish will determine to a certain extent its coloring and certainly its spotting. More hues are to be seen on non-migratory fish, for the silvery guanine coating of the fresh-run anadromous fish suffuses the colors with a silvery finish. The fish's skin is capable of some adaptation to match particular surroundings. This is achieved by chromatophores – color cells which can react to their surroundings, so that a bright, silvery fish introduced to dark overhangs in peaty water will to some extent be able to reduce its brightness.

Parr marking, which helps break the outline of young fish, may never be lost in dwarf races but a constant feature is countershading of some sort, whereby the dorsal surfaces and upper flanks are darker than the lower flanks and belly. Intensity of color may change with the cyclic or terminal onset of sexual maturity, a time when selection of a mate becomes important. Char in particular spend most of the year as discreet olivaceous fish, handsome but subdued, but at spawning time their bellies, backs and fins take on an extra vividness – a flush of pinkish-yellow becomes vivid red-orange and the fins a rich carmine. There may, however, be an element of camouflage about the male Atlantic salmon's mottled reddish brown, a complement to the autumn waters of the spawning beds.

Many writers on fish cite other physical features as grounds for distinguishing one species or subspecies from another. Young fish of one species often show characteristics which they grow out of, so that, for example, the young of Atlantic salmon and brown trout are difficult to distinguish, when they are both small, by the criterion of a 'forked tail,' but the brown trout's becomes square as the fish ages. Length of head as a proportion of body length is also an unsatisfactory aid to identification. A

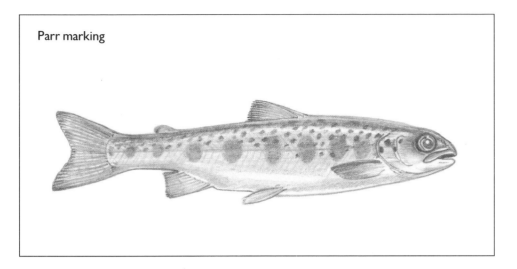

Parr marking

male fish's head is larger than that of a female, and for spawning both the upper and lower jaw of the male develop, sometimes producing the marked kype. Slenderness – even in good condition a char is normally more slender than a trout – can be a useful aid to identification and is often accompanied by other revelatory features. The char is slender, and has a high scale count and a forked tail.

Partly because it is much scarcer than it was formerly, the Atlantic salmon is among the most prized of North America's game fish.

PACIFIC SALMON

Although the commercial value of both the Atlantic and the Pacific salmon has long been recognized, it has taken the Pacific salmon far longer to be noted as a sport resource, and to be pursued with as much dedication as the Atlantic salmon is in fresh water. Probably the staggering quantity of fish in the runs and the disproportionately poor reaction to fly or bait was a disappointment sufficient to turn anglers away. Also, until the 1930s technique and tackle were not up to the demands: Atlantic salmon could be taken in some numbers on floating or just-sink lines with reasonable regularity. But Pacific salmon in the deeper rivers needed the fly brought right down to their level, and the species was considered, through lack of study, not practical to pursue with sport tackle in salt water. Another disincentive was the fact that while Atlantics run all season through (with fluctuations peculiar to specific rivers), and are for the most part acceptable table fish throughout their fishing season, the runs mostly occur so late in the Pacific salmon's life-cycle that the fish can be inedible.

Breeding success

Despite an immense commercial toll, Pacifics still run the rivers in huge numbers. If, like other salmon, they do not 'feed' in fresh water, a number of them will strike – the percentage being probably not very different from the corresponding percentage of Atlantic salmon. The frustration of cast after cast over phalanxes of unresponsive fish can nevertheless bring acceptable success. Indeed a higher success rate and a better quality fish occur in salt water, and hatchery management has recently improved littoral and estuarial fishing by breeding and imprinting a fish which does not deep-sea migrate. In salt water it is a feeding fish, not an impulse striker. Here the scene broadens out, yet the techniques are not fundamentally different from those used in fresh water. It is more a matter of fishing at the right depth.

There are five species of Pacific salmon, two more highly valued than the others: the chinook on account of its potential and often realized maximum size, and the smaller coho with its acrobatics and fierce aggression. Both also run through more of the season than the others, and it is possible to find relatively bright fish in fresh water rather than dark incipient spawners.

Pacific salmon have only recently come to be recognized as a sporting resource. Here a fine coho is netted for the international game fisher Arthur Oglesby.

Chinook

Spawning color

Chinook

The chinook (*Oncorhyncus tshawytscha*) is the largest of the five species, with weights of over 120 lb (54 kg) recorded, though the largest within IGFA rules is 93 lb (42 kg), taken in 1985. Size is often the easiest way to distinguish this species from the others: if the fish is over 30 lb (14 kg) it is probably a chinook, though the average weight is about 22 lb (10 kg). However, its black gums, large body spots, spots on dorsal and tail fins, and narrow forked tail lobes distinguish it from the others. It is stocky, strong and thickset, a log of a fish in the large sizes, and as it matures its silveriness darkens through bronze to a dark, dusky red, with a less dull red tail fin. The lower jaw of the male elongates and forms a kype, and the teeth become fangs.

This species has no set pattern of movement: it may be a parr in fresh water for one year and spend three sea-winters in the salt, or it may return as a 'jack' after one sea-winter out of fresh water, or it may spend more time at sea. Although we can reasonably expect salmon flesh to be red, occasionally the fish has the less commercially valuable white flesh. All die after spawning, which takes place, depending on the river, between the onset of fall and the end of winter. Those young hatched near salt water smoltify quickly, and those hatched in the distant headwaters of the bigger rivers have a longer river life.

As an ocean fish the chinook frequents greater depths than the other Pacifics, but as with coho, retained hatchery fish lose the inclination to head for the distant salt water and remain in the waters nearer the estuaries. They do not put on the great weight of the mighty fish which wander afar for four years or so.

Though accepted as a migratory fish – spawning in fresh water and withdrawing to the sea for its feeding until it reaches maturity – in the Great Lakes the chinook has proved itself capable of taking adequate food and coming to maturity there, and 'migrating' to the inflowing rivers where it stops active feeding. The prolific alewives in the lakes will have provided adequate sustenance, but the true sea-run pacifics are capable of the greater weights. Even so, 'landlocks' of over 40 lb (18 kg) are caught. Coho were also introduced to the Great Lakes, and they too have developed this freshwater migratory urge, with considerable success.

Coho

Coho

Spawning color

The coho (*Oncorhyncus kisutsch*) is three times as numerous as the chinook, but is a lesser quarry as it averages only about 8 lb (3.5 kg) and rarely exceeds 12 lb (5.5 kg). The record, set in 1947, is 31 lb (14 kg). The coho is game, fast, jumps freely, and haunts water layers far closer to the surface than the chinooks would choose. The silver, as the coho is often called, has a life-cycle differing little in detail from that of the chinook. There is a run of precocious males, or 'jacks,' the equivalent of the Atlantic salmon's grilse, and the life span is like the chinook's, depending on how long the stay is in fresh water before smoltification and how soon the mature fish returns from the sea. (They usually return at three years old in the southern part of their range, and at four in the less hospitable north.)

The species seldom spawns far inland – the Yukon is the major exception. This is another species which can be influenced by the hatchery to remain in the estuary, but both these and the wider-ranging fish find most of their forage in the first 30 ft (9 m) of water below the surface. As the spawning season approaches, the females dull, losing their bright silveriness; the males go darker, some showing a red stripe along the flanks, and they develop a kype. The spots on the upper tail lobe distinguish them from chinooks and steelheads or rainbows.

In the Great Lakes their behavioral pattern is much like that in salt water: they range the surface layers in their hunt for forage. Where the forage fish are found depends on the temperature of the water and the intensity of the light, for these factors affect the zooplankton on which the forage fish themselves feed.

Chinooks and cohos both need 'topping up' from hatcheries, as the spawning runs are not successful enough to maintain the populations.

Pink salmon

Spawning color

Pink salmon

The pink or humpbacked salmon (*Oncorhyncus gorbuscha*) is the most abundant of all the Pacific salmon species, and three times as numerous as the coho. It averages 3–5 lb (1.4–2.3 kg), but can run regularly to 12 lb (5.5 kg) or about 30 in (0.8 m) long. Its life-cycle differs slightly from the two species above: it runs in the fall only, spawning in the lower reaches of the rivers, even in tide-water. The fry, as soon as they are able, make for salt water and have no period of freshwater life as do the parr of the chinook or coho. As an indication of this difference, the pink's young have no parr markings.

It differs from the other Pacifics in the male's pronounced humpback and in the thumbprint-sized spotting which is repeated on the tail fin. The pink achieves sexual maturity at two years.

Sockeye

Sockeye

Spawning color

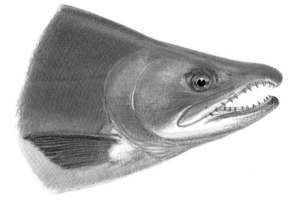

The sockeye (*Oncorhyncus nerka*), the red salmon with the most valuable flesh, is second in abundance to the pink. A stockier fish than the slender chum, it has a broader wrist, a deeply forked tail and a pattern of fine speckling rather than heavy spotting. As a cannery fish the sockeye is taken at an average weight of 5 lb (2.3 kg), although the usual range of weight puts the larger examples at 6–7 lb (2.5–3 kg) and the rod-caught record is 12½ lb (6 kg), established in 1983. This species has plenty of local races and populations and is therefore not in competition with itself. The parr may have two, or even four, years of freshwater life before smolting, and then two or three in the sea. Their weight gain is understandably less rapid than that of the more ardent fish-eaters – in salt water they are less pisciverous and more attuned to smaller food items and crustacea.

There is also a landlocked strain, the kokanee, a fish which seems to reach a maximum length of about 16 in (0.4 m). Though its preference is for the smaller food items, the kokanee may be taken on suitably light tackle – fly or spinner – and is stocked as a sport fish. Often its best role is as a bait-fish for larger stillwater fish such as the lake trout. The kokanee dies after spawning, and has the same total mortality rate as the migratory mainstream fish.

Chum

Spawning color

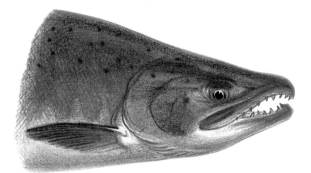

Chum

The chum (*Oncorhyncus keta*) is less numerous than the coho, and the least prized of the Pacific salmon species. It remains debatable whether it is known as 'dog' salmon because it is best used as dog food. The average weight is 6–10 lb (2.5–4.5 kg), although a 33-pounder (15 kg) has been caught. It is a fish with a variable life span: at the northern end of its range it will spawn earlier, and will run up to 2000 miles (3220 km) of fresh water. As soon as they emerge the fry start to head downstream. When they reach salt water they adopt a coastal environment for several months before they head off for deeper waters – below 200 ft (60 m) – in the true salt.

Spawning males turn olive-green with irregular vertical blood-red markings. The teeth become fangs as the fish matures, another possible reason for the species' alternative name of 'dog' salmon.

ATLANTIC SALMON

Perhaps its exclusivity has made the Atlantic salmon (*Salmo salar*) one of North America's most coveted game fish. Certainly it is at its best as a sporting fish in the waters of North America and Canada, although equalled perhaps in Iceland. The reduction in numbers from hundreds of thousands to the mere thousands of today has perhaps lent this fish its attraction.

It is not simply a matter of the salmon's wildness – the North American continent has many waters far from the beaten track and set in incomparable scenery, and there are plenty of wild races of fish well differentiated from imported or stocked mongrels – tradition has a large hand in our affection. In Europe the salmon was seen as bright, strong riches from the sea, with immense primary commercial worth. Its primary value has never diminished, but when it became a 'sport' fish it assumed a secondary commercial value as well. It became an inducement to visitors to salmon-producing areas to contribute to the local economy in food and accommodation, payment for fishing and the employment of guides.

The salmon is a powerful symbol, because the first fish run in the spring, of the reborn year, or of the eternal cycle of rebirth. As the ice goes out, taking with it the last vestiges of winter, in come fresh, bright fish; and as they run, so in the gravels and headwaters the next generation stirs into life.

Size variation

Part of the fascination of a great salmon river is the uncertainty about the size of the fish. Broad, strong torrents are likely to hold deep-bellied heavy fish, the faster, smaller turbulent streams have smaller, torpedo-shaped fish. It is vital that salmon stocks are never extinguished, by massive netting at sea, through the loss of their spawning beds, or even by anglers' selectivity in taking only the largest examples.

The specific name *salar* comes from the Latin for 'to jump'. It would be better if it conveyed the salmon's ability to run as well, for we talk of a 'run', a spring or summer stock, of fish which 'run', or work their way, steadily upstream through the pools and lies toward their spawning grounds. We know something about the 'run' in the latter sense: that the water is high enough to allow access over or past the obstacles, and that the temperature of the water is not so high that the fish suffer for lack of oxygen, or so cold that their metabolism is slowed down so much that they cannot run even if the water heights are sufficient. In the sense of a seasonal stock of fish, the 'run' is altogether more complex. We can determine from the fish's scales its age grouping (see page 39) but we cannot tell why.

Running patterns

For the fishery manager or owner a really valuable river is one which produces prime fish weighing 15–20 lb (7–9 kg), which after their freshwater life have spent two winters at sea and return in the early part of the year. The size of these fish is attractive to the angler, and if commercial netting is permitted (or advisable in relation to abundance) they are of economic importance too. In general, spring-run salmon take to fresh water early in the season so as to be able to reach their spawning beds, which are well upstream. Fish which follow them throughout the year choose spawning beds progressively nearer the sea. The latest fish to run, at the end of the year, may only just make it out of the tides to spawn and as spent fish will be back in the salt within only a few weeks. However, it does not

Atlantic salmon

Spawning color

appear that the collection and hatching of eggs taken from spring-run fish necessarily gives 'springers' later on. Salmon group as parr and as smolts. No doubt some of the smolt groups intermingle in the estuary and the foraging band takes on a common behavior, all returning at the same age, the grilse having spent one winter at sea, or two sea-winters, or more.

Some rivers have basically one run – in June; others a more extended season, with different stocks heading at different times for their spawning beds. Unfortunately the least attractive fish for sport or commerce are the fall-running fish, which cyclic trends show to be superabundant. They will have lost their wonderful silver-and-steel-blue chain mail, but fresh from the sea they can be tremendously strong and dogged fighters not to be discounted. Even so, they are not as attractive as the fresh, bright earlier-running fish.

SCALES AND SCALE READING

Of the various features which can indicate the age of a fish, the most easily studied are the scales. The science is similar to that of dendrochronology, in which the age of a tree can be determined by the study and counting of the growth rings.

Scales are small plates set into the skin of the fish, overlapping and angled backward. They start to be formed shortly after the young fish emerges from the egg, and cover the body but not the head of the salmon and trout-like fish. As the fish grows, so do the scales, and their number remains constant, though there may be variations within the individuals of a species, and the number of scales along the lateral line may be determined as much by temperature at the time of the eggs' maturing in the gravel as by genetic influence.

The composition of a scale is something like that of a tooth: growth is revealed by the laying down of ridges or rings of material at the circumference, enlarging the area of the scale each time. Although some authors have stated that there are a precise number of growth rings each year, a more authoritative view is that the number varies. The spacing between the rings is wide in the summer months of abundant food, and closer when there is less food and the fish's metabolism is slower. Rings which are close together may be seen as darker bands, and the convention is to attribute to each such band a year of life.

So much research has been done on Atlantic salmon and their scales that we use this species to explain how growth and spawning are evidenced. The growth rings are less easily read from the scales of resident fish as growth is less rapid, but the principles are the same.

The average juvenile salmon will spend two years in fresh water: one year where conditions are extremely beneficial and more than two further north in the salmon's range. If we catch it the following summer there will be the dark bands from the winter spent in fresh water and then many more widely spaced rings, denoting the benefit to the fish of foraging in salt water. A grilse caught early in the summer will on balance be lighter than a grilse running later in the year, which will have been feeding longer.

The grilse scales will have freshwater marks, sea-feeding widely-spaced summer rings, sea-winter rings and a reflection of how long it has been at sea in the spring and early summer. The larger of the two grilse mentioned above will have more rings following the sea-winter rings. The grilse is also referred to as 'sea-age group 1+.'

A fish which spends a second winter at sea will probably be larger than the average grilse and if it is an early-running fish it will be classed as a 'small spring fish' or of 'sea-age group 2.' The scales will show one summer, one winter, a second summer and a second winter marking. A small summer fish will have the markings of group 2, but with extra summer rings: it is called '2+.'

The next group is group 3, with another sea-winter recorded. 'Group 3+' are the fish which run later in that year — the 'large spring fish' preceding the 'large summer fish.' One sea-winter later the early group is 'very large spring fish', and with the extra summer growth, 'very large summer fish,' groups '4' and '4+' respectively.

Such are the terminologies for maiden fish on their first entry into fresh water to spawn. If a fish has spawned it is easily referred to as its group, say '1+', to which is added 'S.M.+'. The plus may indicate a long absence or a short absence and this can be told from the rings. The group designation is more accurate than the generalized name, because length of time in the sea does not always result in greater weight gain.

The spawning mark is different from the narrow winter band because it shows erosion of the scale edge. Possibly the stresses of spawning draw material from the scales back into the fish's system.

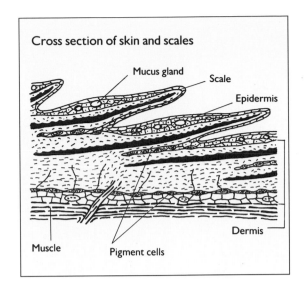

Cross section of skin and scales

Mucus gland

Scale

Epidermis

Dermis

Muscle

Pigment cells

Kelts

Salmo salar and its landlocked kin do not suffer blanket mortality after spawning. A certain proportion, differing in different rivers, survives to run again, the females proving hardier than the males. Some of these kelts return within the same year as their descent, some overwinter in the sea and run in the early part of the year, and some spend more time in the sea before they run again. They return in prime condition, as good as maiden fish, but a more golden tint to their scales, the pattern of erosion on the scales, and heavier spotting on the gill covers and below the lateral line distinguish them from maidens. Anglers with enough experience of catching salmon on rod and line consider that the returning fish are also definitely harder fighters than maidens.

In theory a kelt is easily told from a fresh fish. Although after spawning it recovers quickly to a silvery color, it is a bright nickel – a brittle color not like the turquoise-steel sheen of a truly fresh fish. The eye tends to look downward rather than boldly forward, the tail and underfins may be ragged, the vent enlarged and slightly extruded, and the gills infested with gill maggots. There is neither the thickness nor depth in the cross section and the line of the belly suggests concavity rather than convexity. The head nearly always looks too large. The teeth of a kelt can be large and sharp – altogether more noticeable than those of a fresh 'springer.'

However, mistakes are made: a slit along the belly of a dead hen fish will disclose slender, neat, new egg-strings – milt sacs in the male – in the fresh fish; or a few large crushed eggs still left in the body cavity of the kelt. The flesh of a fresh fish is firm, while that of a kelt is noticeably soft, for its apparent return to good condition seems to be due to a bulking up of its muscle tissues with water. When cut, the flesh lacks the rich tints of recent sea-feeding and is pale pink or even grayish.

Although it may be legal in some places to take kelts, it makes no difference to the morality of killing them. There is no excuse whatsoever to kill them, for a sufficient percentage return to make a contribution, in the face of diminishing runs of fish.

Kelt

Landlocked salmon

Landlocked salmon

There is no doubting the *pur sang* ancestry of the landlocked salmon. Although it has not had the rich sea-feeding that the anadromous Atlantic salmon has, it is as fast, hard and game as the brightest of fresh-run fish. Physically there is little difference: fin-ray counts, lateral-line counts, pyloric caeca. However, the external spots are a little larger proportionately, and more liberally scattered.

On a surface troll, or fly-fishing near the top, particularly in the first couple of weeks after the ice breaks up, the fish take like tigers and fight their hearts out with reel-screaming runs and rodeo-like jumps. Yet their voracity does not make them unselective, and one smelt streamer may prove excellent one day and less than good the next. It may be a trick of light or water color or temperature, but to carry a very limited selection of patterns is unwise. The fish are feeding, the food fish is capable of being imitated – and must be – to overcome the fish's selectivity.

The range of these fish has widened: stocking has taken place in many lakes which did not hold them naturally and if the inflow and outflow streams do not prove suitable for self-sustaining populations, stocking continues. Originally the fish subspecies was classified from those caught in Sebago Lake – *Salmo salar sebago* – but they were also found in other watersheds in Maine and north-eastern Canada. They constitute Maine's most important game species, and though most of the excitement of fishing for them wanes at the end of June when they seek the Great Lakes' depths, they can be taken on insect imitations, wet and dry, as well as wet fly.

The record in US waters is still 1907's 22½-pounder (10 kg), but it is thought that those fish transplanted to the deep, well-oxygenated South American lake-and-river systems, where there is rich food available, may soon top this figure.

Sebago for the most part cannot migrate to the sea: insurmountable barriers prevent it. If there is access, it chooses not to. The Ouananiche, an even more heavily spotted (and proportionately larger-finned) landlock from Quebec, often does have access, but remains a freshwater resident. It is highly regarded as a sporting fish, but as it averages 1½ – 2 lb (0.7-0.9 kg), smaller than *sebago*'s average of 2½ lb (1.1 kg), and rarely exceeds 6 lb (2.5 kg), it is angled for much as trout.

SEA TROUT

The sea trout (the sea-run brown trout) is infinitely closer biologically to the salmon than the Atlantic salmon is to the Pacific salmons. Often, apart from the passing interest, there are sound reasons for distinguishing between the two: one of the species may be out of season or perhaps the angler wishes to release the fish to continue its spawning run. There is a lot to be said for doing this with the larger sea trout. The North American angler visiting various European rivers should be able to make the distinction between the species.

Some of the identification features are determinable at the waterside, some are more scientific. The bankside tests are listed first:

SIZE   If the fish is under 3 lb (1.5 kg), it is unlikely to be a salmon (or small grilse).

SHAPE   Weight for length the sea trout is a heavier fish than the salmon, and a grilse is even more slender than a salmon. A stocky fish of broad cross section is more likely to be a sea trout.

SCALES   The salmon has fewer and larger scales. The test is to count the scales on the diagonal forward from the trailing edge of the adipose fin to the lateral line.
There is 'overlap' where the identity could be either, but there are areas where the fish could only be one or the other.
Salmon: 10 – 13, usually 11.
Sea trout: 13 – 16, usually 14.

TAIL   The shape is all-important. The tail of the fish must be spread as widely as possible. The lobes of the tail of the salmon will be sharper-pointed and the edge will be slightly forked or smoothly concave. The tail of the sea trout will be either square or even slightly convex. Small sea trout, however, often have a markedly forked tail, so this is a test for bigger fish.

DORSAL FIN   Though this fin is positioned at the point of balance on both fish, the number of rays differs:
salmon: 10 – 12
sea trout: 8 – 10

ANAL FIN   The test is that the ray furthest from the body of the sea trout extends the furthest aft, whereas the ray closest to the body of the salmon extends the furthest aft.

Identifying features of sea trout

Line of mouth is below eye

Scale count 13-15 (usually 14)

Square edge on caudal fin

Maxillary extends beyond eye

Tip of outermost ray of annal fin lies nearer to tail than innermost ray when fin is closed against tail wrist

WRIST

What used to be called the wrist is now often referred to as the caudal peduncle. This, the bone which supports the tail fin and its rays, is more pronounced in a salmon, and allows 'tailing' (carrying by its tail). The feature is less pronounced in a sea trout and a secure grasp is almost an impossibility. The feature is also not so pronounced in a salmon grilse; but the overall slenderness of the grilse is a diagnostic feature in itself.

JAW

The fresher-run the fish, the more pronounced is the difference. The sea trout has a larger mouth than the salmon and the bony flange called the maxillary extends beyond the eye. In the salmon this flange reaches the hind edge of the pupil or of the eyeball. However, the head of both males extends and distorts near the onset of spawning and the test is less clear. Close the fish's mouth for this examination.

POSITION OF EYE

Probably an easier test on fresh-run fish. It was propounded by Malloch that the eye of the sea trout is set higher in the skull. The eye will thus be clear of a horizontal line drawn along the top of the mouth. A salmon's eye would be intersected by this line. Since there seem to be no strict rules as to how the line is drawn it is rather a subjective test, made more confusing when a fresh-run fish has to be compared to a stale one.

PARASITES

Both species carry the sea louse, a saltwater parasite with an 'attached' expectancy of three or four days in fresh water, or up to a week when temperatures are very low. Only the salmon is known to carry the gill maggot.

COLORATION

When fresh-run, both species are silvery, with a paler background with darker spotting. The males in both may be tinged browner. If the fish has very few spots on the gill covers and barely any below the lateral line, it is more likely to be a salmon. On a second or subsequent spawning run it will be much more heavily spotted in both these areas. Both sexes of both species darken as they approach spawning: the spotting on the sea trout becomes more pronounced, and spots on the salmon start to turn into vermiculations.

GILL COVERS

The hindmost edge of the gill cover is closest to the lateral line in the salmon, and nearer to the pectoral fin in the sea trout. The shapes to be compared are a segment of a circle and a pointed ellipse. Much variation is found.

TEETH

In the roof of the mouth there is a bony structure called the vomer: the style and number of teeth on its head and shaft are indicators of the species. Some wear and attrition may have taken place. The salmon has larger and fewer teeth, all found on the shaft of the vomer in a zigzag row, with none on the head of the vomer. The sea trout's teeth are more numerous, on the head of the vomer and in a double row on the shaft.

As many tests as possible should be applied as there are areas of overlap or species variation. It is thought that only about one percent might be hybrids, so it is usually possible to make the correct identification.

Further tests are available, though they are hardly bankside recognition features:

GILL RAKERS

Both number and style differ: the salmon has 18 – 22, and they are long and slender. The sea trout has 16 – 18, and they are shorter and thicker.

PYLORIC CAECA

These are the fleshy filaments attached to the fish's stomach and which exude into the gastric tract substances to help digestion. The salmon has 53 – 77, while the sea trout has 33 – 61: there is an area of overlap, and definite areas of determination.

CHROMOSOMES

The genetic make-up of each differs. The salmon has 60 diploid chromosomes and the sea trout has 80.

BROWN TROUT

It has taken a while for this alien to be accepted in North America. At last it has become appreciated as a fish which has a robust enough constitution to take over when stream conditions are no longer suitable for the brook trout, or other native trouts, or in rivers where there were no natural stocks. If at one time it was a competitive interloper, now it is often regarded as ideally suited to its new environs and a very worthwhile quarry. It is a longer-lived fish than the brook trout, ten years being a possibility rather than about half that, and it gains markedly in wisdom as it grows older. This, depending on the fisher, may either condemn it or present a more appealing challenge.

The spread of game fish

American fly-fishing is not a tradition with many centuries of 'science' to back it. In Europe there had long been a huge corpus of information acknowledging trout as supremely interesting sport fish, albeit with considerable commercial interest. Europe was not a land of new settlers establishing a lifestyle for themselves, struggling for subsistence. With time off from what was vital to sustain life, leisure activities could develop in the newly settled territories. Thus the indigenous brook trout could become an object of sport fishing, and their predilection for bright and garish flies, their relative lack of fear, and their predatory curiosity would be their downfall. They were not too difficult a prey. At the same time as styles of sport fishing for them developed, their habitat was being changed, to their disadvantage. Water temperatures were being altered by removal of forestry canopy, drainage run-off was hastened, rivers used in various ways by human populations inevitably became polluted. It was fortuitous that the science of breeding trout in hatcheries was by now reasonably reliable, and those in the know had the will and capability to transport fertilized trout and salmon ova to other parts of the world.

Easy adaptation

North America received its first brown trout in the 1880s, and the fish soon found the waters to their liking, for the temperatures were within their acceptance range – a wider range than that of brook trout. The imports were also more forgiving of pollution.

At the time of their arrival, they had not brought with them their experience of fishing culture. It was hard for American anglers to adjust to their sullen ways: the 'attractor' patterns which succeeded with brook trout seemed to have little attraction for brown trout. Analysis of the diets of the brown trout and the brook trout in the same circumstances and with the same availability of food seems to indicate that the fish choose largely on grounds of least energy expended in collection, with least risk from predators. However, the brown trout's diet may be weighted toward mayflies: subsurface, in the surface film, or on the surface. In such a situation attractor patterns which resemble 'a brook trout's fin' are unlikely to be very successful.

Fortunately help was at hand: in the years when brown trout were becoming widely established, and largely disliked in the eastern states, the Englishman Halford was formulating concepts of 'exact imitation' and of how to fish a surface fly – a dry fly. Much of this new theory was directly applicable to the American scene, for were not the mayfly genera the same in many instances, even if the species did not exactly overlap? *Baetis*,

---

SPOTTING

The brown trout is a spotted fish: the dark back and paler belly give some protection from predators and the overall tinge is golden brown, though this general characteristic varies to reflect the habitat in which the fish is found. At the extremes the fish can be silvery, almost resembling a fresh-run Atlantic salmon, or a dark mahogany in deep, dark, peat-stained waters. The amount of spotting is genetically determined, and different strains and races will produce different profusions and styles.

Spots may be black flecks, covering a few scales only, or broad smudges; they can be surrounded by halos of lighter color than the background. Relatively few will be without some red spots – above or below the lateral line, though the Loch Leven strain is said to lack this characteristic.

Brown trout

Male with hook jaw

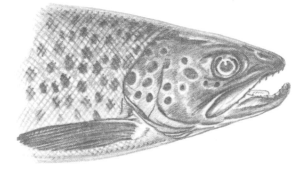

Ephemerella, Ephemera, Centroptilum and many other genera, with their forms and behavioral differences, are common both sides of the Atlantic. But American waters differ from those of England, particularly from those placid streams on which dry-fly theories were formulated and tested. The principles to be applied to the alien trout were now to undergo adaption and improvement by the best American fishing minds. The brown trout could be enjoyed as a finicky, frustrating, challenging quarry, as well as a fish capable of rapid growth and great power. It was a different style of fish from the brook trout and from the rainbow.

European ancestry

The first brown trout to be brought to America were taken from Black Forest stock: von Behr was the host whom Mather visited in 1880. Mather arranged for eggs to be sent, for if the fish hatched they would provide a hardy and attractive alternative in the areas where fishing pressure and deterioration of habitat had made the brook trout scarce. From this early introduction brown trout have been referred to in America as German, or von Behr, trout. Another source of brown trout was Scotland, the strain being that from Loch Leven. At this time the taxonomists were having a field day about fish species and their classification. The Loch Leven trout was genuinely believed, on grounds of various perceptible anatomical differences, to be set apart from other trout. What accounted for this difference was the number of pyloric caeca: 60–80 compared with the more normal less than 46; pectoral fins with pointed rather than rounded ends; and an entire absence of red-spotting, which is seldom missing in the standard brown. The caudal rays are said to be proportionately longer in the Loch Leven than in a standard brown, and the flesh more highly colored. Ray counts are given as: dorsal 12, pectoral 12, ventral 9, anal 10 and caudal 19. As a strain it is widely regarded as having ideal sporting attributes, notably its willingness to take a fly and its more lively play. However, the former quality was considered in Loch Leven before 1850 to be entirely non-existent, and this was a supposition of extremely long standing. But after 1850 the local trout's willingness to take a fly became part of its legend, and in its home waters it was the target of intensive competitive team fishing.

It is unlikely that 'pure' Loch Levens are at all common in their new countries. This is because trout from many sources by now will have made a genetic jumble, capable of a certain amount of plasticity – that is, able to adapt as well as possible to surroundings – yet carrying certain genetic stamps such as style and profusion of spotting.

Coloration

The range of coloration is wide: dorsal surfaces may extend from greenish olive, through tans and sepias to nearly black. The flanks and under-surfaces may be gold or bronze, but often have a tinge of olive, and the belly may be white or cream or even lemon-yellow.

Fins too are very variable in their coloration. The dorsal may contain just a few spots or be plain; the adipose is grayish-brown with usually a red, orange or yellowish tint to its posterior edge. The tail fin might have a hint or two of spotting among the topmost rays, but nothing like the markings of either a rainbow or a cutthroat.

Pectoral, ventral and anal fins also show considerable variation, ranging from almost black to almost white. Very often light passing through the fins and giving an almost golden glow is one of the early aids to recognition when the angler is seeking fish lying in the water. There is a warmth of light emitted that is much brighter than the river bed or surroundings, and is of a brownish gold. The occasional white anterior edging shows little in the water, but may be a noticeable feature in the hand and at a catch-and-release fishery is a way to identify individuals of this species. There are not the vermiculations found in brook trout dorsal and tail fins, nor the

lengthwise stripes as in the grayling's ventral fins. The maxillary extends to past the eyeball, well past it in large, mature males: an indication that this species is adequately equipped to transfer its interest from small insect forms to larger prey like crayfish or bait-fish. Western stream fishers regularly include mouse-fly patterns for the trophy browns, which long ago learned to stay safely in sanctuary until it is time to feed in the most energy-conserving way, when they find a sizeable food item without prolonged exposure.

Selective feeding

The brown trout is the most selective of the trouts. It is, however, extremely catholic in its hunt for food. The whole range of aquatic insects in larval, pupal or adult forms are acceptable at some stage in the trout's life: its selectivity comes from its choosing a specific food form at a particular time and training its eye to detect any flaw in the presentation or the dressing of an artificial. It is also a longer-lived fish than the brook trout, and its acuity of judgement increases with age. It seems to become wise disproportionately quickly, becoming even more critical of the angler's attempts, whether with the minutest midges on size 28 hooks, or large bucktails or streamers. Although most of its diet is taken below the surface, the brown trout's willingness to rise to surface hatches makes it a particularly enjoyable quarry. Its habit of alternately enthralling and infuriating fishers on the great chalkstreams of England is the same in American waters where rich fly hatches are rife and the fish are at their most selective.

Two brown trout, showing a variation in markings and background tone. Both genetic inheritance and environment have a considerable influence on the appearance of many of the species of game fish.

Rainbow trout

Regional spotting variations

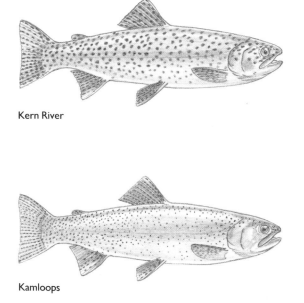

Kern River

Kamloops

RAINBOW TROUT

While the fish taxonomists argue it out, the rainbow trout is a worried fish. Since 1836 it has been used to being classified as *Salmo gairdneri* after a biologist attached to the Hudson Bay Company. Now it appears that it is no longer an American but a Soviet: *Oncorhyncus mykiss*, identified previously by scientists as the Kamchatkan subspecies. So it has lost both the name and the nationality by which we have always known it to the name established by Walbaum in 1792.

Like the brown trout, the rainbow has many genetic forms. A combination of some genetic features produces an easily domesticated, easily reared fish which puts on growth fast at an impressive conversion rate and at a low cost unequalled among other game species. The result is not only excellent table fare easily available from fish farms, but also a fish which may readily be stocked either to waters which undergo serious and depleting fishing pressure, or to waters previously devoid of trout or char but which prove a suitable environment for sport. Such waters are often major man-made reservoirs both on the North American continent and abroad.

The virtues of a good rainbow are its willingness to take a fly, its rough-and-tumble acrobatics as it seeks in bursts of energy to escape the restraint of the angler's line, and its adaptability to waters no longer viable or practical for other species. Though shy on occasion, rainbows are not as easily disturbed as alien browns, nor do they become such specialists in their food forms or as selective as browns. In the wild they can be divided practically rather than scientifically into coastal, migratory and freshwater pure strains. In general, courtesy of confused hatchery planning and management, rainbows are a mixture of differing lineages and behaviors, with a tendency to cross-breed when they can with either native strains or with species-similar cutthroats. Spawning time differs wildly among the strains and races, with barely any part of the year not being a spawning time for either resident rainbows or migratory steelhead.

Steelheads

Imagine a party of Atlantic salmon anglers who have just returned from a steelhead expedition, telling stories of the fish that now stands highest in their affection and admiration. From being salmon fishermen they had to learn fast that these were trout, migratory trout, but with trout habits and 'style,' however large and powerful. A steelhead angler would not allow that steelhead do not feed in fresh water, for the avidity with which they take just about every legal offering is as much an indication as the stomach contents that they do.

Fishers have held these fish in awe on account of their tackle-bursting strength. Those they have hooked on 20-lb (9 kg) leaders have sometimes popped them off like pack thread. However, there is a school of thought which holds that the finer you fish the more hook-ups you get. Fish lost will come to no harm if they do go away with the fly or bait, so now there is an 'ultra-light' school fishing as light as 2 lb (1 kg) with rods designed for both casting light tackle and playing spirited fish without losing too many. The 'lite-liners' attribute their success – with wigglers, eggs and diving plugs – to presenting their bait without arousing the steelhead's suspicions. Then their light tackle presents very little water resistance to cause either a break or a pull-out. Depth must be precise to the inch and round the Great Lakes the steelheader's pulse begins to beat harder when the water temperature hits 45°F (7°C) and warmer.

Widely diverse strains have been taken and planted in the spawning rivers to the Lakes to see if some have a better homing instinct than others, or will run in the warmer water temperatures. The pure, high-river strains have less of a tendency to migrate: there is always some search for ideal spawning, which may mean leaving a quieter river stretch or reservoir for better oxygenated water with a suitable river bed for redd-digging. But limited migration like this is far removed from the anadromous behavior of true sea-run steelheads.

Scale size and thus the scale count along the lateral line are affected by the temperatures of the headwaters of these resident subspecies as well as being part of the genetic make-up. In general more rings develop each year in rainbow scales than in brown trout scales, but there are so many other distinguishing features that this 'difficult' test is not a normal criterion.

Cutthroat

CUTTHROAT

The native trout, the wild trout of the west, cutthroat, widely known as *Salmo clarki clarki*, though now also grouped under *Oncorhyncus*, are somehow more primitive and more natural even than rainbows; and they still exist – just – in a wide range of subspecies. They are close to rainbows biologically and though wild strains of each can live within the same water system without hybridizing, stocked strains often do so, thus diluting and diminishing the quality of the resource.

The coastal cutthroat is widespread with anadromous and resident strains, the resident strain producing the heavier fish, a feature shared with the brook trout. As both the cutthroat and rainbow may have the same silvery-olive background color and liberal black spotting, there are superficial resemblances. However, the rainbow does not have the usually conspicuous red or orange streaks or slashes beneath the line of the lower jaw. Though there is a great deal of variation within the species and the strains of the species, the lobes of the cutthroat's tail are more sharply pointed than those of the rainbow, but the profuse spotting can be found in the fins of both. As the fish mature in fresh water, there is still the magenta/reddish coloring of the gill covers but it is the belly that takes a red or orange hue unlike the rainbow's lateral stripe. The distribution and the size of the spotting vary greatly among the inland pure relict subspecies. Some examples of the Yellowstone cutthroat carry barely any spots until the dorsal fin: then that fin and the back show irregular marking. The adipose, caudal peduncle and tail will be well covered. The greenback, subspecies *stomias*, has spots at least the size of its eye-pupils.

Depending on genetics and environment, the species and subspecies can show quite diverse characteristics, but apart from the chin slashes there is another feature: small teeth at the base of the tongue, the hyoid, or basibranchial teeth. This dentition is a clue to the species' willingness to include fish in its diet.

As cutthroat are largely spring spawners, they are often taken when voracious to put on weight. Bright attractor flies can draw them from their fastwater lies, from which they can put up good resistance. Their diet willingly includes the downstream-surging young of the salmon, after a safe and successful hatching. Live and artificial baits, spinning, bait-casting and trolling in the estuaries all take their toll of cutthroat.

Regional spotting variations

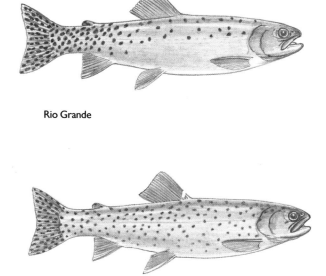

Rio Grande

Lahontan

Golden trout

GOLDEN TROUT

Those who have sought the redbands and cutthroats in their native headwaters run out of superlatives when they encounter golden trout in their eyries at 10,000 ft (3050 m) or so.

Two main 'species,' *Salmo aguabonita* and *Salmo roosevelti*, have close similarities. A further golden trout is found in high lakes and streams in Mexico, the Mexican golden trout *chrysogaster*. Fishery scientists regard this latter fish as a close relative of the rainbow, attributing its peculiarities to a hybridization of a rainbow-like strain × a cutthroat-like strain, eons ago. All, however, have a gloriously golden coloration in their natural habitats, but features of spotting and additional coloration and how liberally they are found, mark the differences between the subspecies.

Aguabonita (*aquabonita*), from the headwaters of the Kern, is often pictured as *the* golden trout. Its colors can be less intense than *roosevelti*, the golden yellow more muted and buttery, the carmine less startling, the color zones on the fins less contrasted. But spots freckle the head and shoulders as well as the posterior surfaces and tail, and this is a most noticeable and constant characteristic. Parr marks give both fish vertical stripes of camouflage, and even when mature they carry them. But brightness of color can be a reflection of the fish's adaptation to its direct environment, and how close it is to spawning. The spotting seems to be a convincing criterion for dividing the subspecies.

Aguabonita is the type which has been hatchery bred and transported to suitable lakes and waters throughout the western states, and some of the new habitats have proved so suitable that fish of 3 lb (1.4 kg) occur, with the record a mighty 11 lb (5 kg), set in 1948.

The Mexican golden trout (*Salmo chrysogaster*), first described in 1959, was not named until 1964. Its scales are not as small, nor the coloration so pronounced, yet the fish has identification features all its own, such as the lowest number of vertebrae (57) and fewest pyloric caeca (10-30) found in the North American trouts.

These fish are now being considered under the genus name of *Oncorhyncus*, having been formerly considered under that of *Salmo*.

(There is another 'golden trout'. Found in New Hampshire, its name is the vernacular term for the char (*Salvelinus aureolus*) but geographically and taxonomically it is not to be confused with the true golden trout.)

CHARS

The two characteristics which are usually picked out to distinguish the chars, the *Salvelinus* species, from the trouts are the different arrangement of teeth on the vomer and the paler spots on a darker background, compared with the darker spots of a true trout. An additional aid to identification is that most of the chars are more elongated and streamlined, with a forked tail, but the eastern brook trout is an exception: its tail is so blunt it is often referred to as the 'squaretail.'

The chars have resident and migratory strains. Sometimes the environment of the non-migratory species is so harsh or lean that it never achieves weights of much over 1 lb (0.5 kg). Some chars – the lake trout, for example – have adapted themselves so well to cold, deep water and a diet of bait-fish that they can reach immense weights, but they are a long-lived species taking many years to mature and then to reach maximum size. There is a wide variation in both the migratory and resident fish. Those left behind and isolated as the ice cover edged north many thousands of years ago, have had time to establish characteristics of color or style. Differences in spawning season and in preference for deep or shallow-water habitat are further justification for their division into subspecies.

The water at the surface flows at all speeds and the fisher must maintain contact with his fly or bait by handlining or rod positioning, all the while allowing it to behave naturally.

Arctic char

Arctic char

The next chars have both resident and migratory populations, unlike the lake trout, which appears to be an entirely freshwater fish. The arctic char (*Salvelinus alpinus*) was named from an example found in mid-European lakes by Linnaeus in 1758, and is now more noted on the North American continent for its anadromous form, returning to fresh water to spawn in fall and winter months. The fresher-run the fish and the further from spawning, the more silvery the overall coloration, but it is typically char, with a bluish/greenish background with large pale spots which are each larger than the pupil of the eye, to distinguish it from the nearly identical Dolly Varden of overlapping range. The tail is more forked than that of a brook trout and the fish may also be distinguished by its lack of vermiculated markings, or the red spots with blue halos, peculiar to the 'brookie.' In particular the dorsal and tail fins are clear of markings. The arctic char is a long-lived fish, maturing at about 5–7 years old and putting on most of its weight at sea on capelin, lance or sandeel. When it enters the rivers, bucktails and spinners are initially offered, though it may move to insects and insect imitations further upstream.

The landlocked char, under the subspecies *oquassa*, *marstoni*, *pluvius*, *aureolus* and other names, are glacial relics maintaining their existence in the deeper and cooler lakes and ponds. They are not much sought after by anglers, and occupy a rather hazardous ecological niche, threatened by transplants of brook trout, browns and rainbows.

Brook trout

Spawning colour

BROOK TROUT HYBRIDS

The brookie has proved useful as one of the parents in hybridization. The splake, a male spotted (brook) × female lake trout cross, can occur naturally, but was engineered to bring about a fish to take the place of the lake trout in the Great Lakes, which was being heavily predated by lampreys. The cross would have otherwise the behavioral characteristics of the lake trout but would grow more rapidly. It is not a mule, as it is capable of reproduction.

The tiger trout is a male brook trout × female brown trout cross. It is a mule but because it grows fast and will take fly or bait more keenly than either parent it is in demand for some put-and-take fisheries. Although the brook trout alone of the pure breeds has vermiculated markings, the hybrids also show this feature.

Brook trout

For the early settlers the eastern brook trout (*Salvelinus fontinalis*) was *the* fishing quarry. In so many ways it resembled the trout of their native Europe that it has struck a chord of affection far stronger than that produced by the 'alien' stocks of brown trout and the transplanted stocks of rainbows. Schwiebert elegantly refers to it as the 'Aphrodite of the Hemlocks,' which gives an inkling of its qualities. The vernacular has given it the name trout; biologically it is a char but one with special features. Instead of the strongly forked tail of usual chars, the fish's tail gives it the soubriquet 'squaretail.' Where the other chars have spots of a pale red or orange on an olivaceous or silvery background, the 'brookie' has vermiculated markings and some of its more brilliant spots are surrounded by blue halos. The intensity of the markings varies greatly. Sea-run brookies hide their brightest coloring with a silvery sheen and lake fish are more silvery than river inhabitants. As usual the male shows the brighter coloring, and this intensifies in the breeding season.

The brook trout is generally a short-lived fish, so if it is to attain notable weights the environment and feed must be ideal. The record fish of 14½ lb (6.5 kg), taken from the Nipigon in 1916, was one of a long-lived northern strain termed *assinica*. From hatchery figures the growth rates are 1 year: 4–5 in (10–13cm); 2 years: 7–8 in (18–20 cm); 3 years: 10–12 in (25–30 cm); 4 years: 14–16 in (36–41 cm). As the brookie is a stocky, compact fish it weighs about 1 lb at three years. It is a voracious feeder with a wide range of food acceptance, from all forms of insect to bait and forage fish.

The species' downfall also comes largely from their curiosity: the wet flies to which they succumbed bore little relation to anything in nature and thus brookies continued to be highly regarded in comparison with brown trout, which fed with greater selectivity. Nowadays a good imitation is felt to be more efficient, so the fancy patterns have given way to more precise tyings.

The brook trout has a preference for cooler waters than the rainbow or the brown. When, on account of improved drainage or agriculture, or forestry clearfell, the average temperatures of the streams rise, the brook trout is the weakest competitor, being found in the cooler headwaters or river stretches furnished with cool upwelling springs; or else it succumbs to the undue pressures of an environment no longer suited to it.

Lake trout

Lake trout

Some features of the lake trout (*Salvelinus namaycush*) are entirely char-like: the markedly forked tail, the dark greenish, olive, gray or brownish back and flank with lighter spotting, and the pale leading edges to the lower fins; but it has extra teeth in the roof of its mouth, once giving it the genus *Cristivomer*. It also has basibranchial teeth at the root of the tongue, a feature of the cutthroat.

The lake trout can attain tremendous weight but its maturity is reached slowly and its life span is long: trophy fish may be considerably older than the angler in pursuit of them and therefore are vulnerable to over-fishing if the larger specimens are kept. Its high speed is necessary as its diet is mostly bait-fish – cisco, whitefish or kokanee – and it is suited only to cold lakes or waters of great depth. Practical barriers to its range or spread are warmer and shallower waters, and it has been suggested that its absence from Asian waters is because there are no suitable waters in the Bering straits area to support a transcontinental crossing. However, there are close affinities with the Eurasian *Hucho* species. A subspecies is recognized, the siscowet or humper or fat, being a deep-water variant of a far greater girth-to-weight ratio and richer, oilier flesh: it is found in Lake Superior, but similarly shaped and fleshed fish have been taken in Great Bear Lake, as well as lake trout with markedly higher-toned coloring.

To match its wide range, the lake trout has a broad spread of names – mackinaw, Great Lakes trout (or char), salmon trout, gray trout, mountain trout, laker, togue, namaycush, touladi and others – reflecting American, Canadian, Indian and French interest. It is a fish of great commercial worth, particularly in the Great Lakes, but on the entry of lampreys the lake trout proved extremely susceptible. Fortunately, a lamprey-specific poison was found and the hazard reduced, but the laker now competes with the rainbow, chinook and coho for the smelt, alewives and other forage fish which make up its diet there.

The lake trout differs from the other salmonids in its spawning behavior. It is not a nest or redd digger: it sweeps around to clear reefs or gravelly bottoms and deposits the eggs to fall naturally into whatever crevices or cover the spawning site allows. It rarely spawns in streams, and spawns in the fall.

DOLLY VARDEN

The Dolly Varden (*Salvelinus malma* or *Salvelinus alpinus malma*) is so closely similar to the arctic char that some taxonomists consider it a subspecies. But differences occur in the size of its spotting: smaller than the pupil of the fish's eye; and the gillraker and pyloric caeca counts. The Dolly Varden has 21-22 gillrakers and 30 pyloric caeca, whereas the arctic char has 25-30 gillrakers and 40-45 pyloric caeca. It is the char of the northwest and west of North America, overlapping the arctic char's range, and in its turn divides into northern and southern strains. The Dolly Varden is normally an anadromous coastal species occasionally disliked for its habit of following more important game fishes to the spawning beds and taking a toll of ova and young. This, however, is a natural predation, not one induced by human agency, and salmon and steelhead stocks have always suffered natural losses from the appetites of other fish species. Size is used to distinguish Dolly Varden from bull trout (*Salmo confluentis*), which is more usually found in the larger inland lakes and waterways: 'doubtful' fish under 12 lb (5.5 kg) are probably Dolly Vardens, heavier fish are bull trout. Bull trout took on specific status in 1978, as 'the characters of the head and cranial skeleton' differ, but these features are not easily made out.

GRAYLING

European taxonomists have always been puzzled by the status of the grayling (*Thymallus arcticus*; formerly *Thymallus signifer*). It is clearly one of the salmonids on account of its adipose fin and other relevant features, yet its behavioral patterns differ from the other salmonids, particularly its propensity to spawn in the spring. In North America this behavioral feature is not really a departure from normal: the wide diversity of spawning runs of the various strains of the trout, salmon and char species is such that spawning extends throughout the whole year.

The grayling is not a major sport fish, but rather an intriguing curiosity in out-of-the-way places. It is a fish the 'bignesse of a trout,' a trout of wild places, which seems to reach a maximum size of about 6 lb (2.5 kg). As it is not a long-lived species, conditions have to be extremely favorable for it to exceed 3 lb (1.5 kg).

The North American graylings were once believed to be four separate species – the Arctic, the Michigan, the Ontario, and the Montana. Evidence of the Ontario consists of two museum specimens, and the habitats of the others have changed so radically for the worse that the Michigan grayling is no more, and the Montana grayling is severely reduced in both its numbers and its distribution.

In appearance the grayling most closely resembles the whitefish, *Coregonidae*, with its coarse scales and a metallic silvery finish. In some areas the name grayling is inaccurately applied to various whitefish, but the immediate distinguishing feature is the high, broad dorsal fin. This fin has at least seventeen rays and apart from size – males are bigger than females – it further helps to distinguish the sexes as it is proportioned differently. In the male the rays are longest at the rear of the fin; in the female, at the front.

Grayling

The grayling's dentition is lightly developed, practically non-existent in some fish, and the mouth small, the maxillary extending barely to the level of the pupil. Although European writers have described it as having a soft mouth in which it is difficult for a fly to take a good hold, failure to hook the grayling probably results more from the structure rather than the size of the mouth – the upper jaw considerably overlaps the lower – and the fish's choice of small food items. Therefore an inescapable problem lies in the narrow gape of the small flies which must be used. Although the grayling primarily offers sport for the fly-fisher, who should be aware that it drifts downstream slightly to take a surface fly, larger specimens can be taken on light hardware such as wobbling spoons or spinners.

European writers have also suggested that the enlarged dorsal fin gives the grayling an advantage in rising to surface food. Its style of rising does differ from that of a trout, which may lie in mid water or higher to intercept floating insects, whereas the grayling has its feeding station near the river bed, usually in shoals, and actively swims up to the surface. The dorsal is thought rather to be part of the sexual display and threat mechanism; strangely, the male wraps it over the female in the act of spawning.

The grayling shows a wide range of tints and colors overlaying an essentially silvery background. The usually darker back and lighter belly may be suffused with bronzy-gold tints, or even olives and lilacs; the dorsal may be tinged reddish or purple, even spotted; the pelvic fins may have lengthwise striping. The amount of black X- or Y-shaped spotting varies.

The derivation of the name grayling is thought to stem from 'gray lines': the species seems to be striated, the way the scales overlap giving an impression of faint parallel gray lines like the flickers of an oscillograph reading, from head to tail. The genus *Thymallus* has been attributed to the fish's scent of the water plant thyme: a connection not confirmed by every nose, yet the grayling does have a natural scent which differs from that of trout or char.

The grayling does not dig a redd, unlike many of the other trouts and salmons, but its eggs will not thrive if the water is too warm. They are smaller, about one-third the size of those from a similarly sized trout, and spawning takes place in May and June.

Mouth of grayling

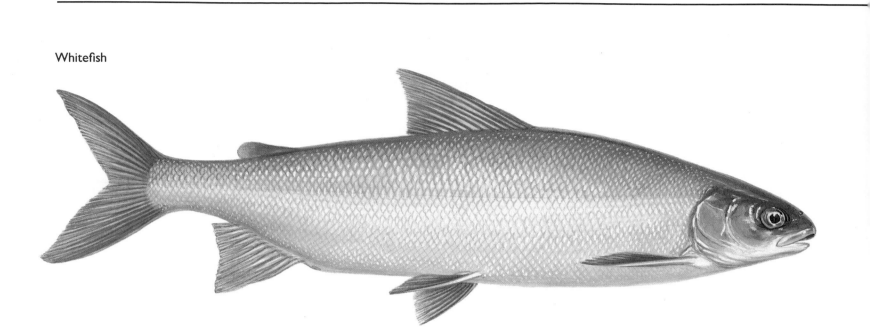

WHITEFISH

The whitefish, grouped under *Coregonidae*, are considered under the salmon heading, though they are not remarkable as sport fish. The species of possible interest to the game fisher are the round whitefish (*Prosopium cylindraeceum*), the lake whitefish (*Coregonus clupeaformis*), the mountain whitefish (*Prosopium williamsoni*) and the inconnu (*Stenodus leucichthys*). The smaller species provide admirable forage for the larger trouts and chars, and the larger species are important commercially if not for sport. The whitefish inhabit waters which other game fish favor, but on account of their weaker mouths and dentition do not progress with age and growth to larger food forms, with the major exception of the inconnu, or sheefish. This has a wider mouth and a maxillary extending beyond the eye, like the predacious trout.

Various writers note that the whitefish can prove quite entertaining quarry to the fly. In the lakes they follow the plankton, and the plankton predators on which they feed, to the surface, and may rise while light levels are low at dawn and dusk. In some areas they are discouraged, being thought a competitor for food with the more favored game fishes, particularly, for food items on the river bed or lake bottom.

RIGHT *Fishing can be companionable or solitary, ambitious or relaxed.*

Inconnu

TACKLE

There is a huge range of tackle available, and ever-increasing international competition has ensured that much of it is of extremely high quality. At the top end of the price range are the lightest yet strongest rods and the smoothest-running reels and lines. Nevertheless, much game fishing is still done with fiberglass rather than graphite rods and with budget lines and reels, and perhaps the majority of fish caught fall to this humbler tackle.

The best store-bought flies are well proportioned and securely tied, so that you can expect to land many fish before the dressing begins to fray or loosen. However, most keen fly fishers tie their own flies. They know the precise patterns they want to use, and can produce them rapidly and more cheaply than they can buy them.

Over the years an item of tackle, particularly a rod, may earn such loyalty from the angler that he chooses to use it even in conditions that do not really suit it, or for fish that are too big for it. However, it is generally best to use balanced tackle, selecting rod, reel and line in accordance with their manufacturers' weight designations.

A nice cutthroat senses imminent freedom. The reel is one of the Hardy 'Lightweight' cage-construction models.

FLY LINES

The line is of prime importance: it dictates the casting range of rods, influences the size of leader and the size, weight and resistance of the flies fished, and is also a factor in determining what reel is needed. Its influence on the success of fly-fishing should never be underestimated.

Lines used to be made of natural materials – horsehair, linen and cotton (and mixtures of these) – length and strength being the requirements. The use of silk allowed lines to be given more efficient shapes, but silk's disadvantages are that it sinks, being heavier than water unless greased, and it rots. It is manufactured by soaking it in a complicated preparation of oil, which with time and use either wears off or becomes sticky. Nowadays silk has been superseded by products of the plastics industries, and whereas lines were formerly designated by size, now they are designated by weight.

Weight is not the same as density, and a particular weight of line is made in a variety of densities, to suit fishing on the surface or at pre-determinable depths below the surface. Both length and shape of line are chosen according to the requirements of casting. Suppleness is a compromise between sensitivity on the water, the line riding the waves and currents as if it is alive, and the aerodynamic properties required of a line when it is cast. The smoothness of the finish is important, and the best lines go through the rings with least friction. Depending on its construction – usually a center core of braided Dacron with a plastic coating to give density, shape and finish – a line may stretch a little. It is claimed of some lines that the problem of stretch has been eliminated, but this is debatable. Color is another variable and is chosen according to the fishing conditions and on the basis of personal preference.

Line weight

Silk lines were measured according to the Standard Wire Gauge. Silk's density was uniform, so size automatically indicated weight. The problem of negative buoyancy, when a floating line was required, was overcome by an application of grease which would suspend the line in the surface film. The great tournament casters found that they could develop different shapes of line by altering and increasing the numbers of fibers woven into the line at stages in its length, and soon a line's taper had to be indicated by the manufacturer for the ordinary buyer. Letters from the alphabet were at one time used to indicate size when plastic lines first took over from silk, but problems arose because a measurement of size was being applied to lines of different density.

We use the American Fishing Tackle Manufacturers Association (AFTMA) standard established in 1961. Lines are numbered for their weight over the first 30 ft (9 m). A variety of shapes may be available for each number, and of densities for each shape.

The most practical lines are #4 to #11, so within this range the widest choice of shape and density occurs.

Shape

A fly line may be level throughout its length, but its casting performance will be less good than lines with other shapes and the leader end of the line will be thick and unwieldy compared with the end of lines of smaller diameter. While the diameter of a level line is constant, the length varies from one manufacturer to another. The description is 'Level', abbreviated

AFTMA Fly-line standards

No.	Weight*
1	60
2	80
3	100
4	120
5	140
6	160
7	185
8	210
9	240
10	280
11	330
12	380

*In grains (1 oz/28.35 g = 437.5 grains). Based on first 30 ft (9 m) of line exclusive of any taper or tip.

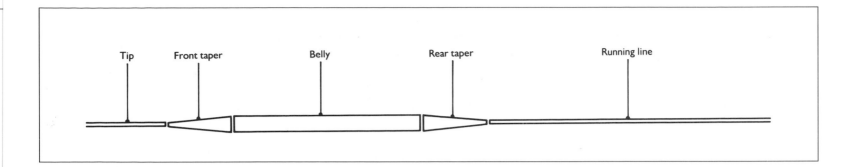

Tip   Front taper   Belly   Rear taper   Running line

to L. Those manufacturers who produce level lines do so without great enthusiasm or market success.

The Double Taper (DT), above, is extremely popular and practical. It casts well and because the diameter is reduced at the leader end it alights with delicacy. The lengths of each section shown in the diagram above are those of one particular maker. Other makers may vary these lengths slightly, and shorter lines will have a shorter central section.

The right choice of fly line and its precise control during casting are indispensable to consistent success.

are m
Bot
the wa
explar
tions
of the
An
and L
its ma
line.
alway
line –
If the
and
preser
caster
style
lines t

Density

The Floating line (designated F) is easiest to handle and causes least strain on the rod when you are picking the line off the water. Floating flies float better because both line and fly leave the surface. However, this is not to say that the line with the next heavier density, the Intermediate, cannot often present a floating fly well, but it may drown it from brief immersion when you are picking it off.

A wet fly or nymph can be controlled easily with a floater as the line can be mended, and weighted patterns can also be used. It is this line's versatility which commends it to many anglers, and if you plan to buy only one density of line this is the best choice.

An example of a floating line is DT5F (Double Taper 5 Floating). The floating element is the plastic dressing which contains minute bubbles ensuring positive buoyancy – 95 percent of water's density, for example. The most expensive floaters also have a water-repellant finish which reduces the line's contact with the water surface. Floaters are the easiest lines to use with on-the-water casts like the roll, although this kind of casting is perfectly possible with lines of other densities.

A floating line has a few disadvantages. First, although it permits line adjustment and control, placing and replacing on the water surface, and so an easy control of the fly's pace, nevertheless wind will belly it on the surface and when it is retrieved it makes a surface disturbance in the form of a herringbone ripple. A floater also throws a substantial shadow, the meniscus effectively doubling the thickness of the line, and in bright, clear, low-water conditions this may make it more difficult to deceive a fish without scaring it.

In order not to lose all the benefits of the floating line yet ensure that a fly intended to be fished subsurface stays submerged, the sink-tip line was invented. In theory it should cast just as well as a uniform-density line, but opinion is divided on this. The format is to have the first 10-20 ft (3-6 m) as some grade of sinking line, this merging into an ordinary floater. Standard shapes are used, most often DT and FT. Companies like Scientific Anglers offer all their sinking densities in the tip – the denser the tip, the longer the sinking section. The designation is SF (Sinking Floating).

The sink rates of a popular range of fly lines.

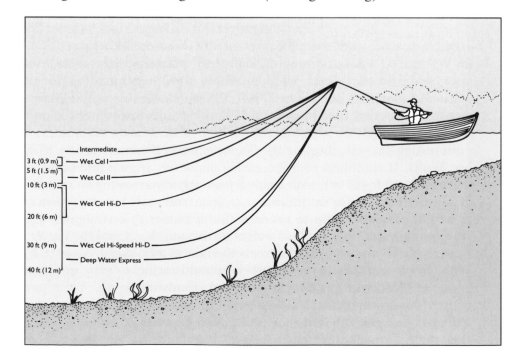

Sink rate

The rate of sink of a line can only be fairly measured on an expanse of stillwater unaffected by currents. Manufacturers generally state the rate of sink of their products, each forever seeking some dynamic marketing name for the lightning speed at which the densest of its lines sinks. The superlatives used by one company may well obscure the fact that a line is not as fast-sinking as a more conservatively described product manufactured by a rival company. It is wise, having checked the brochures, to retain a degree of scepticism about some of the claims. However, the diagram below left is based on the performance of lines produced by Scientific Anglers, a truly reliable manufacturer.

The variation in the figures is because lines of different weight sink at different rates, the lighter ones sinking more slowly than the heavier. Wave and current will effect the sink rate, so that fishing into a current from below will make the line behave quite inconsistently, while fishing downstream will produce an upward force on the line.

Sinking lines

Sinking lines are designated Intermediate, Slow, Medium, Fast and so on. Sinking lines sink – or do they? Those which have a noticeably greater density than water certainly slip through the surface but it depends how fast the current is, how fast the line is retrieved and how long the line is allowed to sink. A further factor is the angle at which the rod is held in relation to the extended length of line.

Fishing a sinking line is a very testing discipline. Too slow a sink makes it difficult to get to fish that are deeper. A line that sinks too fast may be kept high in the water by casting short distances, keeping the rod top well up and retrieving fast. Again, too fast a sink may put the fly into the vegetation on the bottom of the river or lake, but flies tied in the 'keel' or 'weedless' styles and given positive buoyancy may overcome the problem. The line being fished close to the surface may have to be part of a team of tackle to which weighted flies and leaders are attached to achieve the depth required, so that the usual discomfort of casting a weighted fly is unavoidable. However, the permutations are many.

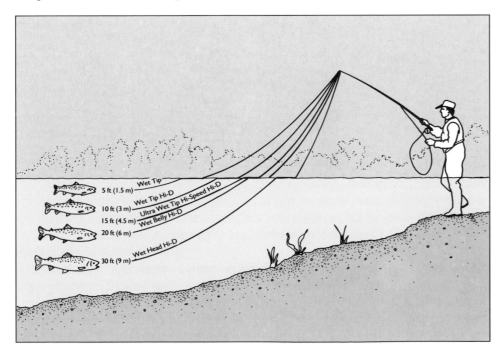

The depth at which a popular range of lines are designed to fish.

CHOOSING A LINE

A good line will serve you well on even an inexpensive rod and reel. The most expensive rod will not achieve its peak performance with a line of inferior characteristics and finish, even if the reel is a one-off master craftsman's gem. I buy the best lines, never trying to economize, as I feel it is much better to economize elsewhere. However, most of us cannot afford the entire range of shapes and densities of line for a rod weight of, say, 6. Typically, about 25 lines are suggested and so some choices need to be made. For example:

1. **Floating**	WF	DT	ST
2. **Intermediate**	WF	DT	
3. **Sink-tip**		DT	
4. **Slow Sink**	none		
5. **Medium Sink**	WF	DT	
6. **Fast Sink**	none		
7. **Very Fast Sink**	ST		

The above is only a suggestion, and since I am more conservative than progressive, and use the roll cast or roll cast with a change of direction more than the overhead cast, I would omit all the WFs. I now have this sort of line coverage, but not in just size 6: it is spread unevenly among a number of rod weights so that even though, being human and fallible, I will probably have left at home what I need most at the river, there is still a good chance that I will have with me tackle suitable for nearly every fishing situation.

OPPOSITE To achieve depth, a fast-sinking line is needed in fast water, a medium sinker in a medium flow and a slow sinker in slow water. A floating line is the most easily controlled.

In practical terms a sinking (S) line will continue to sink, at its own rate (fast or slow), until it hits the bottom or hangs vertically from the rod point, being too short to hit the bottom. It will not find a level where it will 'hover' at perfect equilibrium. Of interest to the fisher is the shape the line adopts underwater, because this influences the path of the fly. The behavior of three zones of the fly line are worth observing: the leader end, the belly and the curve back to the rod point. Density and water resistance are counterforces.

The forces on the point of the line are water resistance and any water resistance encountered by the leader. The downward force is strong on the belly as it weighs more and, having greater volume, overcomes what water resistance there is with more ease. It sinks more readily, but the length closest to the rod is denied this tendency, because it is suspended from the rod top. You might think that with a simple, steady retrieve the wet fly would behave as in the first diagram below. But in fact it would probably perform as in the second diagram.

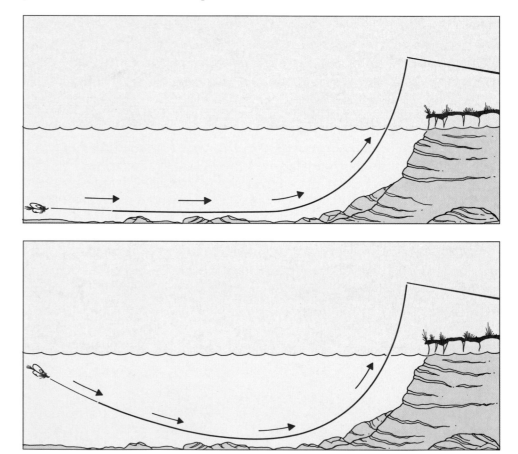

It is difficult to decide if this really matters, but if it does, a lead-core ST which has no taper probably meets the requirement of the angler better than a normal tapered line. An ST cast long and well, with backing peeled immediately into the water so that the line can sink without tension from the rod, may also achieve a result similar to that of the first diagram.

While some fish are taken 'on the drop' as the fly and line are given their chance to sink, and many are caught during the main duration of the retrieve as the fly travels in the path dictated by the line back toward the fisher, most are taken as the fly climbs toward the surface. This is because many aquatic food forms show this natural movement; coming to the surface to hatch, gather air, or hunt food in a water layer above them.

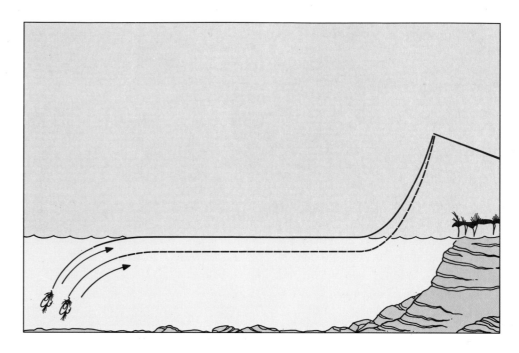

Seen from above, the line's curve is hollow, concave. A convex curve is natural with a floating line, but it is also possible with sinkers, particularly with intermediate and slow-to-medium sinking lines, as shown in the diagram above.

By using a weighted leader and heavily weighted fly you can make the fly end of the tackle sink faster than the point and belly of the line. A steady retrieve will produce a steady curve, and then the fly will travel in a path approximately parallel to the surface until the final lift from the water.

An intermittent retrieve will produce this sort of pattern:

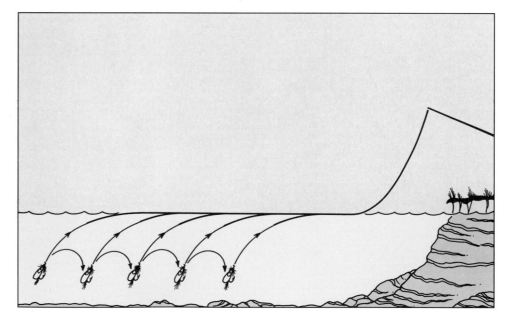

The pull on the line will straighten out the point and put an upward force on the main line which prevents it from progressively sinking. The many combinations of fly weight, leader weight and line density give scope for variations on this theme. This may be a far more taking technique than using the heaviest of lines to achieve the same depth for the fly.

Sometimes the fisher can choose how deep he fishes, particularly in lakes and reservoirs. If he wants a convex or concave curve he knows how to achieve it, and its depth in the water will be determined by how long he lets his tackle sink before he starts to retrieve it. The river or lake bed might be the determining factor, or a temperature zone. By counting the seconds until he hits the bottom, he will know how many seconds less will put the fly at the level of his choice. By counting the seconds to find a temperature layer, he applies the line's sink rate (in inches per second) to his calculations. Once he has established the depth he wants, he can set an electronic watch to give an alarm.

A versatile line

The line designations are I for intermediate, and S for sink, without further indication of rate of sink. The general characteristics described above apply to the intermediate but it is a line with several further virtues. Its density is about that of water, or only very slightly more. Ungreased, it slips beneath the surface, but any current buoys it up so that its sink rate is negated. The result is a line which may be considered a floater yet does not disturb the surface while it fishes round. Furthermore, the reduction in surface disturbance substantially reduces line shadow in bright conditions. The line is not influenced by wind and wave – or at least not to the same extent as a regular floater. Being denser than a floater, the line is of smaller diameter and therefore offers less wind resistance. The line finish also tends to offer less friction to the rod guides. In extreme weather the line is easier to cast and travels faster through the air.

Some makers suggest that their intermediates may be greased to make them float, relying on extra surface tension. This increases their versatility but it is vital to check that the floatant you intend to use is compatible with the line finish.

The intermediate is unlikely to fish more than a few inches below the surface, and line retrieve has the same effect as current, putting an upward force on the line.

Color

The color of line is an area of marketing, hype and supposition, only intermittently illuminated by logic. The logic first: ideally the fisher should be able to see his line and the fish should not. If the line sinks, the fisher probably will not see all his line though he will see some of it, but it should be as undetectable as possible to the fish. If the fish looks up vertically toward the line and the major light source is in turn directly above the line, the line will appear as a dark silhouette. If the light is to the side, the silhouette is less dark. If the principle of countershading (see page 28) is applied the line logically should be the palest practical color – that is, white. If the light source is well to the side and the fish is also not directly under the line, white shows up strongly against any background. On the counter-shading principle, the advantages of whiteness are apparent, and many of us are happy to have such benefit and not worry about the disadvantages. Looking down at and along the line, we see it well – except when looking into the path of the sun, but then it is difficult to see anything in such conditions. Because we can see our line well, we can control its position on the water: we can see if it is where we do not want it to be, and we can accurately reposition it to suit the circumstances. We also know where our leader and fly is, and can detect a take by sight without difficulty.

However, if a manufacturer improves on his best fly line, which is white, with a new and more clever formulation and both are floaters, he will want to market the new line in another color to emphasize the difference. He

---

LINE MARKING

Within the AFTMA graduation system 30 ft (9 m) of WF and DT will weigh the same, within the ± allowance. However, if 40 ft (12 m) is extended, the WF's 40 ft will weigh less than the DT's, as the heavy belly continues in the latter, while becoming lighter running line in the WF. The DT then weighs enough to bring it up a weight category. When even more line is out the weight increases again, while that of the WF barely does so.

Rods generally have enough adaptability to cope with some degree of underloading and overloading. (Underloading is when the weight of the line is not sufficient to develop the springy action of the rod, and overloading is when the weight is so much that the action is overwhelmed.) If you find you are permanently overloading a rod it may be wise to change to another rod a weight category heavier, or move down a line on the same rod to compensate. Within your own fishing style you will find a regular pattern which is comfortable: it will spring from liking a rod's action, favoring a line for its power or its delicacy, and achieving a casting distance which is far enough yet not too demanding. This will mean that you have found the 'right' length of line to pick up off the water – relatively long with a floater, progressively shorter with the deeper-sinking lines.

Although in theory it is clear when to pick up an ST – the knot joining the reel line to the backing rattles against the top ring – it is not as evident with the dressed fly lines, and so it is wise to whip a neat collar onto the line with a few turns of rod-tying silk. This will not affect the line's travel through the rings, but will be felt by the fingers as line is retrieved in preparation for recasting. If the retrieve is fished in until the line is very short, the marker is simply disregarded. There is no reason not to add a further mark, such as a double collar, to indicate the maximum line to be extended when, for example, fishing in the dark in a limited waterway.

Lee and Joan Wulff recommend a further set of line markings. In addition to using adhesive stickers on reels or spools, they use an indelible marker on the point of the fly line nearest the leader to indicate by a code the line's size: six dots for a 6, seven for a 7, etc. They also mark distance: a single band at 30 ft (9 m), a double band at 40 ft (12 m), a triple band at 50 ft (15 m). They can instantly check their line to see the distance at which action took place and then put the fly straight back to the same spot.

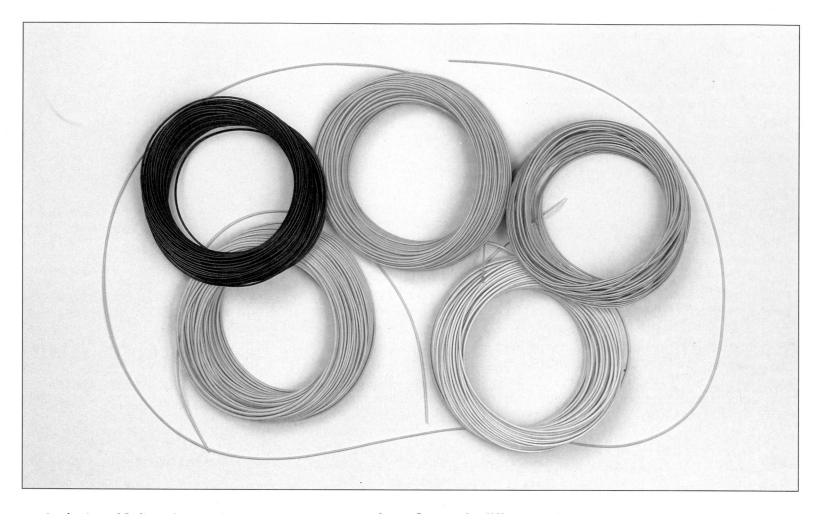

A selection of fly lines showing the variety of colors. Usually the darker the color the faster the line's sink rate, but one manufacturer makes a white sinking line. By using the lines of one manufacturer you will learn to instantly relate color to sink rate.

now produces floaters in different colors more for marketing purposes than because the new color fishes better. But then another line maker feels that *his* line should be yet another color to distinguish it from other makers' offerings, and markets a delicious pale pink line, a color rare in nature. However, for sinking lines, most makers try to find a natural color that will generally not look particularly out of place in the water. Therefore sinkers come in greens and browns, and faintly echo the countershading principle in that the shallowest-sinking are paler than the deepest-sinking.

Saltwater fly-fishers find that white lines can scare sensitive fish like bonefish and permit, so their ideal is a matt gray. By contrast, when strike detection is of the ultimate importance, fluorescent floating lines can be used or sink-tips with a fluorescent floating section. They are certainly visible to the fisher, and for photography, and so make excellent instructional lines for fishing coaching either at the waterside, where the line's behavior can be seen in the air, and on the water, as well as on videos for later discussion and comment.

One maker has recently introduced a translucent intermediate, and although it still poses a slight problem of silhouetting, it should nevertheless take on the color of its surroundings.

Backing line

Fly lines are generally sold in 30-yard (27 m), 35-yard (32 m) and 40-yard (37 m) lengths (or equivalents) as 'full' lines, and in shorter lengths as Shooting Tapers. Standard lengths are generally neither long enough for casting nor for practical fishing, and so line is usually added to the spool, underneath the reel line. Known as backing, this line is not an integral part of the fly line. It can be nylon monofilament with a round or flattened section, or braided. Nylon stretches more than, say, braided Dacron, but can be bought pre-stretched. It has the advantage of a very hard, friction-free surface which is a benefit for casting but is hard to handle when fishing. It is an essential part of a Shooting Taper line. A nylon backing flattened in cross-section is thought to be less prone to tangle. It may be your preference, but I have yet to run comparisons thorough enough to prove such claims. Also available is a braided nylon of rather a loose weave with a hollow core. It still has a good 'friction-free' finish, yet is more easily handled. The British firm Masterline attaches this backing to some of its fly-line ranges.

For Shooting Tapers, my choice is for braided hollow-core line, which floats better than monofilament and so is easier to lift off the water. For full fly lines I prefer a backing of a tightly woven pre-stretched Dacron, although by its nature Dacron has little stretch in it. I cannot see any reason to have backing of a breaking strain less than 20 lb (9 kg), and at this strength the bulk of braided Dacron remains minimal.

A fish may take when the line is fully extended and wish to run further; the backing gives it this chance. It also serves to fill the spool, so that the reel can be operated with maximum mechanical advantage. The pair of diagrams on the right shows the advantage of a full spool. In the top diagram every revolution of the handle gives a greater retrieve of line than in the bottom diagram. Also, the resistance of the reel's checking mechanism is less in the first case than in the second.

One of the reasons for the continued popularity of WF lines is that it is much easier to handle a dressed fly line than backing. However, high-density WFs sink along their whole length, so some innovators splice in running level floating line as a substitute for the sinker's own running line, which makes for an easier pick-up off the water and rapid travel through the guides. This arrangement is also practical when using a 25-yard (23 m) sinker on a big two-hander: it is worth splicing a length of floating line to the reel end of the line before adding backing, to help with the handled pulls of line.

Using a high density WF line into which a section of level floating line has been spliced makes it easier to pick line up of the water to recast.

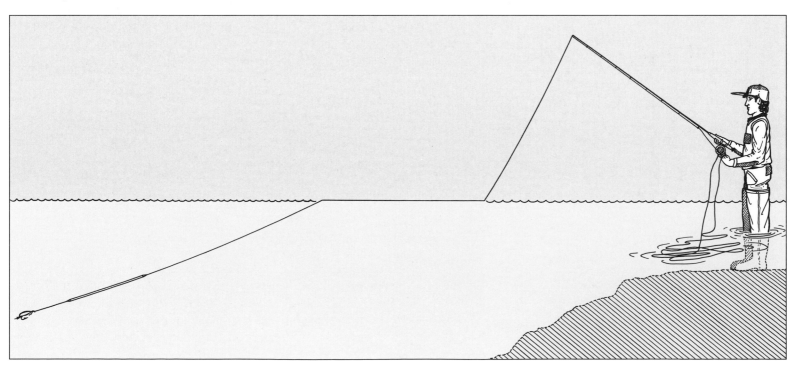

RODS

It may come as a surprise to read that to cast a fly on a fly line there is no need for a rod at all. Yet it gives the first inkling that the dynamics of fly casting are at bottom a matter of the line and its behavior. The next assault on apparent common sense is the assertion that a fair line can be cast by using something as stiff and unwieldy as a broomstick with rings tied to it. But this is simply to reaffirm the ability of the lever to hurl things farther and faster, a fact well known to the most aboriginal of races with their arm extensions in the form of throwing-sticks.

With a good-quality modern rod, a matched line and a tapered leader and fly, even the less experienced fisher should feel that fly-casting is a fairly straightforward business. The modern rod does not make instant tournament casters out of us, but allows anyone to achieve a high standard, in

A well-balanced combination: a Sage Graphite III rod and an Ari T. Hart fly reel.

comfort and without an unreasonable expenditure of effort. Most of the work of the rod is casting, for we may cast at an average rate of once a minute for a large part of a day's fishing. The next greatest segment of time is spent in using the rod to guide the line and fly, controlling depth and pace. Only a minute fraction of time is spent in playing fish, and an infinitesimally short time in striking.

A tool for casting

Fortunately a sweet-casting rod manages to fulfil the other roles most satisfactorily and only in extreme cases do we find a rod design that does not have casting as its main function. At one extreme such a rod is used in ultra-light fishing, where it must have maximum resilience so as not to 'pop' very light tippets. The other extreme is where the biggest of the deep-sea game fish have to be pressured to bring them to boat. The casting characteristic of the latter type of rod is more robust than comfortable.

Since the fisher's contact with the rod is via his hand, the rod handle should not only be comfortable but also of a suitable shape to accept the forces which are transmitted through it. The rod should also be as light as its duties permit. A ten-hour day with an old-fashioned two-handed greenheart of 15 ft (4.5 m), weighing, without the reel, about 30 oz (0.85 kg), puts a far greater strain on the back, shoulders and arms than a modern combination such as a graphite rod and a magnesium-alloy reel, which together weigh less than a third as much. With such equipment, fishing becomes less toilsome and more fun. If the rod is 7½ ft (2.3 m) or less, the material from which it is made becomes less important on grounds of weight alone. However, the great benefit of modern materials has been in the reduction in diameter as well as in weight. This improves the speeds at which the rod can be used, so that it can be forced through the air faster during casting. How much the wind will tug at it will be a factor of considerable importance when considering comfort in fishing.

There is a magic in a favorite rod, the sort of magic that the neolithic hunter must have attributed to his weapons. The choice of rod is entirely personal and the rod seems to have a personality. It is the object of considerable affection and is the recipient of a good deal of faith, all the more so if it is made from a natural material. For that reason split-cane and bamboo rods will continue to be made because for their users their responsive character has assumed greater importance than some of the more impersonal benefits of the artificial rod materials. This is not to say, however, that a graphite rod cannot become an object of considerable affection.

Size and power

Size may play a part in cementing this bond between rod and angler. For a long while my favorite rods were widely disparate. One was a 6-ft (1.8 m), one-piece, six-strip bamboo made specially for me by Sharpe's of Aberdeen, a fair imitation of a rod made by Orvis for Lee Wulff. It was a dry-fly rod for salmon, yet it went everywhere with me and was largely used for trout. There were other trout rods available but my preference was for the one-piece. The other was a 14 ft (4 m), spliced-cane two-hander for wet-fly salmon fishing, which I continued to use throughout the reign of fiberglass and into the dawn of graphite, with its longer, lighter rods.

Not all of us can draw on a wide selection of rods, but fortunately prices

Single-handed (below) and double-handed (bottom) rods showing the most common forms of ferrule.

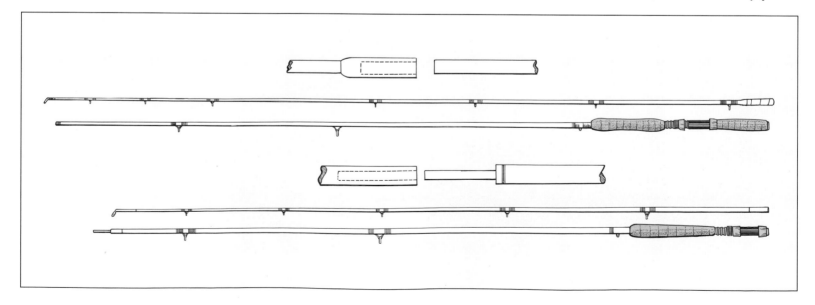

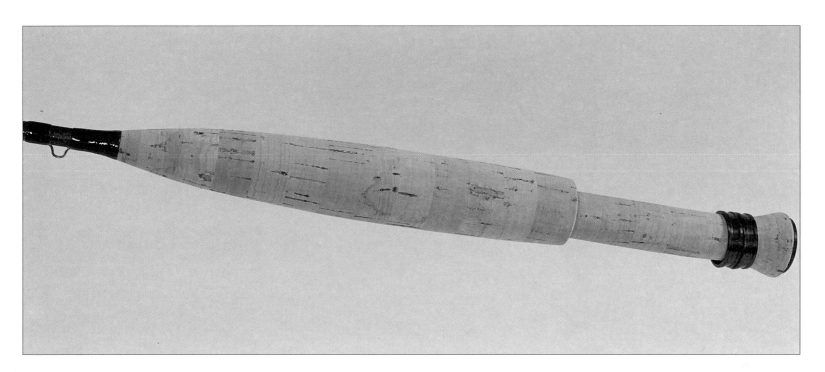

In the very light Orvis #1 the cork grip is tapered to meet the rod section smoothly. This is particularly comfortable for short-distance precision work with the index finger on top.

have remained nearly static. A reputable maker's best graphite rod is the first choice for ever more game fishers, although many rods of fiberglass and other materials are very dependable. If a single rod is bought it will have to do duty for dry-fly, nymph and wet-fly work. It will face extremes of weather and, at one end of its range, challenge 8-12-in (20-30 cm) fish from headwaters, while at the other extreme it may battle with double-figure fish in a run of steelhead or Atlantic salmon. The average rod will take a #6 line, and will perform all the above duties quite adequately. It will command affection, because it will be a good servant. It will present a reasonable range of flies at fair distances, and subdue a fish in a sportingly short time.

By contrast, immensely powerful rods are for powerful anglers; they will be heavier and need heavier lines, and reels large enough to take these bulkier lines. Correspondingly greater strength is required to realize their full potential. In every case, however, what must be found is a rod which matches the fisher's physique and is suitable for the type of fishing expected. Compromises abound. My #1 7½-footer (2.3 m) is light enough to be fished by anyone strong enough to close his or her hand on it, but the style of even the most expert angler will be cramped when a large, bushy fly needs to be pushed into the teeth of a gale. To deceive or to coax fish into taking means being able to fish on occasion with delicacy – at such times the rod must be sensitive enough not to snap off light tackle. It must have enough 'backbone' to bring a fish in with sporting speed.

Holding the rod

Lightness is certainly part of the comfort of a rod; the handle, or grip, is the other part. Occasionally, the pursuit of lightness leads rod manufacturers to pare the grip to such a thin and inefficient shape that it is difficult and tiring to hold. Different-sized hands find comfort in handles of different diameter – a fact which is fully recognized by golfers and tennis-players. The length of the handle of a single-hander should be sufficient to accommodate a large hand without the heel of the palm resting against the reel. The forces in casting tend to 'centrifuge' the rod, tip first, from the grasp, which is why a contour is preferable to a straight cylinder.

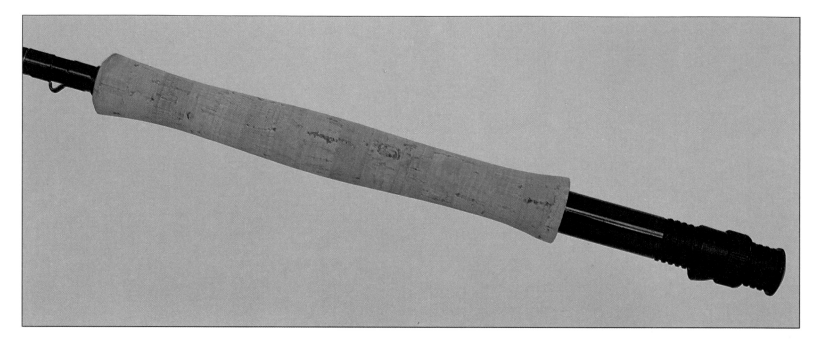

The rod handle and the reel foot. The front part of the foot is inserted into the slot at the lower end of the cork handle and the screw fitting is tightened onto the other. The contouring of the cork ensures comfortable location of the hand and, at the top, the thumb.

The most generally used grip of the rod is with the thumb at 10:30 and the forefinger wrapping round at 1:30, the other fingers curling round in a suitable position to tighten the grasp when necessary. The thumb and the inside of the forefinger take most of the stresses of casting. The shape of the cork beneath them has a significant effect on comfort. I prefer the handle to end with a diameter of about 1¼ in (3 cm). Where my thumb and inside forefinger are applied, I like a slight concavity, and then the cork to taper smoothly toward the reel fixings. This ensures that I always take much the same grasp of the rod, and that the rod will not 'centrifuge' forward. It is neither difficult nor expensive for a rodmaker to alter a handle which you do not like. However, note that a large diameter at the end of the handle compounds a difficulty: while extending the forefinger at 12:00 on top of the handle can improve short-range accuracy, it is, however, at the expense of wrist movement as it is in conflict with the physiology of the wrist and forearm. About half the backward flexion of the wrist is blocked and the forefinger will also have a very uncomfortable posture. My Orvis #1 has a handle tapering down to the diameter of the rod blank. For placing the forefinger on top of the handle it is ideal, but there is no 'meat' for my thumb to press against when I adopt a more normal grip. Any weight in a handle is in the least disadvantageous place, so there is no excuse not to be comfortable.

The reel fittings must be large enough to take suitable reels. This sounds like common sense, but the British company Hardy, claiming its reels (with reasonable care) would last for generations, produced fiberglass rods with reel fittings unable to take its reels of the past twenty years! Thankfully, the company's embarrassment is over, but if you have favorite reels which you are unlikely to want to replace, rather than modify them to suit a new rod it is worth looking for a rod that will accept them. This becomes even more desirable when you realize the interest in and value of 'antique' tackle.

Reel fittings can be broadly grouped into three designs: a fixed slot at the butt and sliding rings to accept the other end of the reel foot; a fixed slot at the base of the rod handle with the fixing rings sliding up from the butt; or the rod section is parallel, and both rings slide, so that the fisher may choose, within narrow limits, where the reel will be fastened.

The least secure system is the latter, which relies on the taper of the reel foot for locking the reel onto the rod. The prudent fisher checks the rings regularly, particularly if the rod is to travel by car in external rod clips. In my view there is little to choose between the other designs. If the fixing is close to the handle and the handle is short, one's hand is permanently against the reel. If the fixing is close to the end of the butt, there may be no room for the rod butt to be pressed against the body for extra leverage when playing a fish without the free turning of the reel being obstructed by clothing.

The reel fixings are made of shaped cork applied over the butt section of the rod, or of wood, metal or plastic. Strength is important in a saltwater fly rod used for the bigger big-game fish, but far less is demanded of the average trout rod.

Rod materials

Nowadays there is one outstanding choice of material for rods. It is the best priced for its performance, and the price has stayed nearly static despite technical advances and inflation. This revolutionary material is graphite (carbon-fiber), the qualities of which are its strength, its appropriate springiness, and its ease of adaptation to the tapers demanded by rod designers. The result is lightweight rods which have a small diameter for their power and length. Given unlimited funds, I would buy new graphite rods for the whole range of my fishing needs, with perhaps just one cane rod, of about 7 ft (2 m) and taking a #3 line, for the pure pleasure of using a rod made from a natural material.

The manufacture of a good graphite rod calls for a carbon cloth of a suitable weave and lay, resins, and a mandrel round which the cloth is laid to produce the 'perfect' taper. After the curing process the mandrel is withdrawn and the rod sections are available for finishing. Most rods are circular in cross-section, and some have a light, regular surface spiralling which is given a coat of varnish, while others have the spiral marks buffed off before they are varnished. The benefit of the spiralling is that the finish is not so brilliant. The use of a matt finish would be an advantage in either case and there may be up to 20 percent more strength with a weight penalty of only 5 percent.

There used to be two styles of graphite rod, 'thinwall' and 'thickwall.' The former needed a larger diameter to achieve the required strength; the latter needed thicker walls to support its slenderness. Modern technology has brought us a thinwall section of such strength that rods are now of the reduced diameter.

An even stronger substance than graphite is used: boron. This is another material which can be made in minutely fine flawless whiskers which are strong and springy. If it is an advance, the amount of advance is nevertheless barely perceptible compared with the advantages of graphite over fiberglass. My own experience is that boron rods feel tip-heavier than equivalent graphite rods. I stress that this is a subjective opinion and that all the rod companies are making constant progress in the design and technology of their products, and in the materials they use.

If the rod is held by the handle and given a vigorous wrist-action flick, it flexes. The butt and middle sections start to move before the tip, which then accelerates to the widest arc and eventually the oscillations dampen down. At one time it was felt that the lengths of a rod's sections should correspond in some way to the dynamics of the oscillations. Pézon et Michel of France produced a number of two-piece trout rods with a butt section shorter than the top section. If Charles Ritz, their designer, was correct in theory, such a

SECURING THE FLY

If the rod blank is being made up for you, make sure that the fly keeper ring is omitted. If your rod already has one, it is worth removing it. On nearly every rod this irksome detail is placed exactly where the rod balances for carrying. The fly lodged there becomes hazardous and the best place for it is down at the reel set, where it will catch on neither hands or clothes.

A folding keeper ring is tedious to erect so that you can hook the fly into it, and a ring standing proud may well snag the line. On a two-hander a keeper ring just at the top of the cork handle comes exactly where your hand moves to hold the rod out while the fly fishes round. If everyone tucked the fly in at the reel seat, there would be far greater safety. However, there is no solution to the problem of danger when a dropper is used. The tail fly is safely contained but the others offer hazard. A rubber band at the extreme end of the butt is a satisfactory keeper when the fly is too small to clip over the reel seat. The band just rolls forward a couple of rotations over the tippet point, so that the fly and its dressing do not come to harm.

A modern rod ring with a low-friction insert. This design is recommended for the stripping (lowest) ring. A double-foot construction may stiffen the rod's action.

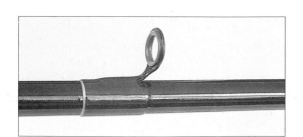

A single-foot guide has the advantages of low weight and little influence on the rod's action.

rod was nevertheless inconvenient in practice, for it was unwieldy when in its case, and the ferrule bung for the butt section had to compensate in strength for the reduced length of the top section.

Sectional design

Nowadays trout rods come in either two or three sections (unless they are travelling rods, 'smugglers', which may be six- or eight-piece to allow them to fit a suitcase or briefcase, and have an assembled length of 8 or 9 ft (2.4-2.7 m)). The two-piece available in lengths of up to about 9 ft (2.7 m), is the more common; longer rods are three-piece. In theory the fewer joints the better, as there is less interruption in the flow of the taper, but, provided the joints are secure and strong, there should be no cause for concern.

Joining rod sections used to pose technical problems: if the rod material was good – greenheart or cane – either the joint had to be a splice or a metal ferrule. The splice called for fine judgement in the rod maker because its overall diameter had to be greater than the diameter of the wood each side of it: too thick and there is a noticeable dead section; too thin and the weakness will result in a break. Metal ferrules are difficult to bond harmoniously to wood, and can be loosened by twisting action in the rod, particularly as a result of roll casting with a change of direction. Nowadays, with graphite, these problems are largely overcome. The spigot system is formed from the rod material itself; it is integral but it still needs to be made to very fine tolerances and allowance for wear is essential.

There are two types of joint. In one the lower section has a protruding spigot of lesser diameter which is mated with the hollow end of the section above. The joint shows no increase in diameter over its length. In this joint the end of the spigot should be smoothed into an easy radius. If the joint were to work loose, a sharp edge would produce a localized pressure point, and could cause the rod wall to fracture. In the second type the lower section ends on its designed taper, and the top section sleeves over it. For the length of the joint the rod's diameter is enlarged.

Rod rings

There is no reason not to have rings (guides) of a good diameter. They must be lightweight and not project in such a way that slack line might catch them. The usual arrangement in a fly rod is for there to be one or two rings more than the length of the rod in feet – for example, 10 or 11 rings on a 9-ft (2.7 m) rod. However, an over-ringed rod slows down the line, and there is more line friction when playing a fish, which may be important when you are fishing ultra-light and fine. A further specific problem is that if either the butt ring or the tip ring is too small it will stifle the flow of line.

Butt rings used to be lined with agate (like line guards on reels) and so suffered from the same brittleness: when cracked the sharp edges wreak havoc with the finish of a line. Nowadays there are line rings of aluminum oxide or some other compound, made by companies such as Fuji, which should not wear out and offer very little friction. The position of the stripping ring matters: if it is too close to the reel, friction is increased when line presses against it, and when line is released to flow through it, it tends to bundle and stifle. If the ring is too far away, it is a long reach for the 'line' hand to gather line. In the latter case it may prove to be particularly badly positioned when the rod is in its 'fighting curve,' as it will be too far up the taper to put a smooth, balanced strain on the rod butt.

The snake ring is of a simple design, being just a twisted loop. The legs, like those of other types of ring, are whipped onto the rod, and there is

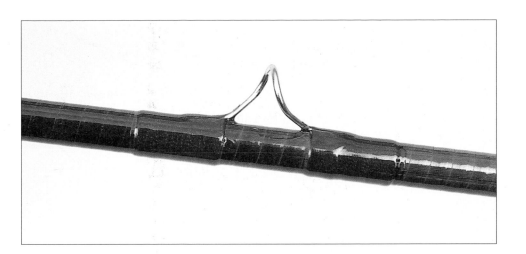

Snake rings flex with the rod and are lightweight. They demand regular checking, since if chromed they may deteriorate and develop sharp edges, and if unchromed they may rust. In both cases damage to the line is caused.

some flexibility, which does not stiffen the rod action as much as a bridge ring, which is less flexible.

Action

The flexion of the rod is described as its 'action.' Our input is at the handle and the impulse travels up the taper from the butt through the middle section and into the tip. A slow or through-action rod flexes like the first rod in the diagram below; an intermediate-action rod flexes like the second rod; and a tip-action rod has a fast taper and behaves like the third rod.

A through-action rod demands less precise timing, but can never be induced to move as fast and transmit as much line speed as an intermediate-action rod. While the latter calls for more precise timing, it is forgiving and comfortable to fish with. A tip-action rod is crisper in feel and needs far more accurate timing if it is to perform to its best. However, even when used below its full potential, it can achieve high line speeds and long distances.

Choosing a rod is a subjective matter, but the novice game fisher who wants reasonable precision and a pleasant rod to fish with will not tax his abilities or patience if he chooses an intermediate or tip-action rod, or something in between the two. It will fish wet flies, nymphs and dry flies in comfort at sensible distances.

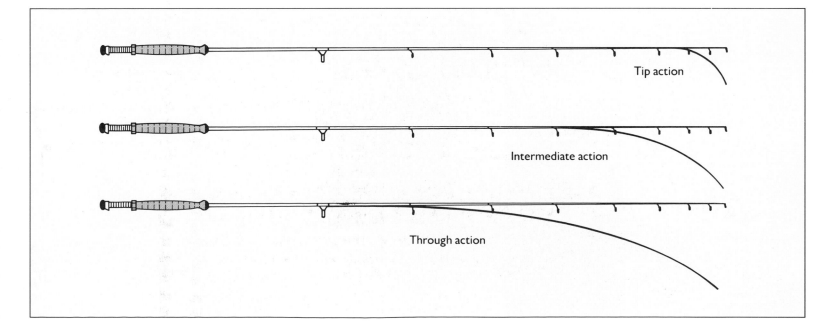

Tip action

Intermediate action

Through action

Bridge rings prevent the wet line from adhering to the rod's surface and so slowing the cast, because they hold the line farther from the rod than do snake rings.

REELS

Technically a fly reel is not needed either for casting or for fishing a fly: a standing line attached to the rod is sufficient. However, a standing line is restrictive in its length and unwieldy, and often a fish is larger than can be dealt with safely by a rod and a fixed length of line. Placing reserve line on a spool which will pay out and receive line, greatly enlarges the scope of fishing. Theorists suggest that a reel placed on a rod is detrimental to the casting performance of the rod, and in Scotland, notably on the River Tweed, the reel or *pirn,* (the Scottish equivalent of a reel but made of wood) was at one time attached to the fisher's waist. Nowadays the general practice is to attach the reel to the rod.

The reel is essentially a container for the fly line and any backing. When a strong fish takes, it permits line to be paid out in a controlled fashion and may provide braking or extra resistance. When line must be regained it is wound back on the spool or drum. The most simple reel is the single-action, in which the handle is attached close to the rim of the spool and each revolution of the spool pays out, or winds in, a single turn of line. Those who prefer a faster retrieve can use the multiplier, which is geared so that a turn of the handle brings back a number of turns of line onto the spool.

TOP RIGHT   *The System Two reel is of the exposed-rim type. It can be braked by palming the rim.*

TOP FAR RIGHT   *A Hardy 'Lightweight', a reel of caged construction with an adjustable pawl-and-ratchet 'click' check.*

CENTER RIGHT   *The Pflueger Medalist, a reliable favorite which is reasonably priced but not of the lightest construction.*

BOTTOM RIGHT *and* FAR RIGHT   *The front and back of the Orvis CFO, a prestigious lightweight single-action reel.*

A modern reel made from polycarbonate for strength and lightness. The frame and the winding mechanism can be separated so that a spool of different line can be fitted.

Features

The foot or saddle   This is what the winch fittings on the rod hold on to. It may be screwed to the reel (make sure the screws are tight), rivetted to it, or cast in one piece with the reel cage or frame. In each case it should be a rigid assembly. Since the foot is at its most slender at its extremities it forms a ramp up which the winch fittings are slid until a tight fit is achieved.

The handle   This should rotate freely every time, whether the fisher winds in or out. It is better if the handle is thicker at the base than at its extremity, as if a loop of line catches over it then the line is more likely to fall away, or can be pushed away with a deft movement of the hand.

The cage or frame   Reels are made from a wide variety of materials, and compromises between weight and cost form part of the design equation. Lightness, as long as the reel remains strong enough, is a benefit, but some of the modern alloys are expensive. Steel is cheaper, but also heavier. Aluminum in its pure state is light but soft, so has to be alloyed. Magnesium, in alloy form, is lighter but more expensive. Polycarbonate materials are both light and strong, and can be mass-produced.

All castings or pressings should be true – a warp or other eccentricity, preventing the spool from running freely, may be encountered among the products of even the most prestigious manufacturers. The arbor or spindle, which is the axle for the spool, must be anchored firmly and its external

The reel foot, also known as the saddle.

A tapered handle on a Hardy Sovereign reel.

An Orvis reel showing the hardened-metal line guard which protects both line and reel from chafing and wear. This reel can be used, without reversal, for both left-hand and right-hand winding.

BELOW LEFT *The System Two reel with its counterweight. A very rapidly revolving spool needs a counterbalance to the weight of the handle.*

BELOW *The reel latch. A small spring in the housing ensures that the spool is located positively. When the lever (top) is pushed to one side the spool can be removed.*

diameter and the internal diameter of the spool must match one another, otherwise the spool will wobble, possibly sufficiently under pressure to foul the rim of the cage. A certain amount of end clearance may be welcome as it makes it easier to change spools.

Line guard   If line is pulled off the reel at an angle it will abrade both itself and the contact point on the reel, particularly if the reel is of a fairly soft alloy. The better manufacturers add a carefully radiused line guard to minimize wear on the line and the reel. Traditionally a line guard was an agate (or other hard stone) ring through which the line could pass with a minimum of friction. Not only was this ring heavy but it was also brittle: if it cracked it would soon shred a fly line. A polished metal ring without the stone ring was then used, but this slightly diminished the practical width of the drum when it came to returning line smoothly to the reel. Therefore most manufacturers decided to screw on a hardened horseshoe in various styles. Check this for smoothness in new and secondhand reels.

The tackle trade used to assume that most fly-fishers are right-handed and that when playing fish they would hold the rod in the left hand and apply their right hand to the reel. Line guards were a standard fixture, but nowadays there is a choice in the matter. Few anglers are truly ambidextrous, and discussion still takes place as to whether the master hand should do the winding or hold the rod. There is more power in a master hand, which means finer nuances of control, as well as sheer strength, so some suggest the use of the master hand for the rod, and the other hand for the reel. They add that no change of hand is needed and thus no possible loss of tension on the line, which might result in a hook falling free. Others prefer to have the extra sensitivity of their master hand on the reel, claiming never to have lost tension or fish when changing hands.

The decision about using the reel right-handed or left-handed must be made when the backing and the line are put on the reel, and the check or brake system and the line guard must be altered, if the design permits.

The spool   The better reel manufacturers indicate how much backing may be added to the different sizes of line so as to fill the spool. A tall narrow spool may have the same capacity as a wide squat design, but there is an important difference in that the tall spool will retrieve line faster as it will be of a larger diameter. However, as the spool pays off line, the overall diameter reduces rapidly, increasing the braking effect.

Brakes   The way to apply the minimum braking effect to a fish which has taken a fly fished on ordinary fly tackle is to point the rod top at the fish and

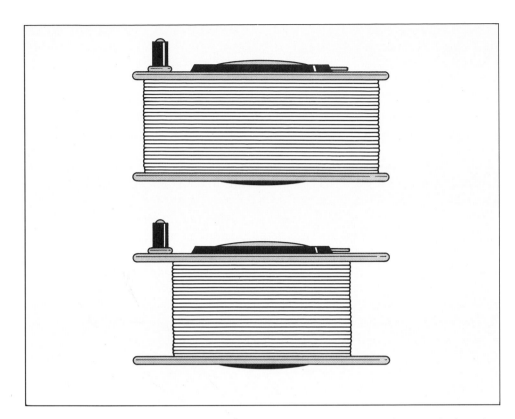

The larger the diameter of the reel the less both line and backing have a small-loop line memory which causes tangles. Also, if the spool is filled to the maximum the retrieval speed is faster than if it is only partly filled.

allow it to take slack line from available coils, the only resistance being that of the line against the rings. However, if the rod is raised, the rings offer more resistance. By using the fingers to control the flow of line, as much resistance as required can be applied. Many fish are caught without line being wound back onto the reel or needing to be paid out from it. The value of playing a fish from the reel is that the line is stored out of harm's way and is to hand for paying out or shortening. There are no obstacles for it to snarl up on, or feet to tread on it. Furthermore, the fisher can easily move around to follow his fish.

Checking mechanisms

The reel's checking mechanism is designed to prevent line being drawn out. Normally it is set at the least pressure that will stop the reel from over-running when line is stripped off it. The less expensive reels have a pawl-and-ratchet check with no method of adjusting the spring pressure

BELOW LEFT *The System Two reel disassembled to show its disk braking mechanism.*

BELOW *A control on the back plate of the reel makes it easier to adjust the brake than does a small, knurled knob set into the rim.*

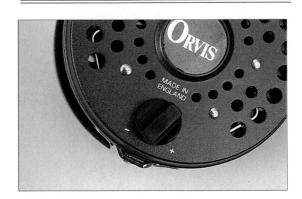

behind the pawl. On some reels the check is set too firmly, but turning the pawl round will enable line to pay off a little more freely. If you do turn the pawl round, you may end up contending with extra check when winding in. More expensive reels have some form of check adjustment, either set in the rim of the back of the frame, or on the back plate.

Not every reel has a 'click' form of check; some have silent braking systems: a felt-padded lever under spring pressure, or a disc brake. The advantage is the lack of vibration, and the smoothness of delivery; the disadvantage, perhaps a matter of preference only, is that the silence does not give a boatman or guide an audible indication of a fighting fish. Also there can be few fishing writers who have not found that part of the fishing thrill they wish to communicate lies in the scream and whir of a fast-running reel. I freely admit that there is a great deal of pleasure in hearing the smallest of Hardy reels make a squeak like a mouse with its tail tweaked, as two pounds of brown trout crosses a wide Spey salmon pool in high spring water – as much as there is in hearing an inexorable click . . . click . . . click as a big salmon angles its nose into the stream despite the massive strain put on it. Heart-rate is well up in both instances, but there is no feast for the ears if a silent reel is used. Braking a fish can be a combination effort: the reel plays its part, while the fingers on the line add their own pressure. Alternatively, the speed of the spool's rotation can be slowed with the fingers or palm of the hand.

Exposed braking surfaces

A reel which has stood up well to the demands of game fishers for the past century is the Hardy Perfect. Fingers can be applied to the entire back of the spool as it is not enclosed in the reel cage. Subsequent designs have an

ABOVE *This Pflueger reel applies a constant check pressure during winding in, but may be variably braked when line is pulled by a fish.*

RIGHT *The Orvis CFO reel showing the cageless construction and the click-ratchet braking system.*

LINE IDENTIFICATION

A good-quality reel is very expensive and rather than buying many of much the same size to accommodate all the necessary lines, it is worth determining what for you is a good average size and then making sure you have enough spools loaded with backing and different lines to meet all eventualities. I like to know what is on each spool, and so on the blind face (the side without the handle, hidden behind the reel cage) I apply an adhesive sticker or write with an indelible marker:
1. the date the backing and line were bought for the spool and put on
2. the approximate length and strength of the backing
3. the line designation
When the spool is fitted into the reel and the reel on the rod, the line manufacturer's adhesive sticker which states the line's specification is all that need be evident. I put this sticker on the handle face of the spool, if the surface is not too perforated with weight-reduction holes. In turn, the reel case or drawbag carries an indication of its contents. If, however, I have only one spool for a reel, I find that the most discreet place for the sticker is on the surface of the reel foot, where it mates with the rod. This does not spoil the look of a finely engineered reel.

exposed rim rather than an exposed backplate, and the palm of the hand may take over from the integral check by producing its own friction. With modern reels of the cage construction, it is possible to apply finger pressure to the body of the line still on the spool or to the inside flanges of the spool. There are advantages and disadvantages in each system. The Perfect is a heavy reel compared with more modern designs. Of these, the exposed-rim kind is more likely to pick up grit, and the reel may press against clothing, giving unwanted braking if the reel is set on fittings at the extreme butt-end of the rod. A reel of the caged design is difficult to modulate with the fingers, and line checked through the fingers can cause nasty burns or cuts if it is a big fish in combination with a strong current.

Beginners have a fatal attraction to stopping a reel running by putting their hand to the handle – fatal because it puts an end to their expectation of bringing the fish in.

Balancing rod and reel

Once it was thought that a reel should balance a rod, that the rod held by the casting hand on the handle should be at point of balance (or where the top hand is, for a two-hander). By complete contrast, the modern theory holds that the lightest possible reel gives the rod its best chance to realize its potential. But what has happened is that rods have become very much lighter than they were, and we use, on occasion, rods that are far longer for their weight than we used to. Such rods offer considerable wind resistance and must be held firmly to keep them steady. The lighter the reel, the harder it is to hold the light rod and reel with an untiring, relaxed grip. There is a time to trade off theoretical casting advantage against greatly increased fishing comfort – in other words, we sometimes put a heavier reel on the rod to balance it, after all!

It seems a human trait to look after something which was made by a craftsman rather than mass-produced, and which was a considered purchase rather than an impulse buy. Whether the little jewel by Hardy or Orvis really has a soul and can be anthropomorphized, is up to its owner. But what is important is not only that it has been better made and that it has lasted a number of generations, but that it is believed in and looked after and given regular attention. Yet I do not consider the reel a particularly important part of tackle for average fishing; for 90 percent of the time it is just a line reservoir. Most of the time there will be little apparent difference between a good reel and an average one, but when a really good fish is on, the water is strong, and neither man nor boat can follow, the best reel undeniably removes one cause of anxiety.

The choice of line color is sometimes a compromise: the angler may prefer to use a bright line that he can see and control, rather than worry that it will be easily seen by the fish.

LEADERS

There seem to be marketing cycles in the fishing tackle trade: it becomes time to produce something different which can receive all the benefit of sales hype. Yet, when tested rigorously, it may not live up to the standards claimed for it, or may not even be an advance on existing technology. Leaders, and leader material, are at present undergoing this treatment.

The leader has two roles: to present the fly with the appropriate force or delicacy, as unobtrusively as possible; and to transfer the casting energy from the rod and line to the fly so that it is delivered precisely. In theory, the ideal leader would be some sort of strand finer than a human hair, of very high breaking strain, of a color which renders it almost invisible in all conditions of light and water, and of adjustable flexibility to help it turn over and present a wide range of fly sizes. However, such demands are in conflict. Different makers and brands can meet one or perhaps more requirements and the fisher will need to investigate accordingly, but what he chooses will necessarily be a compromise which suits him and his sort of fishing.

Nylon monofilament, in its many forms, is the material used for leaders. For its diameter it is stronger than the silkworm gut which preceded it, and gut in turn was an advance on horsehair. As nylon is artificial, it can be designed to be supple, to stretch, to have a shiny or matt finish, and can be tapered. It may also be colored or made nearly translucent. Fine filaments of nylon may be braided.

A current marketing trend is to suggest the use of braided material for the major part of the leader – down to the tippet. Some brands incorporate weight to help the fly or nymph to sink.

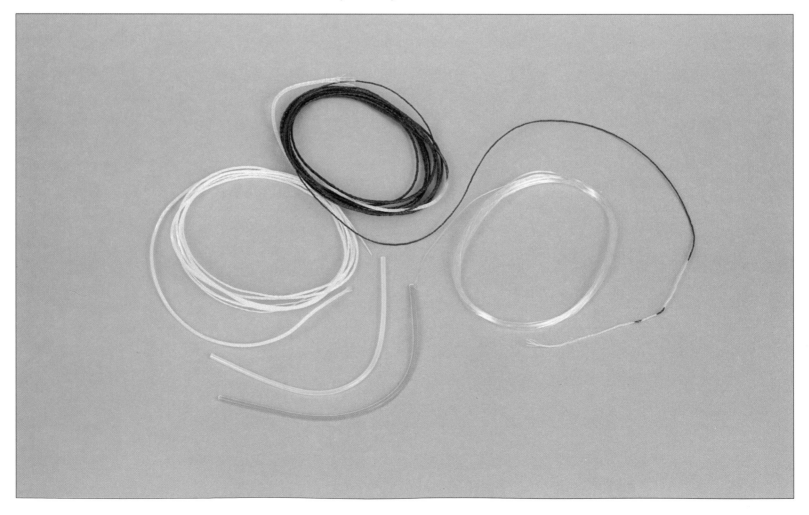

Technical requirements

Let us look at two situations which commonly test the leader: spring fishing for Atlantic salmon in colored water, and midge fishing for trout in the extreme brightness and clarity of high summer and low water. The salmon fisher will be fishing with a sunk line, to put the fly near the river bed and the fly will certainly be large, as the water is cold and may even have extra weight. Water levels in the spring are generally high and on the river in question the average weight in the early months of the season is about 15 lb (7 kg). On this occasion the angler chooses to fish a rod which takes lines of #9, 10 or even 11. The length of the leader need only be sufficient to separate the fly from the reel line. (Although fish have been caught on a fly tied directly to the end of the line, it is not logically the best practice.) A comfortable length is 8-10 ft (2.5-3 m) and the leader will be thickest at the line end – 25-28 lb (11-13 kg), say – and no weaker than 20 lb (9 kg) at the fly. The colored water helps disguise the thickness of the nylon, and the diameter is suitable for tying a satisfactory leader-to-fly knot. With hooks of reasonable size and with a leader of such breaking strain, a well-hooked fish should be brought in after a sportingly short fight.

The tiny hooks used in our second situation – 24s and 26s – are made of very fine wire which will either break or straighten out under extreme pressure or, being so fine, will even cut its way through the tissue of a fish's mouth. The eye will have a very small internal diameter. A leader for casting such a fly needs to be fine, even if the expected fish are of generous size. The knot should be of a size appropriate to the leader's diameter and yet provide a secure fastening. The leader's slenderness brings it as close to invisibility as possible, but its very low breaking strain remains a problem. However, the leader can be cushioned in a number of ways.

Nylon stretches: therefore the longer the nylon the more stretch, so that a long, fine leader is stronger than a short, fine leader. A further benefit is that a greater length of leader gives the fly a more delicate presentation, and the fly is further removed from the much more visible line end. (The sobering disadvantage of an extremely long and light leader is its resistance to being turned over and fully extended.) Further cushioning is provided by the rod: there is no point in using #9 rods and lines to fish 1 lb (0.5 kg) leaders. Use #1, #2, or #3 rods, which have fine tip sections flexible enough, with sensitive handling, to tighten on the fish and play it successfully. Needless to say, the check on a reel should be extremely lightly set, and very smooth in operation, to prevent unnecessary shock to the leader.

Using a tapered leader

Casting energy is transferred to the fly more effectively by a tapered leader than a leader of the same diameter throughout its length. The step down from the end of the line to the butt of the leader should be as smooth as possible. The weakest link is the tippet, and if it is to turn over well a satisfactory compromise must be reached, by trial and error, between the delicacy needed and the caster's ability to turn over a fine, straight section in the prevailing weather conditions. The steps of the taper will again be largely a matter of trial and error, but any knots and joins should be able to pass freely through the rings, and the diameters at each reduction should not differ by much more than 10 percent, as a greater difference produces less secure knots.

The specific gravity of nylon is less than that of water and nylon leader material laid on water will float on account of its own positive buoyancy and the lift of the meniscus. The leader may be rubbed down with a proprietary submersant, for example to help a nymph sink immediately; or polished or greased to ensure that it floats. Otherwise, the nylon is at the whim of the weight of the fly or the play of current.

If, however, a braided leader is used, weight may be incorporated into the braid. Weight can be determined more easily than the allegedly improved transfer of casting power, turnover or presentation enthused about in promotional material. Major tackle companies now offer braided leader material classified by sink rate, using similar terminology to that applied to sinking lines. The braided element of a leader runs from the butt down to the end, and the tippet is monofilament. Braided leader material is proportionately more costly than spools of different diameter nylon or tapered single-strand leaders. Whatever the advantage in theory of a braided leader, it is entirely negated if it has a soft, loose weave.

Deterioration

For its strength, nylon relies largely on the perfection of finish of its outer surface. When knots are tied they should be lubricated with water or saliva as they are drawn up snug, as the friction produces intense local heat which distorts the structure of the nylon. Unnecessary exposure to light, particularly ultraviolet, weakens nylon and so does any form of abrasion – for example, against vegetation during casting, or against rocks or river bed while the fly is fishing or a fish is being played. The minimal cost of routinely renewing nylon is a minute part of expenditure on fishing, and it is never worth trying to make economies in this important area.

All nylon deteriorates with age and it is wise to replace at least once each season all nylon below 10 lb (4.5 kg) breaking strain, even if it has been stored and treated well. If nylon of over 15 lb (7 kg) is kept well, it will last two seasons, because it is normally bought for its diameter rather than its breaking strain. It is best to mark all drums of nylon with the purchase date and the size or breaking strain, or both, by scratching the information into the plastic of the spool.

It is possible to buy spools of monofilament with droppers knotted in at specified intervals. For the benefit of convenience this is not expensive, and the advantages may outweigh any potential disadvantage like lack of taper or the need to trust someone else's ability to tie knots. The use of droppers is a personal decision – to cast a team of four or five flies well is demanding, but the action of a fly on a dropper differs greatly from that on the point and each fly will be fishing at a different depth.

The diameter of the nylon leader butt is two thirds that of the line point. The size of tippet should be in balance with the size of the fly, and there is a rough and ready convention governing this: take the size of fly, say 16, divide it by 4 – the result is 4 – that is, 4X. Use a stronger leader in rough conditions, and a finer one in brighter, calmer conditions (this compensates for the inaccuracies of size which result from fractional results – for example, hook #17 ÷ 4 = 4¼).

Your own practice when making up a front leader may always be the same: adjust the butt to suit the line point and then run a tapered leader to about 10 lb (4.5 kg) breaking strain. Each section of continued taper will step down two X units. If the joining knots are counted it becomes apparent at what breaking-strain diameter the finest section will be. There is another good reason for always buying one maker's specific nylon besides the fact that it ties compatible knots: the diameters relative to the test strains are a known graduation, whereas mixing brands gives problems of diameter and

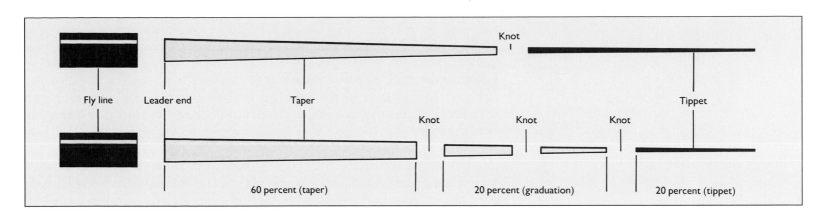

Fly line   Leader end   Taper   Knot   Knot   Knot   Knot   Tippet

60 percent (taper)   20 percent (graduation)   20 percent (tippet)

stiffness. Diameter gauges are available, and no doubt are useful, but if only one maker's leaders are used there is little need for a gauge, particularly if you follow the advice at the start of this paragraph.

You may find the idea of fishing tippets as light as 8X rather daunting. Surely this will be so weak that fish will snap off? However, one commonly employed safeguard is to include a shock-absorbing material like Power-Gum or Shock-Gum in the make-up of the leader. This has a breaking strain far higher than the tippet but can stretch to about twice its static length. Another way to counteract the effect of shock on the tippet is to tie it to braided nylon rather than monofilament. This too has a considerable stretch, maybe four times as much as conventional nylon, and so provides an effective cushion.

An interesting rule-of-thumb guide for a suitable tippet strength for a rod-and-line is to translate the AFTMA number into pounds test: AFTMA #6 = 6 lb (2.7 kg) b.s. and AFTMA #9 = 9 lb (4 kg) b.s., for example. A commonsense guideline for tapered leaders – sections knotted together and gradually reducing in diameter and breaking strain – was formulated in the 1950s and has yet to be bettered: 60 percent heavy, 20 percent graduation, and 20 percent tippet.

LEADER SPECIFICATIONS

In the table below one manufacturer's figures are given; other manufacturers' specifications may differ slightly.

Size	Tip diameter		Breaking strain
	in	mm	lb (kg) test
0X	0.011	0.275	15.5 (7)
1X	0.010	0.25	13.5 (6.1)
2X	0.009	0.225	11.5 (5.2)
3X	0.008	0.20	8.5 (3.9)
4X	0.007	0.175	5.5 (2.5)
5X	0.006	0.164	4.5 (2)
6X	0.005	0.15	3.5 (1.6)
7X	0.004	0.10	2.5 (1.1)
8X	0.003	0.008	1.75 (0.8)

KNOTS

Every knot must be strong enough for its duty and appropriate for the material used. The first knot on a fly reel is that of the backing to the spool spindle. Backing material may be one of the monofilaments or braided. In either case what is important is that this knot should be self-tightening on the spindle. The angler faces a problem if the fish has run to the extremity of the backing. What is most likely is that the weight of line run off will already have caused a break. If not, it will be necessary to be able to wind up both backing and line and regain some control, and for this the knot must be secure.

First tie an overhand or figure-of-eight knot very close to the running end. Were the subsequent overhand knot not to be pulled sufficiently tight this would prevent the line slipping away. Bring the line round the arbor/spindle from underneath: the entry point and the exit point for the line must be through the line guard if there is one. (The choice is made at this stage between right-hand and left-hand winding.) The knot which jams against the spindle is a simple overhand, or an overhand with two turns. It must sit snugly and some anglers prefer two turns round the spindle as well.

Joining fly line to backing

The next knot is that which joins the backing to the fly line. My own choice is to tie a loop in the backing, large enough to allow the reel to pass through it. The loop is formed by making a two-pass overhand knot, keeping the running tail short.

The loop in the end of the fly line is not knotted but whipped. Pare off the coating on the last ½ in (0.5 cm) and do the same 3 in (7.5 cm) up the line. Lay the two bared sections together and whip. The result should be smooth and little greater in diameter than the line with its coating. Varnish the whipping thoroughly. Thread the backing loop through the line loop, pass the reel through the backing loop and draw the knot up so that it is symmetrical. This knot is strong and can pass easily through the rod rings. The advantage is that a new knot does not have to be tied if another line is to be matched with that reel and backing. The usual knot recommended is the Albright with its six turns. Some manufacturers produce lines with backing already connected. In their experience a braid opened up to sleeve the end of the fly line, 'superglued' and whipped and varnished, provides a secure fastening. A variation is a sleeve which fits over the braid when it is pushed up the line.

Also available are hard nylon 'connectors' pierced and tapered at each end with side slots so that the line and backing may separately be given a terminal overhand or figure-of-eight knot, and then pulled back in. They too are sufficiently smooth to pass easily through the rings.

Joining fly line to leader

The next knot joins the fly line to the leader. Ideally this junction should transfer the flow of energy smoothly, the flexibility of the line and the leader being closely in accordance at the join. A needle knot is unequalled for this connection, and is a little more streamlined than the similar nail knot. Five or six turns should be made and a suitable cement or epoxy solution smoothed over the knot so that it will run through the rings without checking, and will not pick up flotsam in the water.

In the section on leaders (see pages 92-5) there is a table showing the

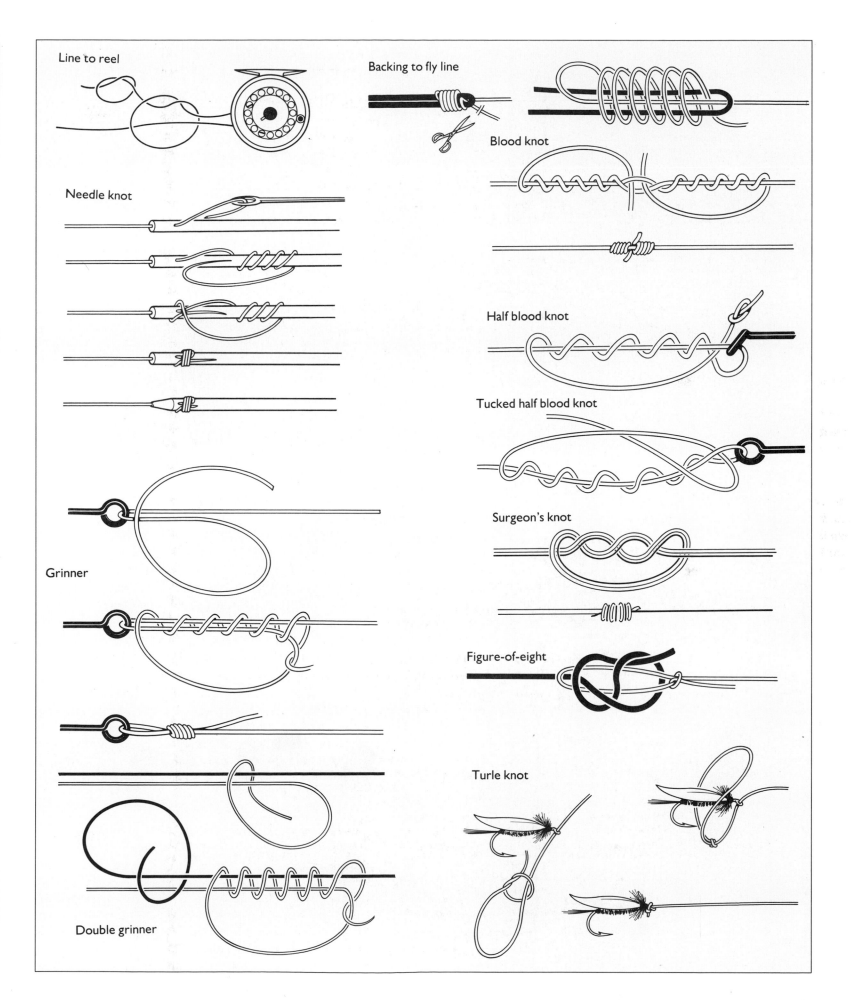

Line to reel

Backing to fly line

Blood knot

Needle knot

Half blood knot

Tucked half blood knot

Surgeon's knot

Grinner

Figure-of-eight

Turle knot

Double grinner

suggested thicknesses to correlate with the line weights. Bought leaders, which are usually tapered, have a loop already tied. If you choose to use a figure-of-eight knot, tied with the end of the fly line, you restrict yourself to using a leader shorter than the length of the rod, because the knot will not clear the rings – it will wind in easily enough, but may not run out. However, using a two-handed rod there will be little problem, as a leader is seldom needed that is much longer than 12 or 13 ft (3.5-4 m). This knot should not have an overhand tied in the running tail: it adds no security but creates a wake or more obstruction in the rings.

Convenience rather than theoretical advantage is important at this stage. A butt length of leader may be needle-knotted to the line and finish about 2 ft (0.5m) later in a loop. Bought or made-up leaders can then be looped straight on. This is the easiest system when your hands are too cold for difficult knots or there is little light to see to tie new knots.

The tapered leader may need a lighter tippet for the best presentation and this join must be as strong as possible. The strongest knots may not be as simple to tie as slightly weaker ones. A sound principle is that a well-tied, weaker knot is more likely to be secure than a badly formed 'strong' and complex knot.

On the whole, the knots designed for the gut which preceded nylon are best altered or avoided. There are also variations in the style and character of nylons which may demand extra turns or other variation.

Joining leader material

The blood knot, or double clinch knot, is one of the best known for joining lengths of leader material. It needs a minimum of five turns to each element and the tail ends should not be trimmed too short. Differences of diameter of over 10 percent are not recommended, though in case of necessity if there is a major difference the lesser-diameter link should be doubled

Playing a fish puts a strain on all parts of the tackle, and not least on the terminal knot that joins the fly to the leader.

before the knot is tied. This is a tricky knot if your fingers are cold or the light is poor: its turns must lie smoothly and be drawn tight with the usual application of saliva. One of the tail ends – usually the thicker – will make the link for a dropper.

A more modern knot, born in response to the technology of nylon, is known variously as the grinner, uniknot or Duncan. It, too, is quite complex to tie with cold fingers or in poor light, but it is strong and probably the best for normal game fishing. A dropper link will be streamlined if it comes from the downstream end of the knot, and will stand out more if run from the top. A disadvantage is the way the leader can be fouled by any weed or algae brought down by the stream. When there is a major difference in diameters the finer diameter may be doubled. A great deal of care is necessary to tighten the knot smoothly.

The surgeon's knot is the easiest to tie in difficult conditions, even if it is not as strong as the preceding knots. The choice of which end to use for the dropper is the same as that with the grinner, and the knot can pick up weed in the same way. If this knot is tied with care, it will accommodate some discrepancy in diameters.

Terminal knot

The terminal knot may be just an attachment, or it may have the duty of holding the fly or bait in line with the leader. The attachment point may be a ring in line with the shank, or may be up- or down-eyed. The ring-eye is best served by either of the following knots – the uniknot or the half-blood, also known as the clinch knot. The uniknot may be tied so that it is drawn up tight on itself, leaving a loop to the ring-eye, or that may be drawn up tight as well. There is no doubt, and it is usually recommended by the manufacturers, that the loose loop is a better form of attachment for plug baits like Rapalas. However, comprehensive testing is still to be done.

ACCESSORIES

The secondary items of tackle make fishing easier, more convenient and comfortable, or more safe. Even so, there is a limit to how much tackle a game fisher finds comfortable to carry when on the move.

The classic 'minimalist' has rod, reel, line, leader and fly all set up. In his pocket he has a spare tapered leader and a spool of tippet material. In his other pocket he has a selection of flies, a few larger, a few smaller, but concentrated in quantity on the most likely size for the conditions. His

self-imposed challenge is to catch fish without using a net, gaff or tailer. The minimalist probably knows his beat well, and its conditions, and is unlikely to regret not carrying something that might prove useful. Compare him to the trout fisher on a stream he does not know too well. The latter will carry boxes and boxes of flies – wets, nymphs and dries; mayflies, terrestrials and lures. He will need spools and spools of tippet material, and spare spools for his reel – intermediate, slow sink, fast sink, and so on. As the burden of his tackle increases he worries more about the choices he has to make. His fishing vest has at least 20 pockets; in one is the list and map of the contents of the other 19. He is more of a pack-animal than an angler.

The well-dressed fisher uses: neoprene waders for warmth in really cold weather, a hat and glasses to protect the head and eyes, boots to protect the ankles, a fishing vest without too many pockets so that he knows what is in which, and fly boxes so that flies wet from use do not soak unused ones, leading to rust and deterioration.

Fly boxes

A hat or a sheepskin patch is a bad location for flies or baits: they rust, or are brushed off, or fall out, so some sort of fly box or wallet is advisable, or a suitable box that will take spoons or plugs or other spinning bait. Some boxes are plastic and float if dropped; others are 'crafted' from anodized aluminum or other fancy materials. You choose according to cost and/or design if you buy them, or use boxes which fulfil the role even though that was not their original purpose.

For salmon flies I like the Wheatey aluminum boxes with clips for single and double hooks. For the flies on trebles I use a tobacco tin with foam lining, and similarly adapted boxes for spoons, plugs and so on. For smaller dry-fly patterns I prefer plastic compartmented boxes and, for the larger, tobacco tins with magnets let into the base or glued in. All these containers fit comfortably into a vest pocket, or a coat pocket, or a kangaroo pouch at the top of body waders. Further flies and baits are kept in a tackle bag or box and left in the automobile if brought at all. Fishing bags I prefer not to carry: the load is borne solely on the strap, as opposed to across the body if a vest is worn and its pockets are evenly loaded, and it can become submerged if you wade deeper than you had planned or noticed, soaking its contents. A bag, however, is a quieter form of storage in a boat, where keeping quiet is essential.

Nature provides us with some very practical dentition: the front corners of the mouth have just the right teeth to bite through nylon, should you lack any other cutting implement. But note that the essence of the bite is a lateral grinding motion, not a vicious vertical nip which could end in

The well-equipped fisher has a dry-fly box with separate compartments that do not crush the hackles. He has floating and sinking compounds for the fly and leader. Gink is a recommended brand, but the natural grease obtained by rubbing the fly on the side of the nose can be used instead to make the fly float. Xink and Leadersink can be replaced with saliva or clay from the river bed, although these are less effective. Clippers or scissors are better than the teeth for trimming leader material. Forceps are invaluable for removing both barbed and barbless hooks. The Orvis Zinger holds small accessories on a retractable string.

chipped teeth. This grinding motion, in a single or series of bites, will sever thick nylon. However, it is far better, as your dentist will no doubt advise, to use clippers, scissors or even a knife, kept on a string or a Zip spring retractor.

Nets, gaffs and tailers

Nets are personal things, and consequently some fishers are determined to prove that the smallest net is suitable for the biggest fish, while others are more pragmatic and take a net large enough to cope easily with all eventualities. I cannot take the former outlook seriously, but concede that a large net is a pain in heavily brushed countryside. In such circumstances I would prefer the battle to be one-to-one – me against the fish – and if it gets off because I was not carrying a net, then the fish won on that occasion.

Gaffs are efficient, but there is for some of us a moral objection about sinking a large hook into the shoulder or flank of a living creature that precludes their use. In the hands of an expert, a gaff is a quicker way of landing a fish than any other as it can reach deep into the water. A tailer is better carried and used by a guide or other companion. It is easy enough to carry 'unset,' but to have to set it while still playing a fish is troublesome, and if it springs before its noose envelops the fish there is the problem of resetting it. Handtailing a fish, beaching and tailing, or reaching for it across its gill covers, are all methods which do not need extra tackle and preserve the one-to-one struggle which for so many of us is part of the enjoyment. For more detailed information on landing fish, see pages 105-9.

Fish which are to be kept must be killed: small fish have weak enough 'necks' for the head to be snapped back, but larger ones need a sharp blow between the eyes or on the back of the head. A priest, kept on a string, saves you having to seek a suitable stick or stone, or a fence against which to strike the fish.

Protection for the eyes

Protecting the eyes may be secondary to the actual fishing, but it is vital. Glasses with polarizing lenses are advantageous as they cut some of the glare off the surface of the water and make visual location of fish easier. They are even more effective in this respect if the brim of the hat or cap is brought right down and the hands are cupped each side of the face. This concentrates the iris to exactly the light levels coming through the lenses, so sunglasses with wraparound sides have a real advantage, apart from providing a little extra protection. Ordinary sunglasses, or even plain-glass spectacles, are better than leaving the eyes exposed. Prescription ground polarizing lenses are the ultimate if you wear glasses, but they are expensive.

Other accessories

There are further items which the game fisher may choose to carry, although they are hardly essential. These include spare spools with different lines, a hook-hone, a carrying bag for the fish if they are to be kept rather than released, a thermometer to check water and air temperatures (to be recorded in a notebook before transcription to the fishing diary) or, when Atlantic salmon fishing, to check if the water is warm enough to need a floating line, binoculars or a monocular to examine insect life in detail at a distance, and floatant or submersant for leaders and flies. Substitutes for both these substances are readily available: the natural grease at the side of the nose is a fine floatant, and saliva helps a fly sink, although not as fast as

---

MEASURING SCALE

Some fisheries have a 'minimum length' regulation. Orvis produces a useful adhesive scale marked in inches which can be stuck to the rod, or you can make your own. Lay a ruler on a hard surface and, by pressing a pencil onto white typewriter correction paper, mark inch or centimeter divisions up to whatever maximum length you choose – say 30 in (75 cm). With care, lay over the markings a straight length of transparent Scotch tape. This will pick up the markings, and can then be pressed along your rod a few inches above the handle. This scale is neat, easy to use and removable, and saves carrying a retracting measure. Some anglers like to know a fish's precise weight and carry a spring balance. But you may have a moral objection to pushing its hook through the fish's gill cover, hazarding the gill filaments, before returning the fish to the water. If so, you may prefer to make easy computations of approximate weight based on a rough measurement of length. For example, for brown trout: 12 in (30 cm) = 12 oz (0.3 kg), 13½ in (34 cm) = 1 lb (0.5 kg), and so on.

proprietary products. Alternatively, you can use the butter or margarine from your sandwiches, or dishwashing liquid.

Finally, we fishers tend to like comfort, so we wear waders to keep ourselves dry and warm. An important advantage of being able to step into the water in waders is that you can feel any temperature changes, such as those caused by cold-water springs welling up from the river bed. Later in the season such places may be the fishing hot spots and so it is useful to be able to locate them with accuracy.

A victim of a dry fly is neatly brought over the rim of the waiting net. A large landing net with a long handle can be very unwieldy in heavily brushed country, but a small net, chosen purely for convenience, is unlikely to be big enough to handle the fish of a lifetime.

ACCESSORIES FOR LANDING A FISH

The expression 'landing a fish' implies that the fish is captured and safe to hand by means of netting, gaffing, beaching, tailing or another method. Logically it is a poor alternative to describing the fish as 'caught,' particularly if you are wading and do not come out of the water!

Netting

When you are planning to net a fish, one simple fact of fish physiology is worth bearing in mind: the fish performs very poorly in reverse. To draw a fish over a waiting net is likely to be a more efficient technique than any attempt to sweep up from behind it with the net. The fish can move forward, yet the net produces so much water resistance that it cannot be forced to follow quickly or responsively. Also, although a fish looks roughly symmetrical front to back, most of its weight is in the front half. If only half a fish can fit in the net it is better if it is this front half. Ideally, a net should have a rim with a diameter at least as wide as the length of the largest expectable fish, and the bag of the net should be deep enough to be closed off by turning it over. There is all the time in the world to wade to the bank, but a still fresh fish might kick its way out of a shallow bag by flexing its tail strongly.

A heavy fish can exert powerful leverage when a long-handled net is used. Reduce this effect by moving the hands down the handle while retaining a firm grip.

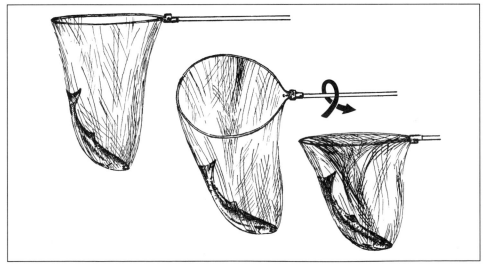

When the net is too small try to enclose the fish's head and shoulders, otherwise with one lusty kick it could be free.

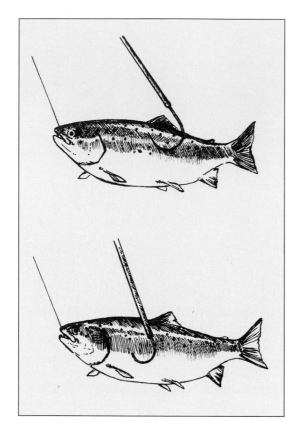

Where gaffing is allowed (and if you have no moral objection to it), it is done most safely as shown in the illustrations above. Avoid the technique shown below.

It can happen, when you are fishing a dropper, that two fish are on. Too shallow a net would make a difficult task almost impossible, that of netting the lower fish. This is a time to come from behind and then scoop up the higher fish to land on top of it. The net may then be turned over.

In a strong current the netting bag may drift around and obscure the rim, a situation avoided by putting a small stone or two into the bag. Any boatman, guide or gillie should wet the net (and weight it as necessary) well in advance of the time he will be expected to net the fish. The net should be in proven good working order. A fisher with any foresight will wet and weight the net as he starts down the pool. When fishing with a guide, there is no excuse for the net's not being of reasonable size and handle length. Certainly, if a boat is used, the handle should be long, whether it has a fixed shaft or is telescopic. The principles of netting remain the same however long the net shaft, but the lifting of a big fish should not be done until the netter's hands are taken off the handle and moved close to the rim. This is another good reason for having a deep bag which can be closed at the top, for there is no need to rush the shift of grip and the lifting of the fish.

A short rod is advantageous when you are bringing in your own fish, and many anglers find that they can net their fish without wading to the bank. Also, the first chances of netting the fish are offered more freely in deeper water, as fish shun shallows if they can.

With the fish safely in the turned-over bag of the net, the tension can be taken off the tackle: it may even be time to pay out line, perhaps to follow the guide who now has taken the fish to a safe place to put aside the rod and remove the fly. It is seldom during the playing of the fish that rods are broken, but in the few moments of landing and just after, particularly when rods are laid on the ground while the fish is dealt with, and then trodden on.

Gaffing

Gaffing is still practised in various parts of the world, and in Scandinavia it is considered the best way of landing their monster Atlantic salmon. The *kleppers,* as they are called, are extremely adept at gaffing the fish's head, leaving the body unmarked. Many people find the gaff entirely repugnant, and would not use it, or have it used for them, ever again, even in areas where it is allowed.

The skills of gaffing are seeing the opportunity, which may occur surprisingly early in the fight even though the fish will be swimming deep, and never tangling the gaff with the line. The usual style is to reach the gaff over the back of the fish, point down, and with a smooth draw pull the point in below the dorsal fin. The handle is shortened by reaching hand-over-hand down the shaft, drawing the fish out of the water. The poor creatures can kick a certain amount, so they must be grasped and killed as soon as possible. Sorry tales abound of fish coming off the gaff point and getting back into the water, mutilated, to their 'freedom'. Some people choose to gaff from underneath, but there is less tissue with which to hold the fish, and the flesh can tear.

There are good proprietary makes of gaff with telescopic shafts and suitable point protectors. When you are playing your own fish the two easiest ways to extend the sections are to hook the gaff round a small limb of a tree or stump and pull; or if no tree is available, the heel of the wader can be placed firmly enough on the hook part to afford a good pull. The handle end can make a good priest, but first close up the telescopic sections fully, otherwise the shaft may be bent and then the sections will slide even less easily than usual.

Landing by hand

Both the head and tail ends of some of the salmonids are suitable for hand landing. Starting with the head end, the two normal grips are insertion of the fingers *into* the gill cover openings and grasping *across* the gill covers. In the first method the parted index and next finger (palm away from the fish) can slip into the gill cavity and take a secure grasp. The fly or bait must be visible and clear of where the fingers will be. I am not sure what trauma this causes to a fish which is to be released. Any damage to the fish which makes it bleed is nearly always fatal and the fragile gill filaments may be damaged. Nor do I know what damage occurs if you reach over the back of the fish's head, in the second method, and press on the gill covers, thumb one side and just two fingers on the other, with the palm of the hand toward the fish's back. If the fish is to be kept the amount of pressure that can be exerted with this grip is impressive. The largest fish I have lifted in this way was a 14-pounder (6.5 kg). The elegance of this method is that the bulge of the head in front of the hand is a positive obstruction to the fish's falling out of the hand backward; the bulk of the body prevents the fish escaping forward, and the muscle blocks on the top of the backbone give the fingers something to hook round. My experience of this grip has been failure-free, yet it is hardly ever mentioned and very rarely in fishing books. It is a valuable grip in any depth of water, though the fish should be up at the surface.

I consider the grip I have described to be a better grasp than that round the tail. Tailing a salmon, the tail characteristics of which afford a grip – the trout's tail slides through the grasp – is more a grasp and a push to aid a beaching maneuver, rather than a bravura lift out of the water. If you do not take a confident enough grasp of the fish, it gives a kick and slides through your hand and gets away. Palm toward the back of the fish, or palm over the top tail lobe: both styles have their advocates. Both grips use thumb and opposing finger (or two fingers) with all the other fingers tightly fisted and cocked out of the way. Wrapping the hand in a handkerchief or wearing a glove should not be necessary, nor even covering your hand in sand, for it is a ridiculous notion that the fish has to be hoisted up into the air where it will weigh all its proper weight.

Tailing combined with beaching is rightly very satisfactory: since the fish's 'gearbox' has no reverse, any flapping pushes it forward. The object of tailing is to take a grasp and help propel the fish on over the shallow transition of water to land, with the fish's weight resting all the time on the wetted margins and then the bank. Tailing will help deal with the problem of the fish, which is nearly weightless in the water, suddenly becoming too awkward for the tension from the rod to continue to draw it on landward, once the full weight is felt as it comes onto dry land. Since no lifting is needed, it is an excellent method for all the salmonids.

The fish on the left above may be grasped early in the fight by a bold opportunist, but the technique is best when the fish is ready after being played. The fish on the right must be completely played out for the technique shown to have a fair chance of success.

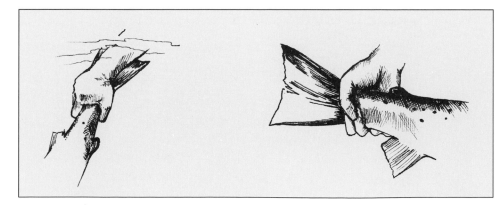

The weakness of landing a fish by the tail is that it can kick. The strongest possible grip around the wrist is needed but the tail should not be compressed.

Beaching

Beaching is most easily done when deep water graduates smoothly at a shallow angle to shallows and then dry land. The ideal material for the lake or river bed and bank is sand or fine shingle. The fish must be tired and not object to being led by rod pressure in the direction you wish. The pressure you put on it, and its own swimming and flapping actions take it safely from water to land, and then the hand is used to push it on to a position which is secure (if it is kept), or where it can be held steadily for the extraction of the hook before being returned.

A bank that looks unfavorable can be adapted: the removal of a few larger stones in very coarse shingle may make a little harbor into which to hurry a fish, or a firmly placed heel or couple of kicks may make a small channel in a mud bank that is too high. Both modifications are best made before you start to fish the pool, although they can be done easily enough while playing the fish when you are deciding where to bring it in.

Tailing

The tailer is a mechanical device of which the potential efficiency is largely outweighed by the frustration it causes. It is not recommended as an item of tackle if you are fishing alone: it is best used by an assistant. The typical tailer has a telescopic shaft down which runs a springy multi-strand wire of considerable thickness terminating in a far lighter and more flexible wire. At rest, the tailer is little trouble to carry; the frustration stems from having

Beaching a fish. In the first illustration the weightless fish is drawn on toward the shingle bank. In the second illustration the beached fish's swimming motion augments the pull of the angler, who positions himself so as to be able to grasp it as soon as possible.

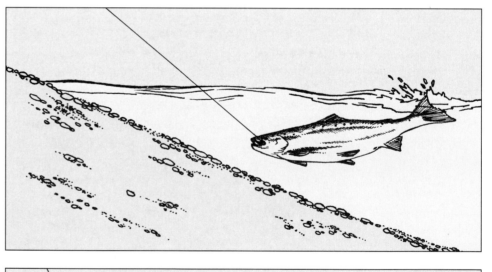

to set it: the telescope extension must be pulled out to its maximum, the wire extended until the shape is as in the diagram on the right. There is a little metal cage which is free to slide at the least provocation or even without any at all. The springiness of the metal loop speeds the cage very fast all the way round until it forms a noose on the fine terminal wire, trapping the fish round the 'wrist' of the tail.

Setting the tailer needs two hands, hands already occupied in playing a fish, and its tendency to 'go off' may mean it has to be reset before the fish is noosed. It is wise to thread your hand through the loop on the handle since it is quite easy to lose your grasp on the handle as the noose is firmly drawn tight, and then the fish goes off again – with the tailer attached.

I have used tailers enough to work them efficiently – enough to convince me I do not like them. They do have a role on 'no-gaff' rivers where big fish are expected, and where banks are so steep that beaching is difficult. The tailer is better operated in deepish water, for then the fish is normally calmer than when it is brought into shallows – though the fish should be at the surface.

Summary

It is easier to land the fish if you are upstream of it. If you are downstream of it and it suddenly stops its effort, directional control of the fish becomes more difficult – the current exerts constant pressure on a downstream fish. However, you must decide whether the current is *too* strong, so at the last moment you can work your way below the fish, and it will be swept down to you. In steady and slight currents, you should have enough control to dictate the path of the fish to your chosen landing method.

The gaff is the only instrument which allows you to take fish from deep water, but the skills of a real expert are needed for this. On all other occasions the fish should be at the surface.

Netting is easier over deeper water than shallow, because it allows the fish free passage over the rim, and the bag of the net is out of the way. Tackle can snag in the meshes, leaving the net caught and the fish free.

With hand landing there is no extension of reach, as with the handles of net, gaff and tailer, so the fish must be very close, and it could take a long time to tire it enough.

Beaching can be done on a long or short line – the longer the line the more give in the tackle, the shorter the line the less the elasticity; and there is an element of hurry in getting to the fish to secure it, so there is further to go if the fish is beached on a long line. If you beach by walking the fish up onto the bank, you will probably be watching the fish and unaware of the obstacles behind you. A bold angler, with a ready assistant, can beach a fish almost before the fish knows it is hooked if under initial pressure the fish turns in to the bank and the transition from water to dry land is an ideal gradient. This method is risky but extremely exciting, and the assistant's timing must be impeccable: to tail and push the fish straight on to safety however hard it flaps. It is a grand way of losing a fish if there is the least hitch or mistiming.

The tailer is better in deeper water. The noose must come up behind the fish without touching the tail before it can be snapped tight, so the fish must be steady and under control. The moment of opportunity must be a long one, rather than a brief instant to be seized.

The best method of landing a fish, but of course not always available, is a very large net in the hands of an able assistant. The next best method, where circumstances permit, is beaching.

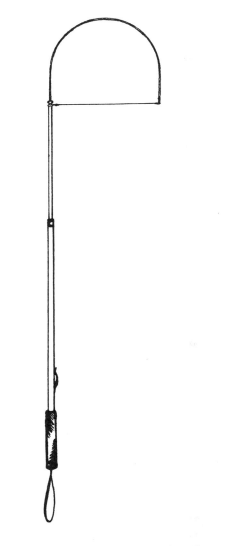

Most tailers have a telescopic handle into which the unset loop can be retracted.

FLY-CASTING

Playing and landing fish have already been discussed in the preceding chapter on tackle because they are so closely connected with the properties of rod, line, reel and leader (and landing accessories) and because fish can be caught on flies simply trailed in a stream or trolled behind a boat long before the angler, particularly a child, has learned to cast. However, the fly fisher vastly increases his opportunities by being able to do so. Furthermore, the casting and presentation of the fly are so involving that they form a large part of the pleasure of the sport.

Most of us experience bad patches in our casting, but watching the line carefully can help to identify the fault.

THE PRINCIPLES OF CASTING

This and the page opposite explain the principles that you need to understand before you can cast a fly successfully. This information is given in some detail on these introductory pages in order to avoid the need to repeat it for each of the casting sequences. It is important that you understand the theory before you move on to the practical sequences themselves.

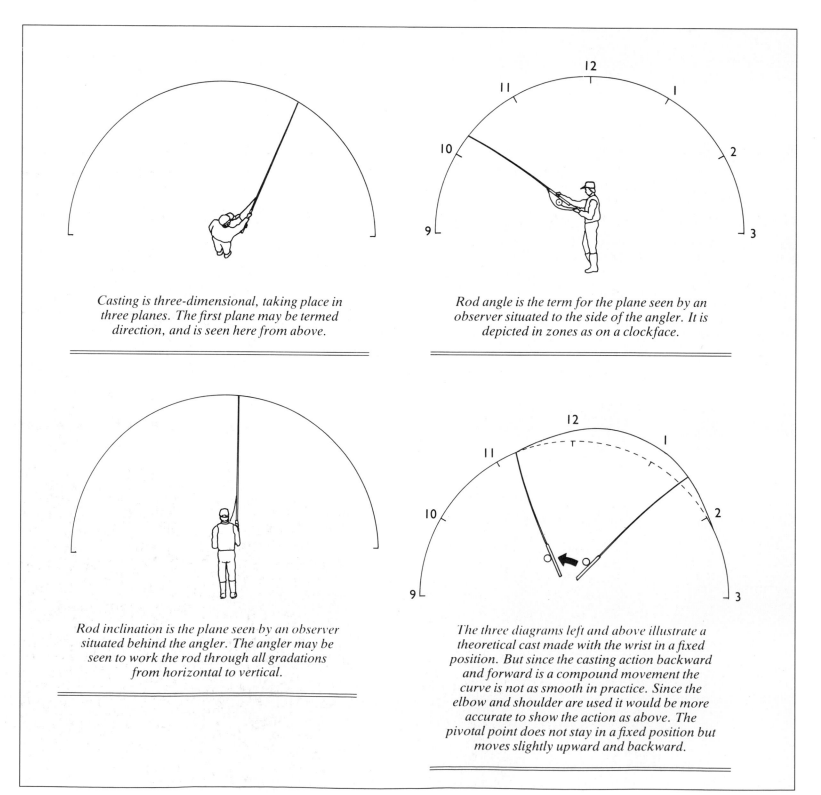

Casting is three-dimensional, taking place in three planes. The first plane may be termed direction, and is seen here from above.

Rod angle is the term for the plane seen by an observer situated to the side of the angler. It is depicted in zones as on a clockface.

Rod inclination is the plane seen by an observer situated behind the angler. The angler may be seen to work the rod through all gradations from horizontal to vertical.

The three diagrams left and above illustrate a theoretical cast made with the wrist in a fixed position. But since the casting action backward and forward is a compound movement the curve is not as smooth in practice. Since the elbow and shoulder are used it would be more accurate to show the action as above. The pivotal point does not stay in a fixed position but moves slightly upward and backward.

LEFT *Wrist movement alone will energize a rod sufficiently to cast a fly. But when it is combined with elbow movement the effort of casting become much less localized and greater distance can be achieved. By using the shoulder hinge as well, the rod's travel can be extended, allowing better positioning of the line, and spreading the effort of casting over as many muscle groups as possible. Wrist and elbow complement each other, the wrist adding precise and forceful acceleration to the impetus or direction already given by the forearm. The finish to any power stroke is the 'snap' from the wrist, especially on the forward casts.*

The extended forefinger stops free and comfortable articulation of the wrist. Movement of the wrist adds 'snap' to the rod's action and is normally part of the complex series of movements that constitute single-handed casting.

The classic thumb-near-the-top grip can deliver plenty of power and allows controlled articulation of the wrist.

Roll cast

There are two groups of casts: on-the-water casts and in-the-air casts. The variations within the groups allow for different fishing conditions, but in all casts the rod is used as a lever and a spring, and weight is provided by the line.

In all casting the caster must feel that the rod is really working, flexing. The best cast to learn first is the one which emphasizes this feel: the roll cast, the basis of all on-the-water casts.

The roll cast is the simplest of casts but it must be made on water. Practice on grass is ineffective since grass offers very little friction to the line, whereas water does, particularly in a current, and this friction is needed to make the rod flex. In this cast the rod is first used as an instrument to place the line where it is required, then there is a single application of power and the line 'rolls' forward.

The energy for this cast comes from the rod's flex: the forward thrash puts energy into the line close to the rod point which rolls on down the line until it is fully extended. For the beginner, the tackle with which to try this cast is a rod of 8–8½ ft (2.4–2.6 m) with a #6 or #7 floating line. The versatile double taper, or the triangle taper, is better for roll casting than the forward taper or shooting head.

Pay out about 30 ft (9 m) of line through the rings by pointing the rod tip at the water and waggling it so that the current draws the line away. Still facing downstream, grasp the rod handle firmly and let the upper arm hang down straight from the shoulder. The lower arm bends from the elbow so that it projects horizontally in front at 9:00. The closer the rod tip is to the water at the start of the cast, the more potential rod movement is available.

The rod tip is brought up to a position above and behind the caster. The line hangs from the rod tip only as far behind him as the rod is angled backward. The fly cannot go further back with this style of cast. To raise the rod to this position the elbow has bent and the hand has been raised to the level of the ear. The rod is angled back. When the rod was brought back and up it was inclined slightly to the right, but its path forward will be more vertical. Wide lateral separation between the backward and the forward path is not necessary, but some is recommended.

In response to a *powerful* forward thrash with the rod overhead, the line has to follow the rod tip, and with rolling energy it extends in the direction of the thrust.

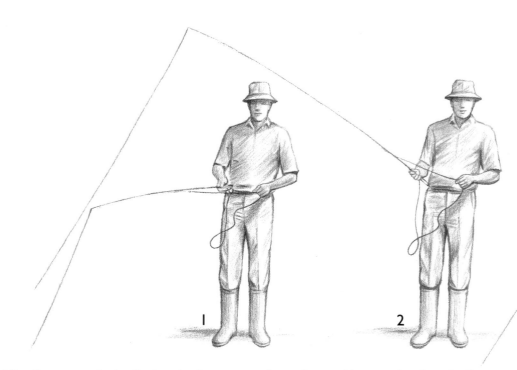

After the power stroke the hand relaxes back to a position a little higher than at the start of the cast, with the forearm parallel with the ground.

If the angler teaches himself to roll cast downstream the current will pull the line taut, so that there is a steady resistance from the line against which he powers the rod on the forward cast.

He can also easily learn the discipline of getting the line under control as soon as the cast has landed.

The line is held between the finger and thumb of the rod hand, to:
- stop the current drawing off more line than is required
- detect a strike by a fish
- add pressure to the line if it has to be wound back onto the reel, so that it lies evenly and smoothly on the spool
- act as one of the ways to brake a fish that is being played.
- act as a line guide while the other hand manipulates the line during the retrieve. This discipline is common to all casts – roll, overhead or any of the variations – and should become automatic.

The roll cast allows little variation of direction. By inclining the rod to the right as it is brought up to the casting position,

the angler avoids a tangle when the line goes forward. But if he wanted to place the fly further upstream the path of his forward cast would cross the line on the water, risking a tangle. So the roll cast can change direction only to the angler's left, not to his right. (See bottom diagram on page 117.)

The roll cast is not only one of the easiest to learn – it is also one of the neatest, as there is no back cast. Since the fly can never be more than about a foot (30 cm) behind the angler, he can fish with a cliff or dense vegetation right behind him. Whereas line speed equals weight in in-the-air casting, in the roll cast water resistance applies a similar load to the rod, so that respectable distances can be achieved, provided enough power is applied in the short arc between 1:00 and 11:00.

If the power *is* provided by the angler the rod really comes to life in his hand. He can feel the surge of its energy as it unrolls the line and in turn comes to rest, no longer flexed. That feeling he must store in his memory, for this is the sensation the rod will transmit on both the forward and back cast of the in-the-air casts, which are commonly referred to as overhead casts.

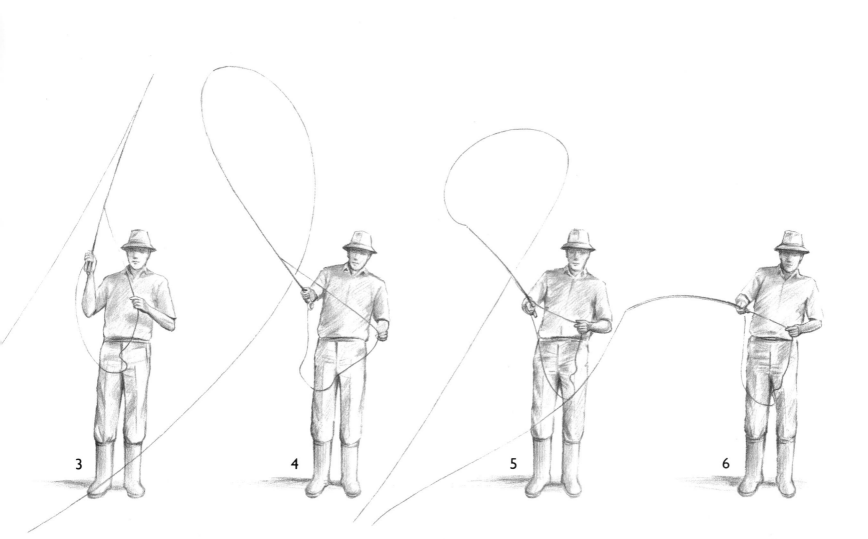

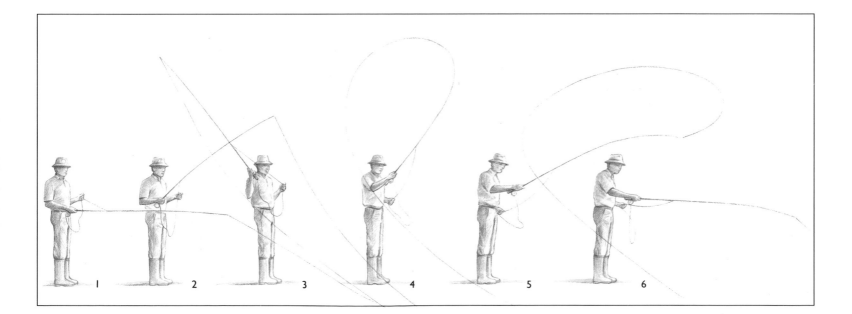

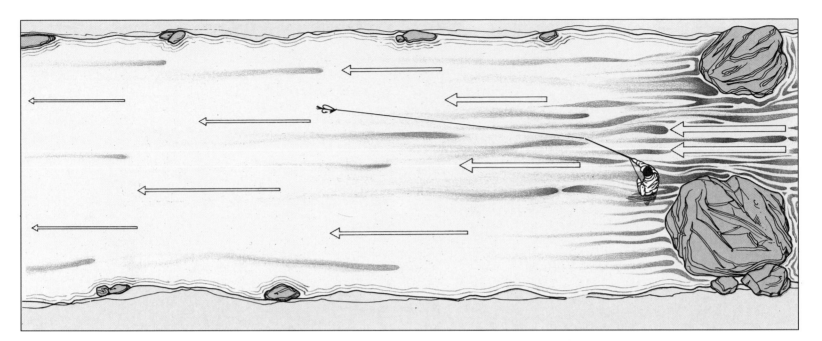

The advantage of learning to roll cast straight downstream is that the current pulls the line straight and the water resistance adds a little 'weight' to it.

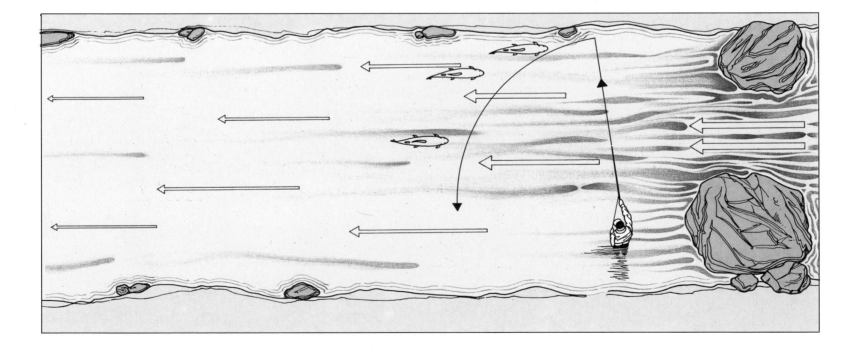

The splash on the left is where the line has been placed. The forward stroke, which is from a vertical plane at the shoulder, shows how in the roll cast the line does not tangle with itself.

When the roll cast has delivered the fly to the far bank and it has swung around, it is very difficult to roll cast again without the line tangling with itself. See pages 122–3 for the solution to this problem.

Overhead cast

The basic in-the-air cast is the simple overhead cast. This differs from the roll cast in that two power phases are necessary, and thus the roll cast has an attraction in that it calls for less energy. However, it is similar in that it is best practised on running water, casting directly downstream, since the current straightens the line and gives it 'weight.' The easiest line to start with is a floater.

The cast should always be a smooth, flowing action. There are no sudden surges of energy, only acceleration phases merging into power phases. In the pick-up phase the line is accelerated from the water until the rod reaches about 10:00, when the grip on the handle is tightened and the rod is given the power application learned in the roll cast, directing the line backward and slightly upward. The power zone is short, and as soon as the power is delivered the grip can be relaxed. The power stroke has made the rod flex, driving the line behind it.

In the illustrated sequence the rod starts low to allow the maximum upward movement. Since the power is in the arc between 10:30 and 12:15, the line is thrown upward at the back, which helps defeat gravity. The line must have time to extend at the back, but not so long that it loses its tautness. The rod has flexed backward and the caster can feel the line pull on the rod tip. It is now time to make the forward cast.

The grip is tightened and the arc of forward power is from 1:00 through 11:30. Then the grip is relaxed and the rod tip is allowed to drop down to a more peaceful angle through about 10:00.

All casting is aimed – by using, for example, a bubble on the water's surface, a floating leaf or a fleck of foam – and the forward delivery must be carefully judged to achieve exactly the distance wanted, with the minimum of wasted energy. The fly must be directed above the water because the forward cast must counter the pull of gravity, and the power phase to drive the fly forward must be strong enough to extend the line, leader and fly. Therefore the target is *above* the bubble, leaf or fleck of foam.

A length of line picked off the water is easily cast for practice. But this is restricting and not much use for fishing, because the angler needs to retrieve line by shortening it to make the fly work or to keep in touch with it as it floats downstream toward him. The line should be taut when it is picked up off the water

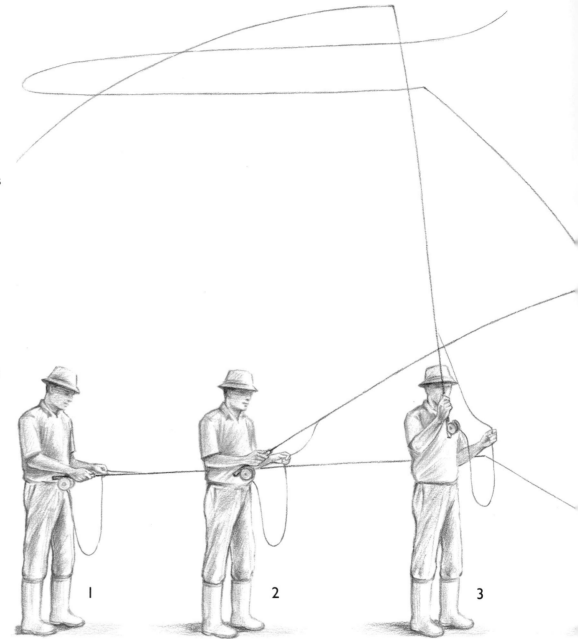

for the cast.

If the angler puts more power into the back cast than is necessary for the length of line in the air, he makes the line go faster, effectively giving it more 'weight.' If he also puts more power into the forward cast, he has the benefit of that 'weight' also, which is strong and fast enough to

pull along extra line behind it.

The release of the line occurs at the end of the forward power stroke, at the same time as the grip on the rod handle is relaxed. This technique is called 'shooting' line, and when he has learned it the caster is well on his way to mastering the art of overhead casting.

4

5

6

The point to aim at in the forward cast is
above the water since it is necessary to
counter the force of gravity.

Back cast

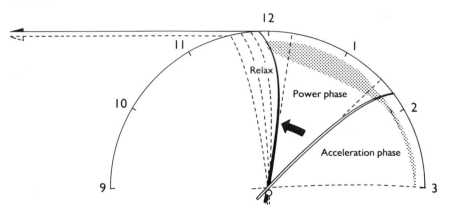

Forward cast

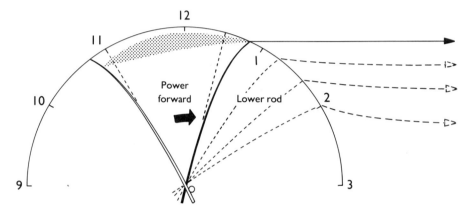

False cast

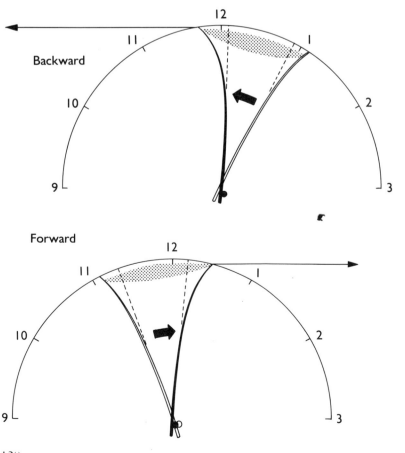

The illustrations on the right show the phases of the backward and forward cast in the overhead cast as performed by a right-handed caster.

Overhead casting is not usually as simple as pick-up, back cast, forward cast and delivery. To be able to extend enough line in the air, and to give it the required pace, it may be necessary to 'false cast.' There is a power stroke backward, followed by a power stroke forward, then backward, and so on until sufficient momentum has been gained and a final forward cast and delivery are made. The back cast, in the upper diagram, is the same as that already learned, and throws the line high and crisply. The forward cast, in the lower diagram, throws the line up and forward, with the rod tip remaining high, ready for another back cast.

A wide loop, top, creates more air resistance and is therefore less efficient than a narrow loop, above.

If the wrist, elbow and shoulder all articulate fully, the line's backward path will be slightly separated from its forward path.

Roll cast with a change of direction

In the preceding pages casting has been shown as being in one direction only, the back cast and the forward cast both being in line with the target. However, it is nearly always necessary to make a change of direction from the point which the fly reaches when it has to be picked off, so that it can be redirected at the target. This change of direction may be as much as a right angle, and sometimes even more.

We have seen that a roll cast will tangle with itself, so we amend the position of the line and the rod as we cast so that the line will be to the right of both the target and the rod for the forward cast. We introduce some positioning movements before we cast, and the more rod movement that is available the easier it is to place the line where we want it.

This cast is one of the most effortless and tangle-free styles, and can also be used in confined spaces where the overhead caster would find his back cast restricted. This on-the-water cast with a change of direction is also known as the Spey cast.

1 *The rod tip starts low.*

2 *To pick up line the rod tip is raised until the rod hand is level with the face.*

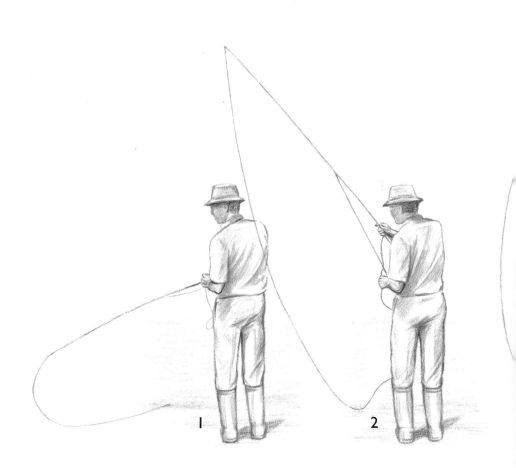

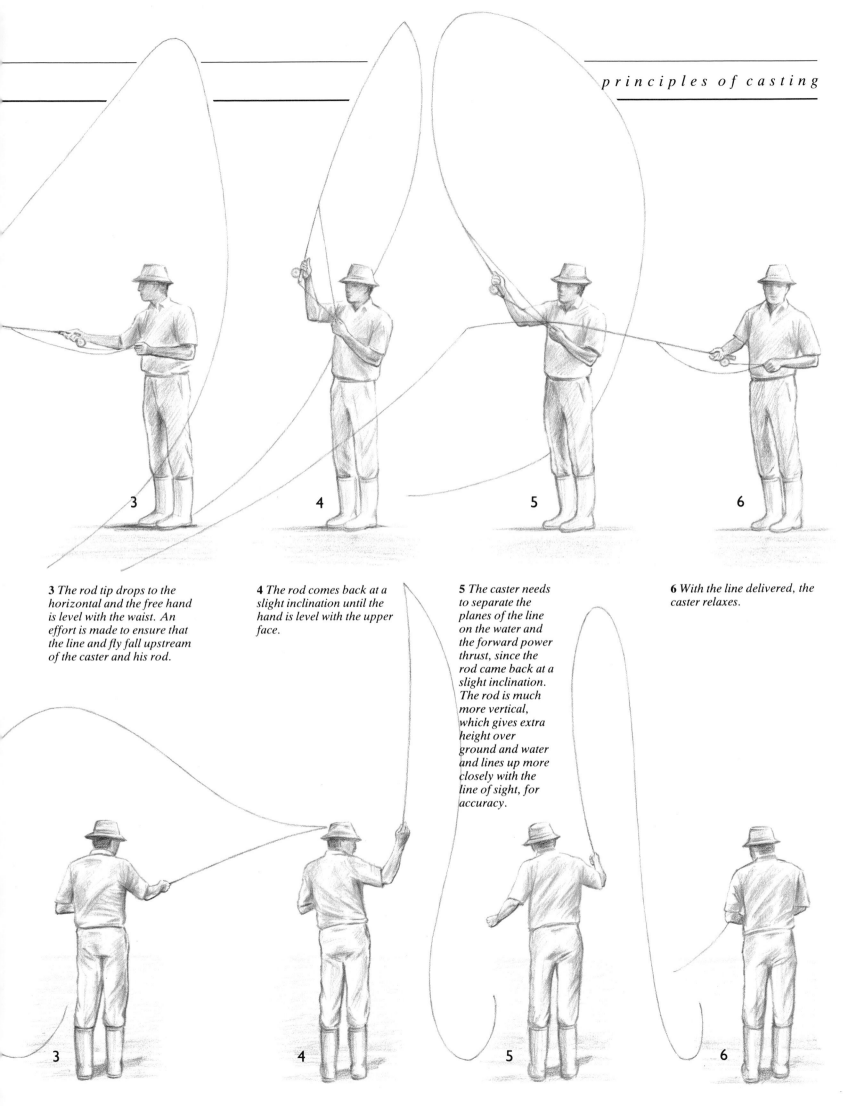

3 The rod tip drops to the horizontal and the free hand is level with the waist. An effort is made to ensure that the line and fly fall upstream of the caster and his rod.

4 The rod comes back at a slight inclination until the hand is level with the upper face.

5 The caster needs to separate the planes of the line on the water and the forward power thrust, since the rod came back at a slight inclination. The rod is much more vertical, which gives extra height over ground and water and lines up more closely with the line of sight, for accuracy.

6 With the line delivered, the caster relaxes.

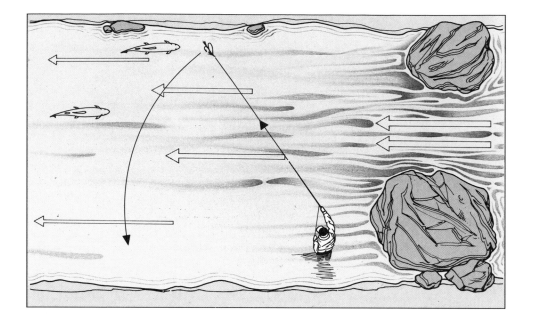

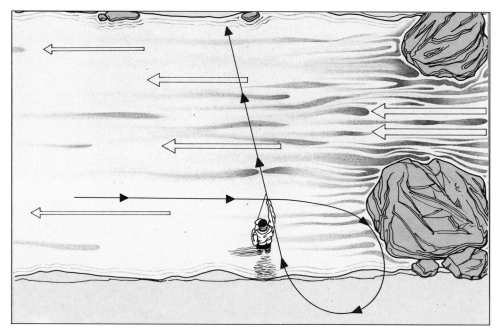

Change of direction in the overhead cast

Both accuracy and efficiency are badly affected if the overhead caster picks up his fly from straight downstream of him to cast it square across. The path of the line in the air will be very different from the direction in which he wishes the fly to travel. But by redirecting his rod on the pick-up – still keeping his line taut – he minimizes the wide discrepancy of direction. The path the line now follows is far more efficient, and when only a small change of direction is wanted, the procedure is: align the rod in the direction of the target and then pick and cast normally.

A compromise is often made in which the angler directs the pick-up halfway between the expiry of the cast and the target, picks the line off into a false cast and then realigns it in the direction of the target. This uses more effort – four power strokes – and so may not commend itself. It also presents the line near the target fish, risking scaring it, so there is a lot to be said for minimizing the number of false casts and always trying to keep them out of the fish's field of vision. As always, it proves necessary to find a compromise between the ideals of casting and the demands of fishing.

In the diagram top right the target fish is opposite the angler, but the current sweeps his fly round in an arc. In the diagram center right a pick-up from below him is very awkward, while in the diagram on the right the change of direction is even more extreme.

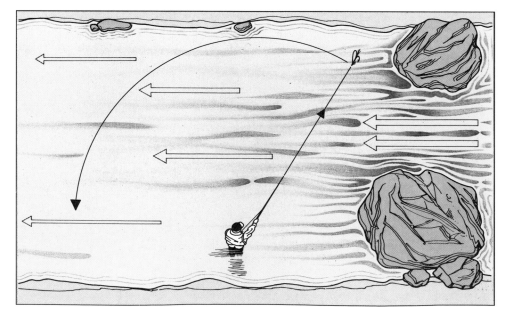

Side casting is the best solution when the backcast is made impractical by bankside vegetation.

Single haul and double haul

When you try to cast further the line encounters greater resistance, and the Charles Ritz concept of 'high speed/high line' starts to make sense. Tournament casting champions seek very fast line speeds. The average caster benefits from their approach, and the first thing he notices about it is how they use their line hand. This seems to have almost as much movement as their rod hand, its duty being not just to keep the line taut but actually to pull on it. This pulling or 'hauling' helps to impart high speed to the line as it extends in forward and backward casts from the rod tip. These movements are the single haul and the double haul.

Attendance at a casting class is recommended.

Single haul

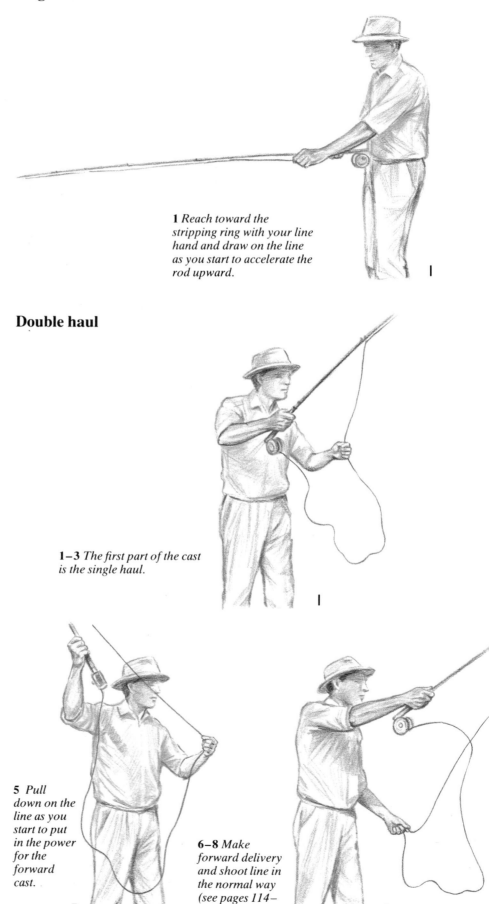

1 *Reach toward the stripping ring with your line hand and draw on the line as you start to accelerate the rod upward.*

Double haul

1–3 *The first part of the cast is the single haul.*

5 *Pull down on the line as you start to put in the power for the forward cast.*

6–8 *Make forward delivery and shoot line in the normal way (see pages 114–15).*

5

6

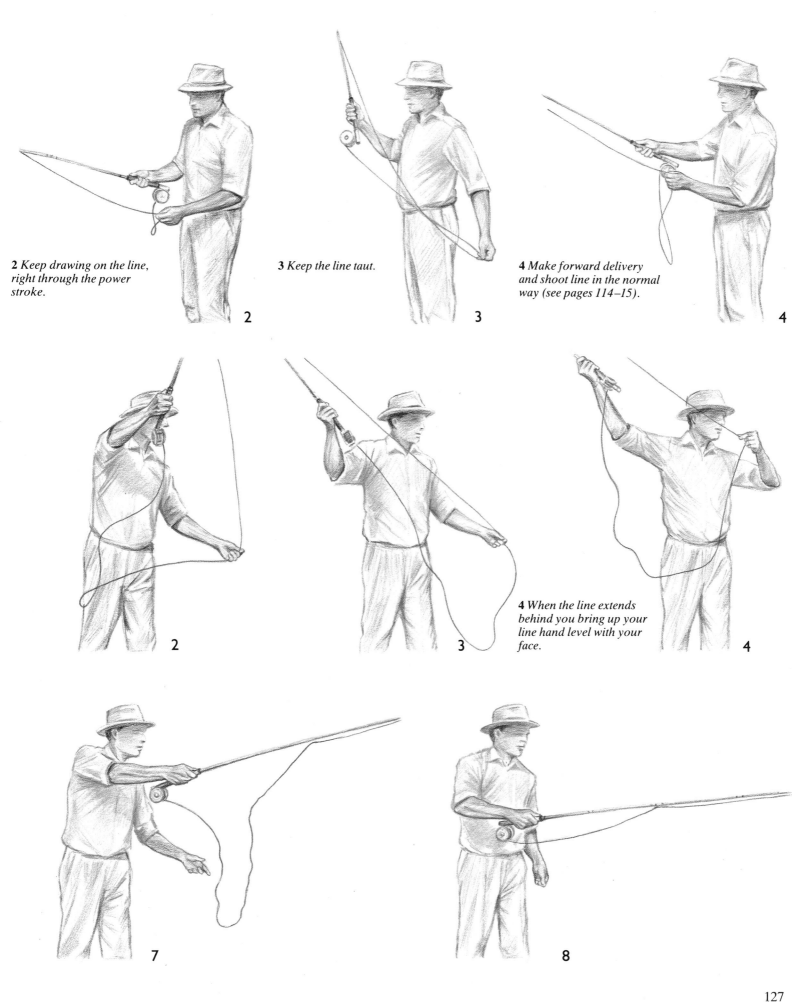

2 *Keep drawing on the line, right through the power stroke.*

2

3 *Keep the line taut.*

3

4 *Make forward delivery and shoot line in the normal way (see pages 114–15).*

4

2

3

4 *When the line extends behind you bring up your line hand level with your face.*

4

7

8

Two-handed overhead cast

The dynamics of the two-handed overhead cast are no different from those of the single-handed, but line speed cannot be increased by hauling since there is no free hand. Line speed nevertheless remains important: there is a limit to the length which can be picked off the water, aerialized and recast, so distance is always achieved by shooting line.

The upper hand introduces the power, the lower hand helps support the weight and restrains the movement of the bottom of the rod, for if this is not controlled the rod loses its springy quality and vastly increased effort by the caster is needed. The more widely separated the hands on the handle, the greater the control.

The path of the lower hand is from the side of the body just in front of the hip at about waist level, rising diagonally across the torso to reach its highest point at the expiry of the power stroke in the back cast. The lower hand is then level with the bottom of the right armpit. This position is held as the line extends behind, and the hand works its way back to its original position during the forward power stroke and delivery. The lower hand's forearm should remain in brushing contact with the body throughout the cast. If the lower hand strays forward during the power stroke of the back cast, it causes the rod to act solely as a lever, not as a lever and a spring.

The secret of two-handed casting is to cut to the minimum the energy put into the cast. Weight is transferred from the front foot to the back foot during the backward power stroke. Weight remains on the back foot as the line extends, and then the transfer to the front foot is synchronized with the forward power stroke.

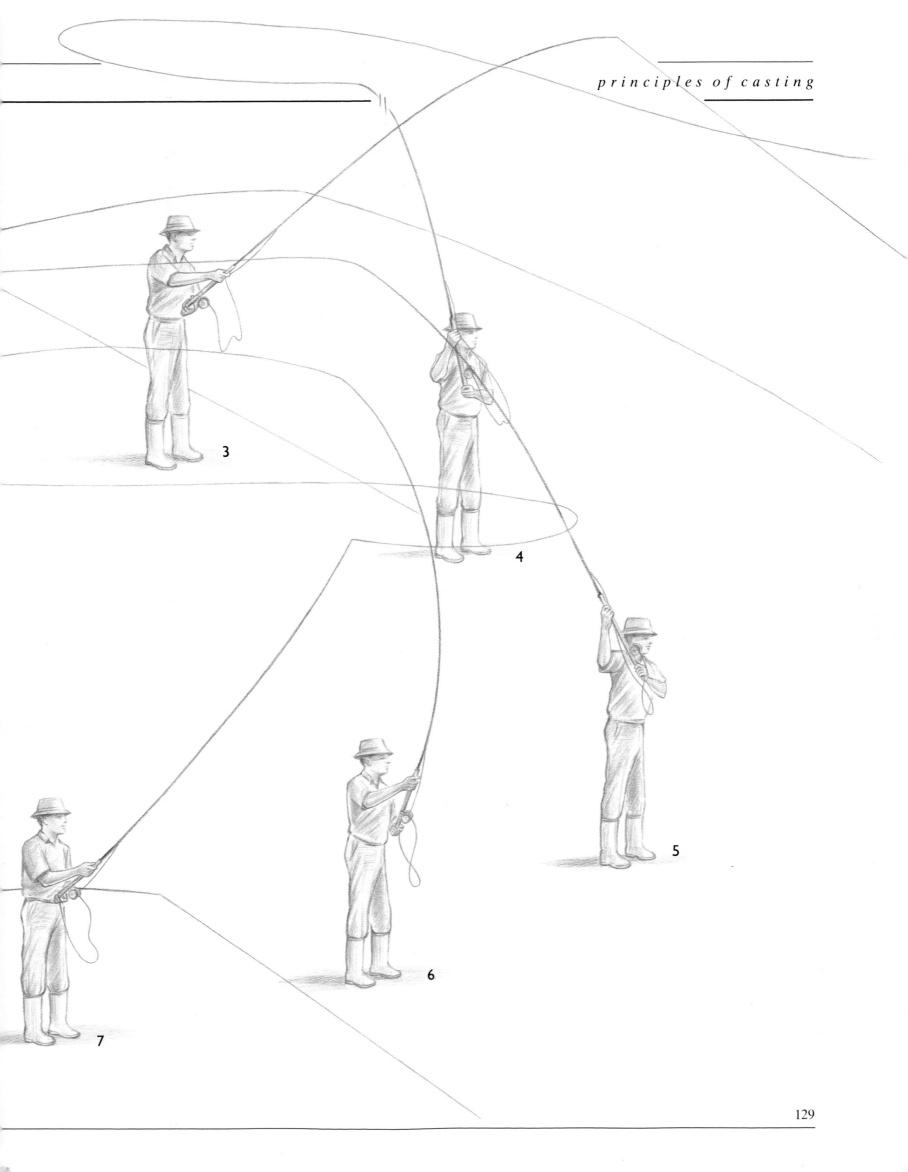

3

4

5

6

7

For two-handed casting either the closed stance or the open stance may be adopted. For the right-handed angler, in the closed stance, above, the right foot is forward and in the open stance the left foot is forward. There is some inclination of the rod in either stance, but an open stance allows a greater range of rod movement.

In two-handed casting there is more weight, more mass and more inertia, so the caster's weight transference is all the more important. The sequence of drawings on the right shows, from the front, the travel of the hands in the two-handed overhead cast.

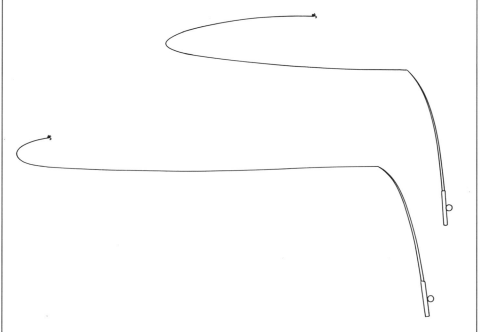

It takes more energy to redirect an inadequately extended line, above right, than it does a well-extended line, right. Much of the fatigue experienced by users of the two-handed rod comes from haste to start the forward cast.

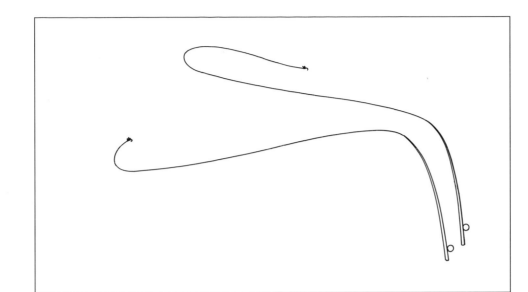

Since a long rod will always pick off a longer line than a short rod will (two-handers are 12–20 ft/4–6 m long), often a considerable length of line is in the air. This must be sent fast and high on the back cast, above left, because it must have time to extend, left, before the forward stroke. The caster's timing must take into account this delay and the fact that gravity is all the while pulling the line down. Delivering the back cast at an upward angle is therefore logical because by the time the forward power is being applied gravity has pulled the line down to horizontal or just below.

The grip on a two-handed rod should be very light; much lighter than on a single-hander. The lower hand merely traps the bottom of the rod to prevent it straying out of control. The upper hand feels pressure against the inside of the forefinger during the power arc of the back cast, and pressure is applied during the forward cast by the thumb. There is no need for a powerful grip, and a light one leaves the other fingers free to allow or check the line shoot.

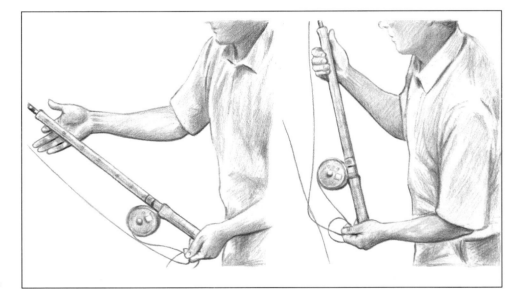

If the lower hand reaches forward during the forward cast and delivery, it is termed 'pushing.' This adds no power to the cast and indeed weakens it since the arms are much weaker at full extension of all the joints than when held close to the body. An analogy may be made with holding a sack of potatoes with outstretched arms or close in to the body. The former is impractical, the latter comfortable.

131

GENERAL OBSERVATIONS ON FLY-CASTING

It is possible to cast without a rod or with a rod as stiff as a broomstick, but it is much easier with balanced tackle, particularly when the rod and line have corresponding AFTMA numbers (see page 63). Enough has been said in the section on rods for the beginner to understand that a rod is more than just a lever.

The mechanics of casting
A simple analogy may be made between a rod's casting action and the performance of the pole used in the pole vault. The run-up gives some energy and then checking the foot of the pole transforms the pole into a lever. Since the pole bends under the force of being checked it adds its spring to the momentum produced by the run-up and to the leverage its length allows. Since the top of the pole wants to straighten out, it also drives past the point of straightness, continuing to give energy and to push. The perfect pole is designed precisely for the speed and weight of the athlete, just as the rod is for the line. The dynamics remain constant whether the caster is right-handed or left-handed. This chapter has been written and illustrated for the right-hander. There are considerable advantages for casting in being ambidextrous, but it is still generally easier to learn with the master hand and then transfer the skills to the other side.

Increasing speed
A fly line is the weight that makes the rod work, but this weight is carried along the line's length rather than compactly as in a spinning or bait-casting lure. The caster wants his line to have speed because increased speed means increased weight, which makes the rod work better and gives him the distance he requires. A comparison may be made with a rifle bullet which weighs 100 grains (6 gm) at rest but travelling at 2800 ft (855 m) per second has 1710 ft-lb (2545 kg/m) at 100 yards (90 m). Speed also counters the force of gravity, which is all the time trying to pull the fly line down to earth. Charles Ritz, the Swiss hotelier, also taught casting, calling his style 'high speed/high line,' and if this result can be achieved for a modest expenditure of effort the fly fisher achieves his desired distances and keeps the fly safely away from himself in all his in-the-air casting.

A fly rod will only pick up a limited length of line from the water. Floating lines are easier to pick up than sinking ones, which are progressively more difficult the faster their sink rate. Also, the shorter the rod the shorter the pick-up. Too long a line is therefore difficult to cast because the acceleration phase on the pick-up takes so long that there is not the time or the movement available to put in the proper power stroke. Consequently, the line does not travel fast enough or high enough to make a good back cast. This is why experts like Lee and Joan Wulff mark their fly lines (see page 71) so that they can see or feel the ideal length that they can easily pick up and power.

Length of line out
Ideally a longish line is picked up, and additional line shot through the rings on the forward delivery. However, in practice, retrieving the fly will have shortened the line too much and a false cast, shooting some line (before the delivery cast that shoots additional line) will be necessary. Having too long a line in the air is very hard work and good timing is needed to keep it fast and high enough. The line is clearly too long when the caster works ever harder for ever less appreciable effect.

There is much to be said for choosing as long a rod as will suit your purposes, rather than the shortest that will do so. Not only is casting easier, but also the line on the water is more easily controlled.

Stance
Stance is how the feet are placed. For right-handed anglers, the closed stance is with the right foot forward; the open stance is with the left foot forward. In the closed stance the rod hand is held comfortably in the line of sight. The right toe points at the target and the right shoulder is also slightly turned in that direction. This is the stance to learn on, for it gives the best chance of casting accuracy. If we imagine the closed stance diagram, above right, from the side, we see that this stance limits the amount the rod can travel backward. The angler's head is in the path of his rod and his shoulder joint is not flexible enough to allow much movement. If he tends to put in too long a power stroke on his back cast he will bruise his knuckles on his face. This is a useful stance to cure this bad habit and is valuable as the line of sight is 'through' the rod butt. The rod can be seen (and corrected) if it goes out of line with the eye and the target.

In the open stance, above, note the separation between the line of sight and the rod hand. However, there is a wider

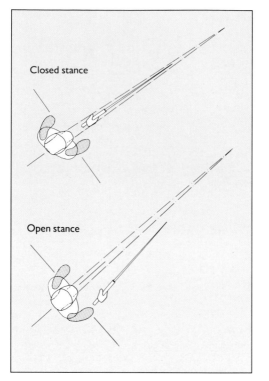

Closed stance

Open stance

range of movement than with the closed stance, and as soon as they have acquired some proficiency with the rod most anglers adopt the open stance. The wider movement comes from: greater articulation of elbow and shoulder; rotation of the body – slightly sideways for the back cast and swinging the right shoulder forward on the forward cast; and weight transfer is more emphatic over a wider movement. It is important to give yourself as much room as possible to develop the power needed. However, since there are more movements to coordinate than in the closed stance, with the result that mistiming is more likely, the open stance is not the one with which to begin learning to cast.

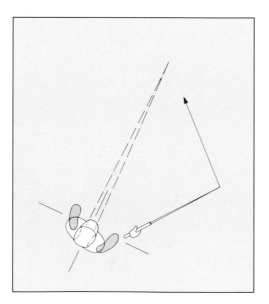

Weight transfer

In discussions of casting, weight transfer is seldom considered in depth. For the beginner it helps establish an understanding of timing. The sequence is: the front foot pushes the ground to transfer the weight onto the back foot as power is applied to send the line backward. Weight remains on the back foot as the line extends on the back cast, and the back foot then pushes the weight forward again during the forward power stroke.

In total comfort the body has tilted slightly forward of center and slightly backward of center. This body movement has imparted extra movement to the rod, which is beneficial in loading it and making it flex, and in delivering power. In its way it helps timing.

Not every stance permits weight transfer from foot to foot but it may be possible to make some body movement when seated in a boat or kneeling, and this will add a little power to the hand, arm and shoulder action.

When a two-handed rod is used weight transfer is even more important as the rod and line masses are very much greater. Wherever possible the 'front-back-front-straighten-up' sequence should occur.

Change of direction

If all casting were simply a matter of directing the fly at a target and then casting and recasting to the same target, choosing a stance would be easy. However, usually there is the need for a considerable change of direction, so that what is comfortable and relaxed at one stage in fishing later develops into an unnatural twisted and strained position.

The direction in which the angler should face is a compromise, an average position between the extremes so that a simple small twist of the torso to his right is comfortable, and then he can reverse the rotation past the straight-ahead position, to his left, as the fly swings round downstream. In the roll cast with a major change of direction this is particularly important since the angler will need to turn upstream to see where he is placing the

The compromise, for extra comfort, has lost some of the benefit of weight transfer from front to back to front again.

line in preparation for the forward power stroke. His most comfortable stance will be with his torso square to his target and his feet also pointing in that direction.

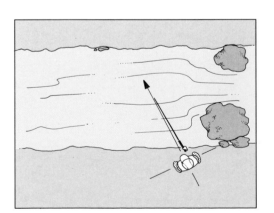

By adopting an 'average' stance the angler can turn comfortably from left to right.

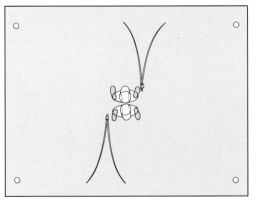

A horizontal cast seen from above. See where the angles are: parallel to the ground, wrong timing will cause loss of direction; power applied too soon on the back cast will return the fly to the left of the target; power too late, to the right. Using targets for the horizontal forehand cast and the backhand cast, practice false casting

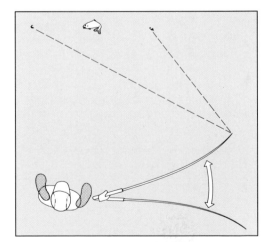

to make the fly do what you want it to. There is no need for the fly to land, so you can practise anywhere with enough room for a short line. This exercise teaches you to deliver the fly accurately on both the forward and backward casts.

Backhand casts

There is no reason not to adopt any inclination of the rod if you choose. For example, a horizontal inclination to put a back cast beneath overhanging vegetation, or to keep the fly as far as possible from you in a strong wind, and so on. However, you may have to increase line speed to counter gravity, and accuracy is more difficult to achieve when the plane of the line directed at the target is widely separated from the plane of the line of sight.

It is to some extent possible to cast horizontally with a roll cast, although the essence of the roll cast is the unrolling energy of the line and this is difficult to achieve with a backward lift and a forward thrust in nearly the same plane, parallel to the ground. Extra inclination away from vertical keeps the fly further away from the caster and so this may form a useful part of the repertoire despite some loss of efficiency.

Power and direction come from movement of the elbow, and flex and control from the wrist. The shoulder joint has no duties. Note that the palm of the hand faces the target in the forehand horizontal cast, and the back of the hand in the backhand cast.

COMMON CASTING PROBLEMS

A defective power stroke in the back cast can be analyzed in various ways:

1 An imprecise power phase, and one which continues past 12:00 or 1:00. This is caused by a long arm movement with no conscious division between the power phase and the relaxation phase, or by the wrist 'breaking' (bending over weakly) at the end of the power phase.

2 A precise power phase but too late in the clockface.

3 A power stroke put in too early. This makes the line project nearly vertically on the back cast, allowing little chance of a satisfactory forward cast. The rod has no travel available that will project the line *forward* rather than *downward*. When intentional this cast is called the steeple cast and it has the advantage that the high back cast may clear obstructive vegetation or a cliff behind the caster. The forward cast must be a conscious scoop upward, to try to transfer a downward force forward.

4 The power phase of the cast may be excellent but if the line is allowed to extend for too long a time gravity pulls it down and tautness in the line is then lost.

5 Another fault is to start the forward power stroke before the line has extended enough behind the caster. However, an advantage is that since the line does not reach very far behind, it may avoid vegetation or another obstruction.

No cast, even a false cast, should ever be made without a target, but as we have seen earlier, the fly must be aimed at a point above where it is to alight. How much above, depends on the wind direction. A wind from behind will make the fly straighten out and fall delicately from a relatively high target point. A head wind demands a faster line and presentation and less compensatory height above the water, otherwise the fly will be blown off course. In the roll cast and the roll cast with a change of direction the rod must deliver the powered line at an upward angle – not downward or horizontally.

'Pushing' has already been described on page 131. It causes the cast to lose all 'snap' and finish, but the habit is very easily detected: the angler ends the day with an aching back. All his casts end with his leaning forward, arms extended and back convex. It is difficult to cast efficiently with a convex back and the most comfortable posture calls for a concave back. This casting fault occurs among users of both single-handed and two-handed rods.

What has gone wrong?
Sometimes you feel you are not casting correctly when your fly fails to extend and reach the desired distance. It may not be a casting fault. A heavy fly on light tackle will not cast as easily as a light fly, and the line needs to extend longer on the back cast, so gravity has more time to pull the line down, and line speed is also lost. Do not expect to cast so easily in such a situation.

Using a floating line in a strong contrary wind can prove frustrating because the air resistance is so great. The line inevitably has a large diameter for its density, so that it is difficult to drive against the wind. With a single-handed rod you can speed the line by hauling, but this is not possible with a two-hander. Again, this is not a casting fault. Changing the line to a slicker-finished, smaller-diameter Intermediate may bring better results since the line will move faster and have less wind resistance, while fishing the fly at a not very different depth.

Wind knots can be very frustrating. Using the roll cast (with or without a change of direction) largely avoids the risk of them, and also demands less effort since it has only one major power stroke. This style of casting should not be thought of as specialized and of limited use. It should be a freely adopted alternative to the overhead cast.

Chapter

4

CATCHING

GAME FISH

What a splendid arrangement: fish experience hunger and so are vulnerable on account of their need to feed. 'A fish only needs one cast: the cast which catches it.' The skilled fly-fisher might indeed with one cast take his fish, having identified the food form or what might attract it and having presented the fly at such a depth and pace that its unnatural aspects were overlooked because of all the properties which made it appear natural. Yet, if we could cast well enough, gauge distance in all weathers, identify the food form and find the perfect level and pace it to such a degree of perfection each time, we would cease to fish. In reality, part of the mosaic of our skills will be a tile less than perfect and when the fish is caught it is not after one but many casts. Just occasionally the fish acts out of character, losing its selectivity and discretion, its fear and its self-possession, and going crazy – then the fisher is the amazed beneficiary. But this jackpot may in fact be the reward for years of homework, for better fishers have consistently better catches than bad or inexperienced ones, though luck can keep a beginner's appetite whetted.

Fish on! – playing a fish from the bank in Montana. The fish took, the angler tightened the hook and, with the rod well up, uses a combination of strength and delicacy to play the fish to submission.

There are times when the river seems dead: not a fin astir, not an insect hatching. The expert studies the flow, the eddies, the accelerated currents, the sluggish boils, and wonders how his line and leader will behave on them from this vantage point, or even from over there. It is barely a conscious thought, this weighing up of possibilities, but when the first flies struggle off the water, not only is the angler ready for them, he is also observant enough to spot the fish starting to move, and can gauge from their lies the size of the fish likely to be rising there. The homework which makes fishing look easy is like the perspiration said to be the major portion of genius.

LOCATING FISH

We need to find our fish without scaring them, and if they are feeding, identify the food they are most likely to be feeding on and then present our imitation of it as naturally as possible. If they are migratory, we need to put our lure before them in the most attractive way, to convince them to take it. We have the mechanical skills, and we know the properties of the tackle; it is now a matter of knowing when and how to apply this knowledge.

First of all, it is important to realize that if you can see fish they can probably see you. To walk to the exact spot where you expect to *catch* a fish, and then to peer in, is a poor tactic. Start with a wide overview of the river or lake at a vantage point which is not directly in the line of sight of the fish or where they can associate you with danger. Hearing may be as valuable as sight, so you lose the advantages of one of your senses if you choose to watch from the nearest and noisiest white water, when you could be watching and listening near placid pools. Equip yourself with polarizing sunglasses, which help cut the glare, and binoculars (or a monocular) if you like to see detail at a far range. The first place to seek fish is out of the water, for some migratory fish betray themselves and the school with which they are running by leaping clear of the water. A flash of silver, an almost subliminal flicker, may catch the eye at a distance at which surface disturbance cannot be spotted.

Surface disturbance
Surface indications of fish take many forms: (a) the 'porpoising' head and tail of running fish; (b) just the back arching up through the surface – another sign of running migratory fish; (c) various kinds of direct feeding from the surface, normally called rising (the splash of running fish is often described as rising, though they are not coming to the surface to feed); (d) nymphing movements, which are waves or ripples or surface breaks at the surface, though the fish is taking subsurface food forms like nymphs and larvae. Also, migratory fish may hump and swirl as they shift in or compete for lies; (e) the departure wakes left by fish which you have frightened. (There is more about scared fish on page 144, but (e) can be used to advantage, although you will have to wait for the fish to recover enough courage to return to its taking lie and start feeding again (if it is a resident-type feeder) or respond again to a lure (if it is migratory).

Subsurface indicators
Below the surface you may spot a fish by: (a) an abnormal flicker of light that departs from the usual rhythm of the water and weed flow; (b) obvious

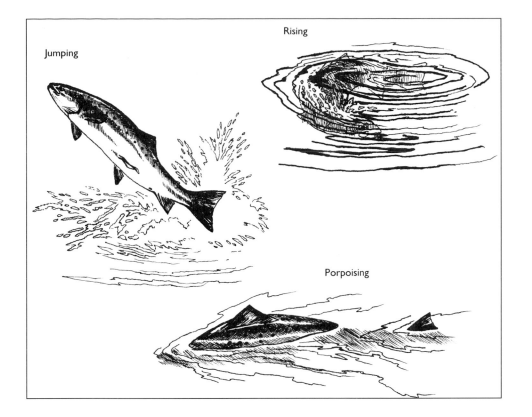

Jumping

Rising

Porpoising

Telltale signs of fish: a fish jumps clear out of the water; a school of migratory fish betray their presence by porpoising or head-and-tailing as they enter the pool; and a brown trout produces concentric rings as it rises to an insect on the surface.

movement which, on closer observation, turns out to be a fish; (c) luminosity – animate objects of some size seem to emanate a warmth of color, a hint of translucency, which inanimate objects do not. Again, suspicion is confirmed by closer, and often long, observation – it is often a hunch based on experience; (d) translucency – when light passes through a fin or tail, giving a color tone that is at variance with its surroundings; (e) in strong sunlight the shadow of the fish may show more strongly than the countershaded fish, particularly in shallow water. It is disconcerting to find the fish is all but invisible, apart from this tell-tale sign and the white line of its opening mouth as it inhales water to pass over its gills. This is particularly a feature of Atlantic salmon in stained waters.

Other ways to find fish
Not all water has a calm enough surface to permit the fisher to see far into it. His own experience of the species will help him choose likely spots to fish, and on an unfamiliar river he should be able to rely on his guide's knowledge. He will use his eyes and ears to detect the splash of a jump or the sipping as a trout nips insects from the surface, as well as relying on his own or 'borrowed' experience. If not much is happening, it might be because he is too early or late for a hatch. Examination of the surface (binoculars are again useful) and the use of a small fly net for taking a sample of what is coming down in or on the water may give him a clue as to which flies will hatch. Whether these are inhabitants of well-oxygenated water or live in the quieter flows of the pools, the use of a fly net is a worthwhile habit to acquire, and the big names have written about it – Vincent Marinaro and Charles Brooks among them – and it has a long history on the other side of the Atlantic. With some knowledge of entomology (see pages 12-18), and the evidence gathered by the fly net, it might be possible to predict what hatch there will be and where it will take place. If no insect even approaching maturity is enmeshed, it could be that subsurface fishing will be the most productive method. Then the sense of

feel will come into play, for you will need all your sensitivity to detect takes, and tighten on them. Don't forget that you are fishing 'blind' when you fish deep: the action will probably be too far away, the water impenetrable to sight. But careful searching of the water by fishing will find the fish.

Finding fish in rivers

A few basic principles:

1   Fish face upstream so as to be able to breathe with ease and the current brings food to them, on the surface or below the surface.
2   A fish uses the least energy required to obtain food with maximum ease.
3   Smaller fish are less conscious of squandering energy, compensating for this by having a different metabolic system: they eat more, proportionately, and use the food they gather more efficiently.
4   Large fish tend to have a much tighter feeding zone than small ones.

Exceptions to these principles are as follows:

1   There may be eddies and back currents, in which case fish will still head into the current, but will face downstream or at other variance to the main flow.
2   Big fish may forsake deep, safe lies at night and roam shallows for large food items.
3   Some fish cruise, feeding in a much enlarged zone.

In cold water, fish choose slower water as feeding lies, since at lower temperatures their metabolism slows down. In warmer weather, with higher water temperatures, they favor currents carrying more free oxygen, and have wider feeding zones. When it is very hot they seek the coolest water and expend as little energy as possible, adopting restricted feeding zones.

Finding fish in stillwaters

The basic principles are :

1   In large stillwaters good lies and territories are less specifically established, whereas areas of smaller stillwaters may be jealously guarded and the regular haunts of good fish.
2   The fish have to swim to find the food: it is not swept to them while holding a relatively static lie.
3   There is a wide range of depth at which they might be feeding. Only surface indications are visible to the angler, but serious feeding can take place from a few inches below the surface to right down on the lake bed.

Exceptions to these principles:

1   There may also be highly localized hot spots on account of a combination of food, shelter, depth and water temperature.
2   Inflow and outflow streams will give a stillwater the equivalent of a river current. The wind also gives the surface a directional drift, and fish spend some time working upwind, before dropping back and working upwind again.
3   The depth at which fish feed is largely controlled by light and temperature: they have to adapt to the pattern set by the food pyramid, going where the food is to be found.

There may also be marked seasonal changes and migrations: for example, as spawning time approaches, fish congregate toward the selected areas, for feeding becomes less important at this time. The places where the inflow streams debouch will attract fish, before they start to run the streams to spawn.

The Neversink River, much written about by Edward Ringwood Hewitt, the founding father of American nymph fishing.

The Yellowstone River, home of browns, rainbows and wild cutthroats. This is a well-documented water in the first and perhaps the best known National Park, which receives more than 2¹/₂ million visitors a year, many of them to fish.

AVOIDING SCARING FISH

Locating fish is a skill that comes with experience, but it is equally important to learn how to avoid scaring them. A frightened fish is rarely a taking fish, though occasionally a persistent threat may change the fish from fearful to aggressive, so that it turns on the plug or bait which is destroying its peace of mind. Enough records exist of Atlantic salmon hounded with plugs or spoons eventually taking the bait, to confirm this exception to the rule. There is also a wider effect: a scared fish will subtly transmit fear to otherwise unfrightened fish. By turning and fleeing it will directly spook other fish which previously were unaware of any danger.

Downstream and upstream approaches

The fisher working downstream brings himself gradually into the vision of the upward/upstream-facing fish. His threefold hope is that his presence does not cause fright, and to this end he keeps a low profile and makes his movements as steady as possible; that the fish which do not like his presence will move aside without infecting other fish with fear; and that the pangs of hunger or the attractiveness of the imitation food item or lure which he is offering will overcome the fish's instinct for self-preservation. A trout tends to move away if it is ill at ease, while migratory fish may just settle a little closer to the river bed. If a fish makes no major physical adjustment, it may nevertheless make a total mental adjustment: to refuse to take.

The fisher working upstream benefits from not being as directly in the fish's vision as his downstream counterpart, but he has the problem of locating resting, lying or non-taking fish in the line between him and his target fish. They themselves will become frightened and spread their fear by working up the pool which is yet to be fished. One solution is to catch the intervening fish and release them to hide where they will not cause trouble, or to disquiet them enough so that they move off without being really frightened.

The downstream-casting fisher's fly will have searched for the fish before any tackle, or the fisher, approaches it. The upstream-casting fisher always faces the risk of his line or leader being seen before the fly.

The hooked fish and the lost fish

Sometimes the fisher is able to avoid scaring the fish he has hooked. So slight is the restraint and so well hidden is the fisher that the fish finds itself drifting over an outstretched net without even feeling the hook in its mouth. The pool in which it is caught remains undisturbed. It is not just the ability to play a fish which marks out an experienced angler, but also his overall awareness of how he can keep pristine the areas he is yet to fish. Hustling or 'aquaplaning' a fish downstream suits the upstream-casting fisher, while convincing a fish to head into the current to fight upstream of him, suits the downstream-casting fisher. If the fish has to go up and down the pool, it is better if it is the antics of the fish alone which scare the other fish, rather than that such antics be combined with an over-evident fisher. The novice makes sure of the fish he is playing as a priority and will only then, if at all, worry about the disturbance. The more experienced fisher plans from the start not to disturb the water, yet does not lose his interest in his fish – a more mature emphasis.

It is rare indeed for a fish that is lost after hooking or simply rising to return to feeding shortly after it has regained its liberty. Even just touching the fish on the strike can put him down for the rest of the day. Tightening technique is discussed on page 153, and an understanding of the problems of setting the hook may save you from losing fish in this way.

RATIONALE OF FLIES

To give an overview of the scope of fly-fishing, the diagram below shows the broad types of flies and the ways in which they can be used. Deceiver flies are those which by intention and design represent some natural food form. Attractor flies are those which should stimulate curiosity, predation or aggression in the fish – enough for it to strike. The information applies to both rivers and stillwaters.

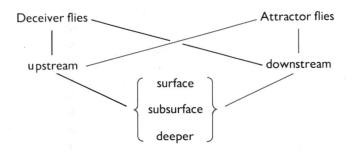

The chart on the left shows the general applications of attractors and deceivers. Attractors are not just sunk lures.

In the simplest terms, a good fly is one which catches fish. To do this it must have certain broadly defined characteristics in addition to being a practical hooking device. These are as tabulated on pages 146-150, regardless of the individual pattern of the fly.

An Atlantic salmon taken on a tube fly. Bright colors are used for fresh-run migratory fish. The tube fly's size is determined by how cold and fast the water runs.

145

Dry fly:

it floats
it lands lightly (if needed to)
it has the right size;
        shape
        color
        translucency
        texture
        posture

First row: Black Humpy, Alder, Light Cahill

Second row: Pale Evening Dun, Brown Tentwing Caddis

Third row: Dark Hendrickson, Letort Cricket, Green Drake

Fourth row: Bivisible, Black Ant

Fifth row: Gold-Ribbed Hare's Ear, Inchworm, Polywing Spinner, Red Quill

Wet fly:

it has/can be given the right movement
it has the right 'footprint'
it sinks (weight can be designed in)
it has a good 'entry'
it does not spin
it has the right size
        shape
        color
        translucency
        texture
        posture

First row: Black Gnat, Dark Hendrickson, Light Hendrickson, Grizzly King

Second row: Picket Pin, Hornberg, Silver Doctor

Third row: Adams, Leadwing Coachman, Red Quill, Queen of the Waters

Fourth row: California Coachman, Parmachene Belle, Royal Coachman

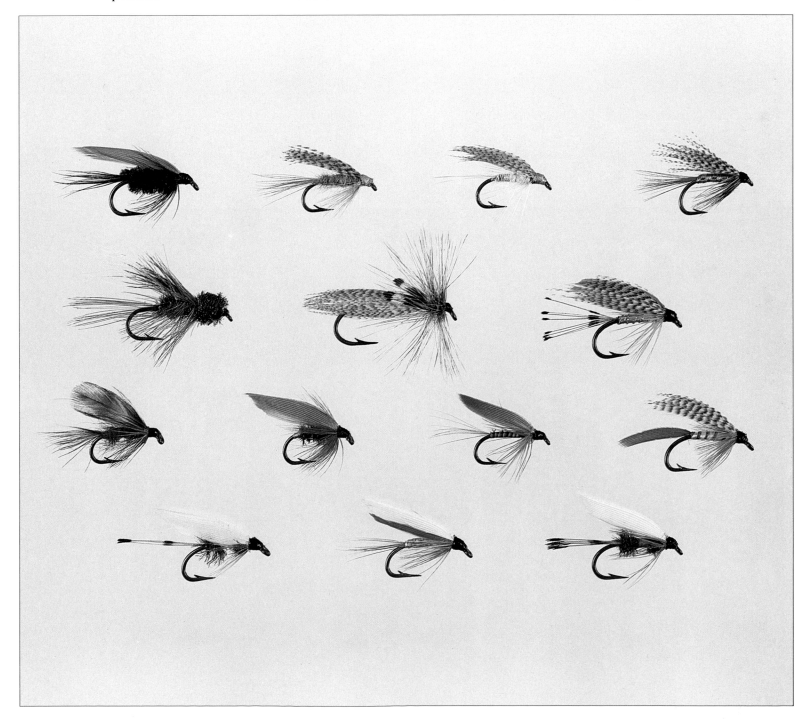

Nymph/larva:

it has/can be given the right movement
it sinks (weight can be designed in)
it floats (if needed to)
it has the right size
        shape
        color
        translucency
        texture

First row: Tellico, Casual Dress, Otter

Second row: Olive Emerger Nymph, Dark Brown Sedge Pupa

Third row: Zug Bug, Prince, Orange Sedge Pupa

Fourth row: Light Cahill, Mosquito Pupa

Fifth row: Ted's Stone Fly, Perla, Montana

Sixth row: Hare's Ear Nymph, Early Brown Stonefly Nymph, Orvis All-Purpose Light Nymph

Seventh row: Black Nymph, Damselfly Nymph, Orvis All-Purpose Dark Nymph

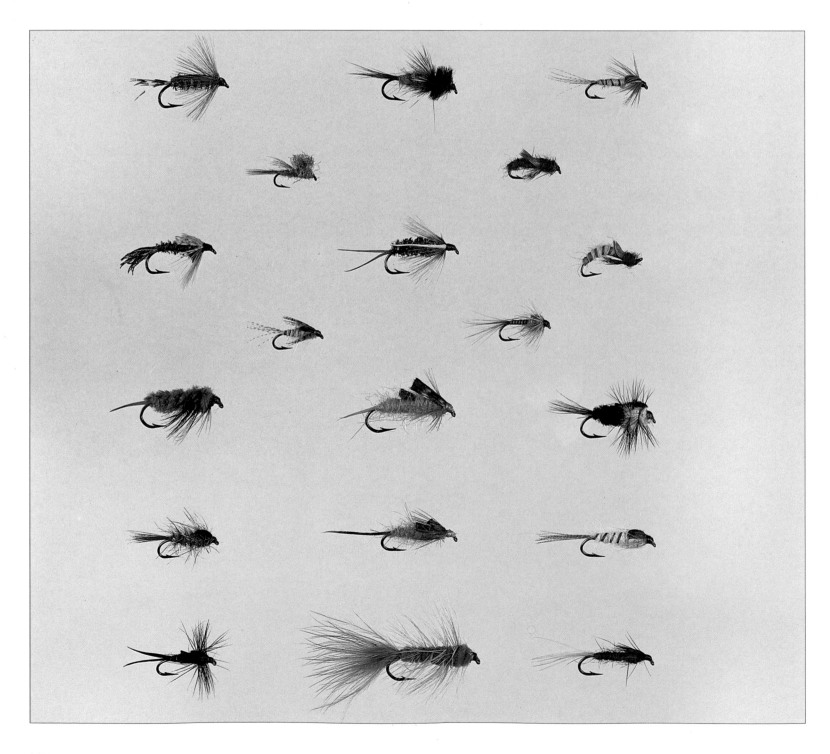

Bucktail/streamer:

it has the right posture
it sinks (weight incorporated)
it floats (if so designed)
it has the right size
       shape
       color
       translucency
       texture
       posture
it has/can be given the right movement
the dressing should not wind round the hook bend

First row: Black Matuka, Olive Matuka

Second row: Thundercreek Shiner

Third row: Orange Hairwing Muddler, White Marabou Muddler

Fourth row: Yellow Marabou Lure

Fifth row: Golden Darter, Silver Darter

Sixth row: Light Spruce

Seventh row: Black Nose Dace, Black Ghost

Eighth row: Zonker

Atlantic salmon flies

First row:　Garry Dog, Black & Yellow Waddington, Hairwing Dusty Miller

Second row:　Hairy Mary, Thunder & Lightning, Akroyd

Third row:　Silver Doctor, Black Maria, Silver Blue

Fourth row:　Shrimp Fly, Blue Charm, Hairwing Thunder & Lightning

Fifth row:　Willie Gunn (tube fly)

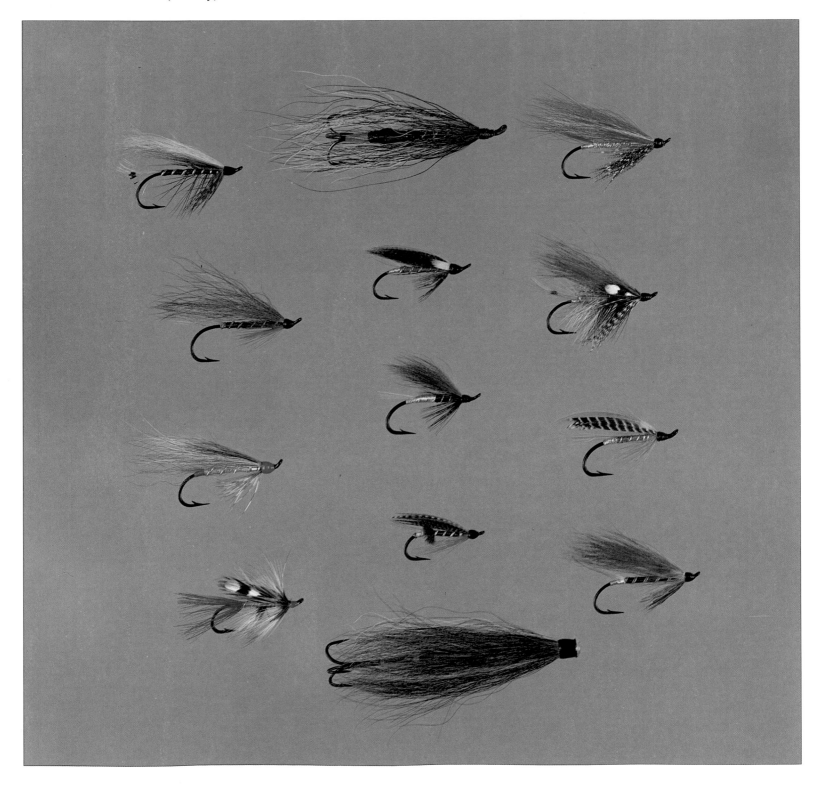

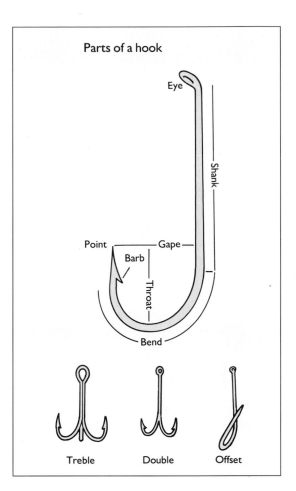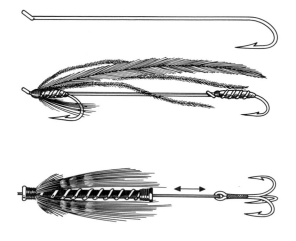

HOOKS

To be a practical hooking device, a hook must take a hold and that hold must be secure. A hook must be strong enough and of a suitable weight for its application. Hooks vary in:

- size
- shank length
- weight of wire
- style of eye (or no eye)
- color of finish: black
  bronze
  silver
  gold
  blued

- bend shape
- having a barb or no barb
- having a point in the same plane as the shank or offset
- having a cross-section of wire
- being single, double or treble

There is little we can do to disguise the bend and gape of the hook. Too much fly dressing round it masks its efficiency, yet unsupported by dressing it is an unbalancing and unnatural appendage. The fish must be sufficiently blinded by the other deceits/attractions of the fly to disregard the exposed portion of the hook.

There is some advantage in choosing down-eye hooks if tying the pattern is made easier: or in choosing an up-eye on smaller hooks because a down-eye would mask the gape.

Characteristics of hooks

Many compromises are available, and indeed inevitable, when you are choosing a hook: between strength and fineness of wire, shape of the wire and bend, ease of tying dressings onto it, the shank length, the presence or absence of a barb, and so on. Most manufacturers do their best to provide wide ranges from which we can select those we consider the most suitable.

Within the range of standard patterns it is usual to use light wire hooks for dry flies and heavier hooks for wet flies. Increasing the hook weight within practical limits saves having to tie in extra weight for deeper-sinking patterns. Some insects have long bodies, and for these it is best to use a long-shank hook, or build a body that extends beyond the standard hook shank. Egg patterns demand a short shank, wide gape and gold or silver hooks. Bucktails and streamers pose a problem: they mostly imitate small fish and so may be 4 in (10 cm) in length or even longer. A very long shank puts exceptional leverage on the hookhold in the fish's jaw, so an articulated basis for the tying is superior and may also be easier to cast, being lighter.

Non-standard hooks are designed to fish upside down – for use with specialist dry flies, or, with a longer shank and stouter wire, to fish well sunk – yet not catch up on snags or aquatic vegetation. A further advantage is that fished point upward they have a better chance of getting a hold in a vulnerable part of a fish's jaw.

Points should be short and sharp, and stay sharp. Barbs should be cut near the point of the hook and no deeper than is necessary to hold the fish securely. The temper of the wire should be a balance between being too soft, and thus straightening out under pressure, and being too hard, and cracking under pressure. Some hooks are also 'forged': the wire section is flattened round the bend to give extra strength. Those who fish brackish or salt water use stainless hooks.

Lee Wulff recommends tube flies. The body can be as long as required and yet remains soft, while the hooking properties are excellent.

THE STRIKE OR RISE

It does not take much effort by the fisher to set the hook. Often the fish's strike is sufficient and by the time you sense the fish has taken, it is well enough hooked. The migratory fish, particularly Atlantic salmon, when presented with a wet, downstream-quartering fly (see page 154) do not eject a fly or bait which 'feels' wrong as fast as the resident feeding fish, but the angler's usual response is to bring the rod up into a fighting arch.

Insect feeders may have taken and be gone by the time you are beginning to be aware of their interest. You will have to tighten at any flick or sharp movement detected underwater, say at your nymph, and take up the slack and tighten as a nose comes up for your dry fly. On the whole, bigger fish are more leisurely and it is indeed possible to tighten too fast: before their jaws are closed or they have tried to take the fly or bait into their mouths. In dry-fly fishing, the fly must be watched: in wet-fly or nymph fishing the

The fish is downstream of the angler: a vertical strike or even upstream (to his right) will give him less chance of hooking his fish than if he strikes to his left. However . . .

. . . since this angler is downstream of his fish the likelihood is reduced of his pulling the hook out of its mouth when he strikes.

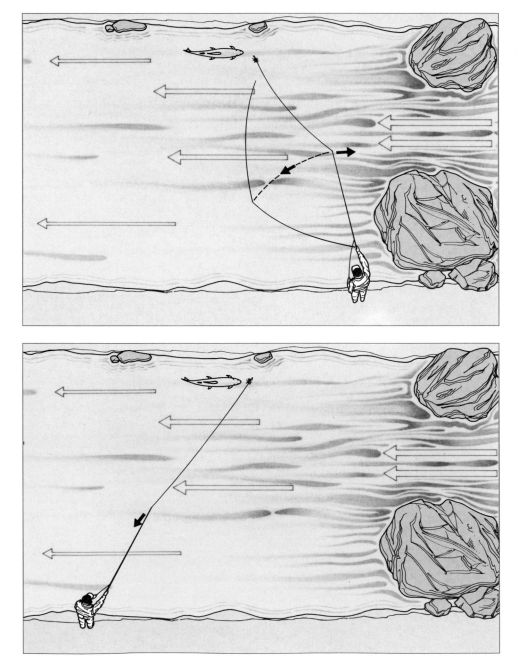

general area of the fly is known so it is a matter of watching for movement toward it.

Tightening on a fish to get a good hookhold is more efficient on upstream than on downstream casts, as the tendency when fishing upstream is to pull the fly into the fish's mouth, while downstream it may be pulled out. If a very long line is cast, reaction time down the line and leader is slower than on a short line. In theory you should be as close as possible for this increases your control over the casting, the presentation, the tightening and then the playing of the fish. But since you also need to be as far from the fish as possible so as not to scare it, a compromise must be found.

Nearly to hand. The hookhold is least secure as the fight draws to a close; a worrying time if the take was tentative and the presentation downstream.

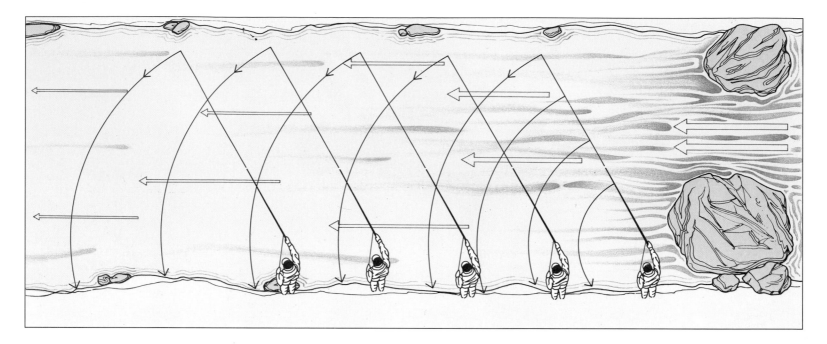

The usual down-and-across-river style of presentation of a wet fly, nymph or lure, a technique known as quartering. Each time the fisher starts in on a pool or stretch he casts progressively longer lengths of line until his regular working distance is achieved. Then he works downstream, taking a couple of paces between casts.

PRESENTATION

The way the fly is put before the fish, from the moment it touches the water, is the art of presentation. The first principle is that you must always have a target, even if you are searching the water without a specific fish or specific lie in mind. Using a target – a leaf, a bubble of foam, the edge of an eddy – keeps concentration at the necessary pitch and ensures that no part of the water is overlooked. The next consideration is the way the fly lands on the water. The tournament champion may throw the furthest, fastest line, falling ruler-straight, but he will find he catches fewer fish than the apparent bungler whose line as it drifts out is slack, with subtle curves in both line and leader. The latter angler has intentionally given slack, so that his fly can travel at the pace he wants for the occasion.

My dry fly for trout, I want to float at the pace of the water on which it is resting. My wet fly for Atlantic salmon, I want to start fishing across the river at a precise angle from the time it touches the water, otherwise I am sacrificing to inefficiency part of the length I have cast. The requirements are widely different. The following section illustrates the wide variety of methods of presentation.

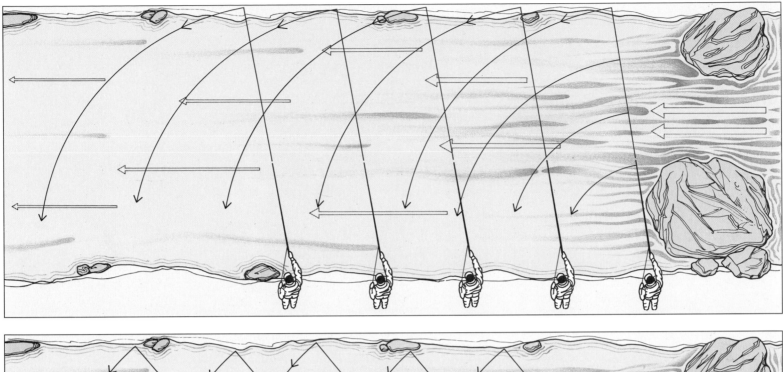

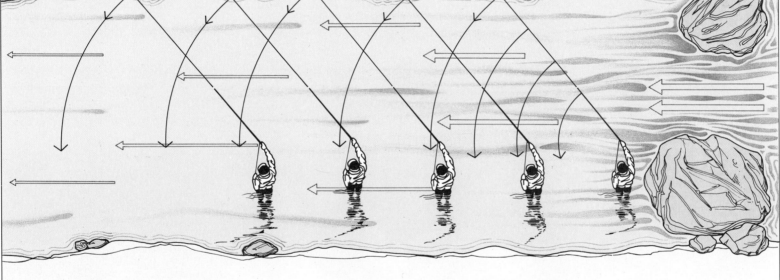

ABOVE   *Wading gives the angler more control over his line and fly near the far bank.*

TOP   *The same principle is followed as in the illustration opposite, but to avoid intimidating the fish that are close in, the angler adopts a position farther back from the water's edge.*

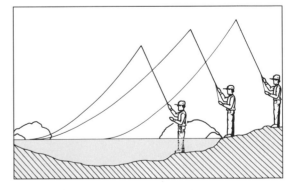

Bear in mind that usually you have the choice of wading, fishing at the very edge of the river, or fishing well back. Each can have its benefits, depending on the circumstances.

155

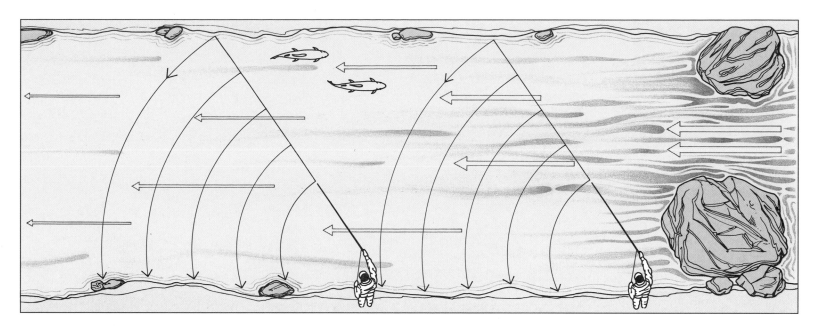

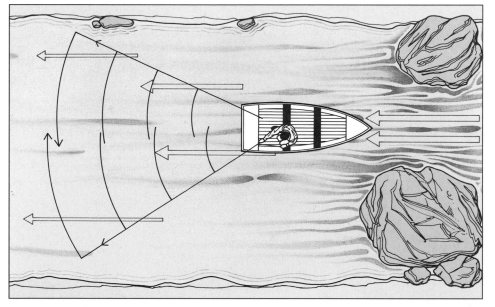

The combination of steady progress and accurate casting leaves only a little water unfished. Even so, these fish would have little chance to see the fly.

More thorough coverage is gained by using the pattern above, but having the boat moved downstream to a new controlled position for working-length casts, and then moved again. The rope tied at an angle from the bows makes the boat maintain its position in the current.

A 'drop' in a boat. The water is covered thoroughly toward each bank and downstream, and then the boat is repositioned to repeat the process. However, as in the case of the bank angler below left, some of the water is never fished.

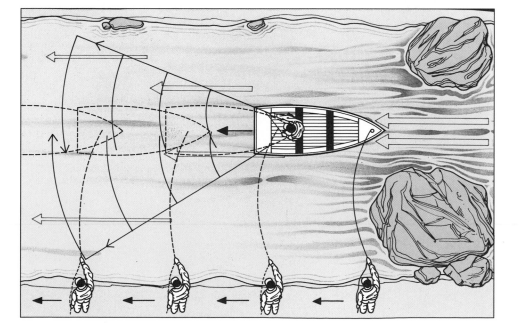

Casting for brown trout and daytime-feeding sea trout.

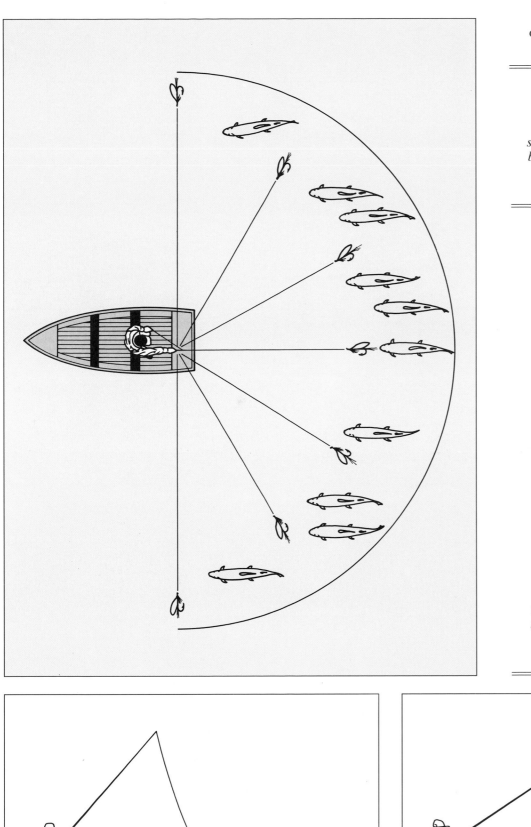

OPPOSITE *A salmon angler takes a shore break after a morning's hectic sport.*

LEFT *This diagram is more theoretical than practical, but it demonstrates that a fly presented to either side of a boat and swinging round below it, has the chance of being seen by many more fish than will see it if the angler presents it immediately below him.*

BELOW *On a stillwater a short rod limits the length of line that can be worked back in the very surface film. A longer rod holds up the fly and line much better.*

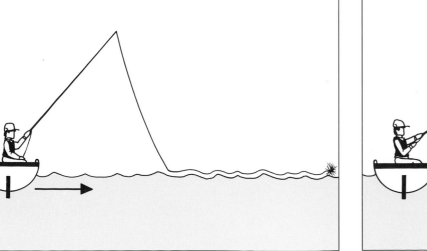
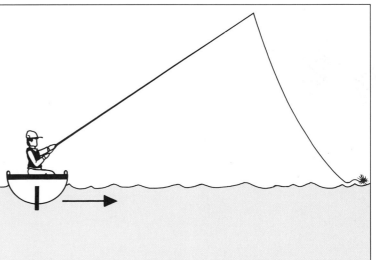

If you cast out to the side and while the boat drifts downwind pay out extra line, by the time the retrieve is started the fly path forms an attractive curve. If the line is a sinker (below) it will also have had time to reach some depth.

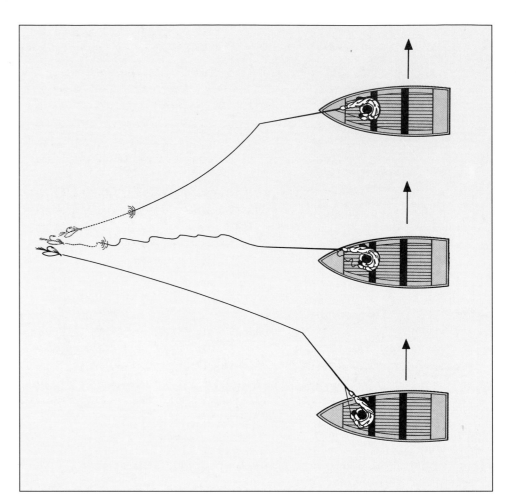

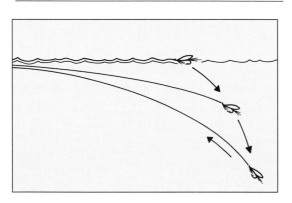

THE RETRIEVE

The action of working the fly or bait back to the fisher – known as the retrieve – is an important part of its presentation to the fish. Let us look first at insect retrieves. Insects with gills, legs, tails and antennae produce a certain amount of natural movement even when they are not actively swimming or crawling or hatching. Therefore, in order for the fly to be effective, some sort of movement should be integral in the tying materials to represent this 'static' movement. ('Active' movement, on the other hand, is determined by line density, current flow and manipulation.) The correct retrieve may be a 'dead drift,' which allows the current to control the active movement, while the materials which constitute the fly contribute the static movement. Other types of retrieve will raise or lower the insect, or make it cross the water on or below the surface as the circumstances require. Nature has a law which relates the maximum speed possible to the size of the creature. Very small creatures moving at top speed are slower than larger creatures moving at top speed, and so insect imitations have a practical maximum active speed.

Retrieving shrimps and bait-fish

For shrimps, the static movement is unlikely to be enough, so a carefully regulated 'hopping' rise and fall may induce the right active movement to bring the inert artificial to life. Sea shrimps and crustacean larvae imitations should be given active movement in imitation of their natural, saltwater models.

Streaking for safety, a bait-fish can move quite rapidly, but in general wounded creatures appear more vulnerable, so the fastest bait-fish is not necessarily the best choice. Charles Brooks used 'dead' minnows, gave them movement and then let them drift (or float) at the mercy of the current. A 'dead' minnow is also one which falls through a school and flutters on downwards. Some fish cut into a school of bait-fish and then circle around looking for the wounded ones. A little movement, an arching or a twitching, by a wounded bait-fish, can be imitated if the 'dead' presentation fails to attract a strike. If one type of retrieve fails, try others, giving each a reasonable test.

Adding weight

Bait-fish imitations encompass two kinds of fish: those which are free-swimming at all depths of water, often in shoals; and those which are solitary bottom-livers, free-swimming very little. The first group consists of sticklebacks, shiners and dace, fish with a tall-oval cross-section. The bottom-livers are the sculpins, whose design presses them to the river bed. There is in certain circumstances some justification for adding a very small amount of weight to the leader, so that a sculpin imitation can be twitched across the river bed in stops and starts. As a result, with the tension off the line, the fly should settle or hover for a moment at the lowest levels of the water.

In general, inanimate objects, such as sticks, fragments of vegetation, gravel caught in the current, do not have either the static or the active movement which attracts the fish's attention. The movement may even be so critical a factor that the rest of the representation – however good or bad an imitation – is not even judged by the fish. Therefore a good retrieve has great importance in fly-fishing and is also what successful bait-fishing and spinning depend on.

OPPOSITE *Three fishing at once from a boat is more stupid than brave. Long rods casting not too long a line work the flies back in the wave tops.*

161

For some of us, fall, resplendent in its rich medley of colors, is our favorite fishing season, poignant with the knowledge that the season is nearly over.

DRY-FLY AND SURFACE FISHING

Its title might suggest that this section is repetitious, but though both types of fishing take place at the surface, dry-fly fishing is a particular style and technique of a far narrower scope than surface fishing, which sometimes has many similarities to wet-fly fishing.

The brown trout which were brought to America in the 1880s were much the same as the British fish, but the American rivers were certainly not all like the hallowed chalkstreams of southern England such as the Avon, the Test and the Itchen, where the dry-fly style of fishing has its origins. For American waters George La Branche produced a rationale for the dry fly which, leaving aside advances in tackle and innovations in fly patterns, remains a milestone in fishing literature and as full of truth today as when he set it down in writing in 1914. La Branche's code was developed for fishing the faster turbulent waters.

The American and the British code are both styles of dry-fly fishing, the essence of which is to induce a feeding fish, or a fish willing to feed, to take an insect imitation on the surface. The insect might be a mayfly, a caddis or a stonefly in particular among the aquatic insects, and the imitation of the mayfly is considered by some to be the epitome of the sport. A floating fly may also represent some terrestrial creature, like an ant, inchworm, jassid or beetle. The problems of imitation and presentation do not differ markedly between the use of aquatic and terrestrial insects, but it seems that most enjoyment comes from the perfect tying of the artificial and then from the perfect presentation of the mayflies and their acceptance by the fish, in sight of the fisher.

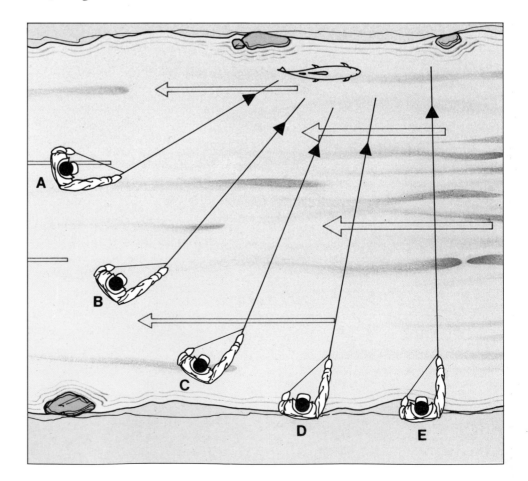

Angler A has the least problem with drag but the most difficulty in putting the line and leader over the fish. It is better for B, but the leader is still too close to the fish. C and D are nearer the ideal position, yet they may be in the periphery of the fish's field of vision. The problem of drag is increasing and E has the most difficulty with it, although he has the easiest cast.

The British style

The essence of this style is to observe until a suitable fish can be seen feeding, and then to seek to identify the food form on which the fish is concentrating. An imitation of that food form is then placed with the utmost delicacy in front of the fish – upstream. The fly resting on the current drifts down 'dead drift' – that is, exactly at the pace of the surface it is resting on – and its natural behavior and appearance deceive the fish into taking. Part of the interest lies in knowing exactly where the fish is, either because it is visible to the fisher, or because its regular rise forms indicate its precise locality. The big advantage in fishing upstream is that when the fish takes the fly, the pull on rod and line that tightens the hook into the fish's jaw comes from an advantageous angle.

The fly must float in order to appear natural, and the line, which should be a floater, must not be perceived by the fish. The leader must be as unobtrusive as possible: if the fish does see it, it must not distract its attention from the fly. Furthermore, making the line or leader land across a fish's back is not recommended, since it usually frightens the fish enough either to make them move off or put them off feeding until their confidence is regained. A fish's confidence can also be lost if it sees the fisher. If he fishes upstream, he is better placed out of the fish's direct field of vision (see page 174) than if he faces the fish as does an average wet-fly fisher. He must also keep the flash of the rod out of the fish's vision, and should direct his false casting (see page 120) off target for this reason, before he places the fly in front of the target fish. He should be aware that shadows from himself, rod and line may be sufficient to put the fish off the feed and that clumsy wading (if wading is necessary) will certainly not be in his favor.

Natural behavior

When the fly alights, it must behave naturally. The mayfly duns settle with wings clapped together above their backs like the wings of resting butterflies, and usually drift down in this rest position, shuttlecocking slightly with the wind. The perfect 'dead drift' is usually the best method of presentation, but in two ways the fly can have unnatural movement in relation to the water surface. Both phenomena are called drag, and either is usually sufficient to dissuade the fish from taking. Drag occurs either when the fly is moving faster than the water on which it is resting – when the pull of the current on the line or leader puts tension on the fly and pulls it across the water; or when the fly lands on fast water and the line and leader on slower water. The fly is then restrained from moving in a long drift at the pace of the water on which it alighted. This is a less common occurrence and seems not to have quite so much of an ill effect on the fish. La Branche refers to this as 'retarded' drag, and a line or leader hung up on the rocks or a weed bar will produce a similar result.

At some stage the fly drifts past the fish, which for its own reasons has not taken it. The fisher must lift it off to dry it with false casts, and re-present it. Drag must be kept to a minimum, until the fly is far enough away from the fish for the fish not to notice any disturbance caused by picking the fly off. A common error is to lift the fly for a re-presentation much too close to the fish or its lie: sometimes a fish drops back or circles for another look.

Casting upstream ensures that slack is always being put in the line and leader, which helps deal with the problem of fast drag described above. The squarer the cast across the river, the more taut the line becomes as the drift of the fly lengthens and line may have to be paid out and rod top moved to adjust the line with mends to prevent the drag.

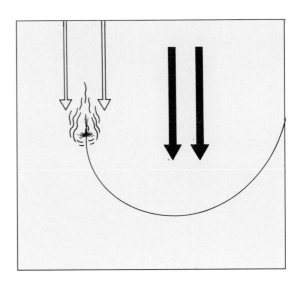

Drag

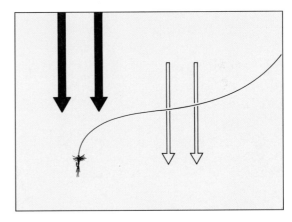

Retarded drag

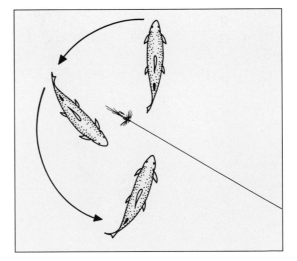

It makes sense not to lift the fly off for another cast until it is well past the chance of being taken, since the fish may circle to take a second look at it.

The American style

The American style of dry-fly fishing, developed by La Branche and Hewitt, incorporated all the principles of the code which crossed the Atlantic in the books and writings of Halford, and added to it, to suit the different conditions. The differences lie in North America's wider range of insects, the greater turbulence of the streams and rivers, and the fact that the fish might not show as rising fish – as fish taking surface food. Yet a well-presented dry fly can often produce better fishing than equally well-presented subsurface flies.

It is more difficult for a dry fly to float on turbulent water, since it can be drowned by the waves or pulled under the surface as it is picked out for casting and re-presentation. Either the tying must use superlative materials or the design must move away from close imitation to a compromise between adequate imitation and good buoyancy. The next move is to increase the fly's visibility to the fisher. A partially floating fly in rough water is very difficult to keep an eye on, and although a good floater in a natural imitative color is easier to see, it is still not easy. Therefore it may be worth creating contrast of color so that you do not have to strain to see the fly. The trade-off is between a better ratio of fish attracted and hooked and the loss of the chance of just a few fish that find the fly suspicious.

Benefits of fast water

Fast water offers advantages in that the fly is less precisely observed by the fish because of the surface distortions; and the fish, because of the pace of the water, has to determine rapidly whether it will have the fly or not, because it will soon be swept away. Thus, if the fly floats, can be seen as 'acceptable' by the fish and kept under close observation by the fisher, the technique is successful even if 'exact imitation to a specific fish selectively feeding to a specific type of insect' is no longer the code. These turbulent streams are usually far less rich in their mayflies hatches, so that fish, being opportunists, tend to accept a wide range of food forms. The fly that is an exact imitation, with perfect floating ability and easy visibility to the fisher, may be an ideal, but you can compromise without much loss of efficiency by using all-purpose mayfly-style patterns with size and color variation, and likewise caddis or stonefly patterns. If the fish are not actively rising because there is no recognizable hatch, they may still be prepared to come to the surface and take.

Fish seen in the water (and not scared) may be tempted to the surface by a carefully presented repetition of casts, with variation among the artificials, until they come 'on the fin,' show an interest and decide to take. Alternatively, the water may be fished blind, the fisher casting again and again into likely lies and back eddies, ready to tighten as soon as a fish comes up.

Dead drift patterns

Dead drift

Much dry-fly fishing is 'dead drift,' in which the fly comes down at the pace of the water on which it rests, and no 'active' movement is given to it. Some 'passive' movement might occur too, owing to the nature of the tying materials. A caddis is seldom a static insect when it falls on the water – its wings are abuzz and it may scurry across the surface. Passive movement in an artificial may be produced by using a hairwing, rather than stiff strips of feather, to give the idea of wings aflutter, and active movement can be induced, producing drag, to represent the scurry across the surface.

'Active' movement can be very subtle – the minutest twitch and the heckle fibres bend and flex, and return to the status quo; the surface is not disturbed and the fly has not changed place. Or the fly can be walked on its hackle points over the water, without causing drag, which disturbs the surface. On lakes in particular these minute movements can cause a wondering fish to wonder no longer, and to take firmly. More pronounced active movement, inducing drag, and intentionally disturbing the surface brings us out of the dry fly codes and into surface fishing.

Surface techniques

We have already seen that a bob fly can prove eminently successful. It is best at the surface, hopping and skipping like an egg-laying caddis or other such insect, and its action, in combination with its fair imitative representation of a food form, will attract fish. A single fly may also be fished in this way, by using dry-fly tackle and working the fly faster than the water. Swift handlining-in is necessary if the fly is cast upstream, and suitable adjustment is required at the other angles. Remember that it is progressively less easy to hook a fish the further downstream the fly is.

It seems contradictory that drag on a 'dead drift' fly will deter the fish from taking, yet considerable surface disturbance from a fly may stir the fish into a savage strike. However, it is so, and flies of wet-fly, dry-fly and streamer and bucktail styles fished and skipped on the surface can be very killing for both migratory and resident fish.

Techniques for keeping a fly working on the surface – dibbing (dibbling) and dapping – are described on pages 218-221. Other techniques are like downstream wet-fly fishing: the fisher quarters the water as shown on page 00, making sure that the fly remains in the surface either by altering the knot, altering the fly, or using a fly which offers plenty of water resistance and little weight. Logically, the use of a floating line makes surface fishing easier, but a high rod point and manipulation of the line can keep a fly fished with a sinker up on the top.

Surface flies are not normally the first choice for migratory fish. However, when water temperatures exceed 60°F (16°C) and the temperature consistently rises during the day, a dry fly or surface fly can be more

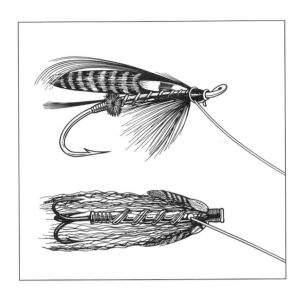

In the first Atlantic salmon fly above, making a second knot behind the eye stops the fly sinking properly so that it creates a surface wake. In the second example, threading on a tube fly by making a hole behind the head produces the same effect. Other flies can be similarly adapted.

Active movements

Fishing a dry fly downstream. Angler I has the best and longest drift with the least potential drag, provided the line and leader can pay out. He risks being seen by the fish, but the fly is seen before the leader. If the fish does not take, the leader and line pass over it. The difficulty lies in picking up the line for the next cast. Also, if the fish does take, it is very difficult to hook. Angler H is better placed: he can control the drift, the fly is seen first but with care he can conduct it past the fish if it does not take, and he can pick up the line without disturbing the fish. But it is still a bad angle for hooking. G and F's positions are more prejudiced by drag, but the hooking angle is better. (E's position is discussed on page 165.)

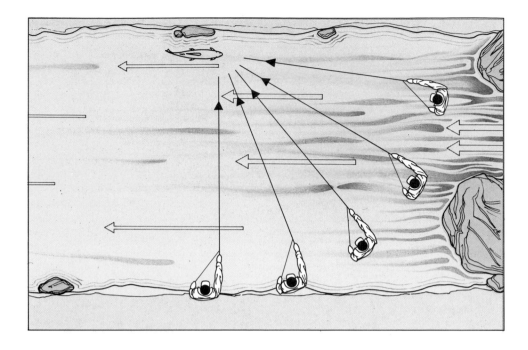

catching than traditional wet methods. It is usual to choose less disturbing forms of surface fishing such as dead drift in preference to induced-action forms. This is probably because the fish are progressively more likely to be spooked, so it is illogical to use the most disturbing techniques first.

Fishing position

The easiest dry-fly fishing is from the most comfortable direction, taking into account the likelihood of being seen by the fish, scaring it with your shadow or tackle, and drag; is the most practical position for access and for backcasting; and is not too badly affected by contrary winds. It can be a beneficial tactic to fish from a difficult position, when you suspect the fish knows where a fisher always lurks. To fish from the other bank, or downstream, may find the chink in a very educated fish's armor.

The usual method is to fish a floating fly on a floating line with a leader tapered down to a suitable tippet strength for the size of fly: stouter for rough conditions and finer for bright, clear conditions. Large, bushy flies with lots of air resistance need a stiffer tippet (which nearly always means larger diameter), particularly in head winds. Although a leader may be partly greased to fish a nymph, the general practice is to hope the tippet does not float in the surface film since this enlarges its apparent diameter and throws an accordingly larger shadow. Therefore dry-fly leaders and tippets are not treated with floatant, and may even have 'sink' applied.

Delivery

Nature's ways provide a rough guide to the appropriate style of fishing. Small, lightweight natural baits alight delicately. A hopper, a mouse or a frog will land with a plop, and then kick and struggle. A fish selectively interested in, for example, hoppers will perhaps react to a 'plop' delivery as far away as out of its direct feeding zone, while a silent delicate hopper delivery would not catch its attention, even within the feeding zone.

Some fish will move a long way to feed, usually when the water is comparatively warm. Fish move less far when the water is cold, or when it is near the maximum temperature they can live in. Accurate delivery is thus a benefit. Many rising fish demonstrate a zone in which they pick up food; they move ahead or sideways within an oval, and then within that oval

choose a particular area just to right or to left. Very occasionally they may drop back or circle back, and take, and then swim back to their feeding position. Surface-feeding trout usually hold themselves near the surface, and with a change of fin angle and only a small swimming impulse direct themselves to the top, to take the selected insect.

A salmon, when it rises, or comes to a wet fly, tends to swim to intercept

ABOVE   *The sequence shows a typical trout rise to a surface fly.*

BELOW   *A salmon, more than the other migratory fish, swims 'through' the take, twisting slightly to do so. The illustrations on the left show the lack of vertical flexibility in the salmon compared with its greater horizontal suppleness.*

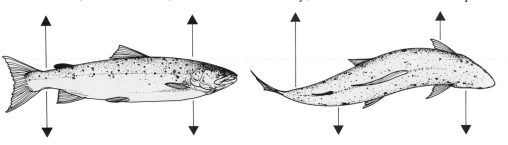

169

On some rivers June is the best month: fly hatches are regular and there is the challenge of matching the hatch and then presenting the choice of artificial as delicately as possible.

OPPOSITE *The brown trout was first established on the East Coast. Here an angler lands a 15-in (40 cm) brownie in a typical New England setting.*

it. The fish has little ability, owing to its skeletal arrangement, to flex vertically, but is much more flexible horizontally, so it often turns slightly on its side to take a fly on or near the surface, and keeps swimming as it heads down again and then circles back to its lie.

A grayling tends to lurk near the bottom and actively swims to the surface to 'rise.' Its zone is much narrower than that of a trout, and its rise shows downstream of its lie as the current draws the fish backwards slightly. It then returns to its feeding lie. The hypothetical zone might be drawn as in the diagram below. The taking point is by the rise form. This is not to say that the grayling has a zone of vision of this shape: its visual range is typical of game fish. A problem arises when a fish adopts a 'groove' in the water – a flow held constant by current and eddy which may nonetheless rhythmically eddy its position in the pool, so that there is not a fixed, accurate indication of the fish's position.

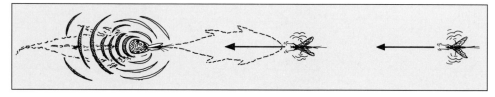

A typical grayling rise seen from above and from the side.

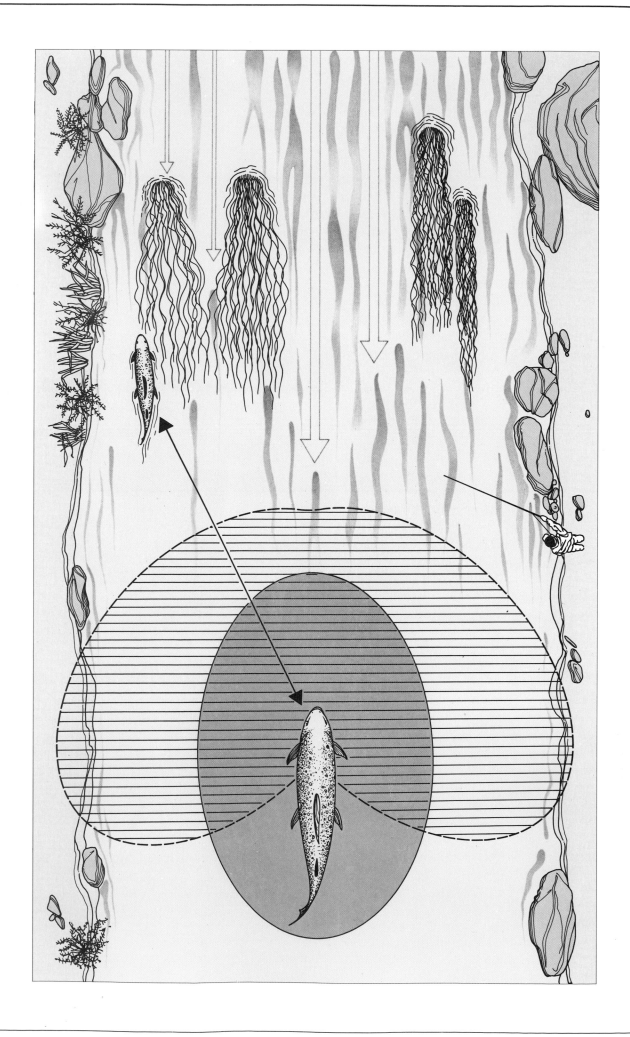

The feeding zone of the fish near the lefthand bank is within the oval of the enlarged detail. Its field of vision, however, maybe as large as the whole of the shaded area.

A practical approach

Provided you obey local fishing regulations and the law, there is nothing to stop you making your fishing as challenging for yourself as you like. When you eventually succeed by your own methods, the prize is immeasurably sweeter. Nevertheless, most of us find difficulties enough in fishing the easiest way we can. The following illustrates the process of problem-solving in dry-fly fishing.

A trout is lying in a small bay with the river bank to its left and trailing weed in front and to the right side which just interrupts the surface. The current is weak in his bay, but stronger to the right of the weed bar. Near the angler, there is another weed bar. The fish is rising freely to small mayflies on the surface. The diagram on the left shows the oval zone in which the fish is prepared to feed, though his field of vision covers a different area, or different areas depending how close the the surface he is. The field of vision may be the whole of the shaded area. The problems are those of presentation and drag. A floating mayfly should not move faster than the water it is resting on. Presentation must be singularly delicate because the fly has no place to land but close to the fish. Terminal tackle must therefore be fine, but there are weedbeds near the fish from which it may have to be pulled, which calls for some strength in the tackle.

Seeing but not seen

The angler in the diagram on the left is in no risk of being visible to the fish if he is careful; and he has few difficulties in seeing the take, since he is fishing the surface. He might resolve part of the problem if his fishing code allows him to change position. As it is, he must land his fly in the run between the weedbeds and his leader must have stacked up in loose coils upstream of the fly so that the fly can drift down naturally without swinging on the arc made where the leader catches on the weed bar. The entire leader must not be dragged by the main current, because the line if cast straight will immediately be pulled fast downstream, and will pull hard on the leader. So the cast will be a shepherd's crook, curling downstream with a soft, underenergized landing, and the line will have been given a lazy-S wriggle so that it falls in a sinuous series of bends which the current will take a moment to straighten out.

Accurate delivery

The delivery must be spot-on. It is extremely difficult. Cross the river, cast the line over land, with the leader only on the water, and the fly can be dropped within the rectangle in which the fish is known to feed, reducing the problems. If drag did not matter, the problems are again reduced. Try a sort of imitation which is succulent, plausible for the water, and which naturally makes a disturbance in the water. Try a fluttering sedge pattern. The dry-fly ethic is preserved. But the fisher's code may have demanded from him 'exact imitation,' so that fishing a sedge would be 'cheating.' The following alternative could also be seen as cheating: a dragging nymph may appear much less unnatural than a dragging dry fly, and a change of tactic may be justified. Take a longer walk and work upstream of the fish on its own bank and float a dry fly down the little channel to it, but expect more difficulty tightening into it, as the strike is upstream — that is, out of the fish's opening mouth. The problem offers a wide enough variety of solutions to delight those who enjoy the skills of fishing, and the weedbeds of one river can in another easily be rocks or ledges, which present their own problems.

CAN FISH BECOME 'EDUCATED'?

In a gamefishing context 'education' means fish learning about obtrusive anglers and poorly presented flies, and the latter in their turn are inaccurate as representations, so that in time the fish become extremely difficult to deceive. Mere repetitive casting might not 'teach' the fish; it might even convince it that there is a hatch, but in case fish do become accustomed to style and presentation, it is worth trying a different position to fish from, or wet fly when dry fly is the common practice, or a nymph or streamer, or even trying for the fish in the early morning or late evening, when the light values differ. The fish may also be more susceptible at the very start or near the end of a hatch, and becomes more and more suspicious of imitations during the main bulk of the hatch — in short, more 'educated.' Too stout a tippet very often causes the fish to reject the fly, whereas a dead, drift dry fly on no tippet at all is so very often taken without hesitation that the fish's 'education' has simply caused it to be suspicious of something as unnatural as any tippet.

WET-FLY AND NYMPH FISHING

So much of the diet of fishes is taken below the surface – in fresh water and in the sea – that there is some justification for fishing the wet fly about 85 percent of all fishing time. It is a thorough and three-dimensional method of searching the water, as well as a method which can be aimed at target fish or lies. What is a wet fly? Some say a wet fly is a submerged insect, some a nymph or a 'bug,' some an item of curiosity, some even that it is just an attractor. Analysis of catches seems to show that the traditional winged wet fly is less efficient than the nymph/bug creations and the bait-fish imitations in the forms of streamers and bucktails. What is undeniable is that since so much of fish diet is taken below the surface, proficiency with a wet fly is a necessary skill if you aim to be an all-round fisher.

Speed of fishing

In rivers, the direction of presentation is nearly always downstream: the pull of the current works the fly across the water in an arc until it is hanging downstream of the fisher. The speed of fishing is important in wet-fly fishing, but since the term 'speed of fishing' has three meanings, let us pause to consider these.

A trout-rich river in Maine.

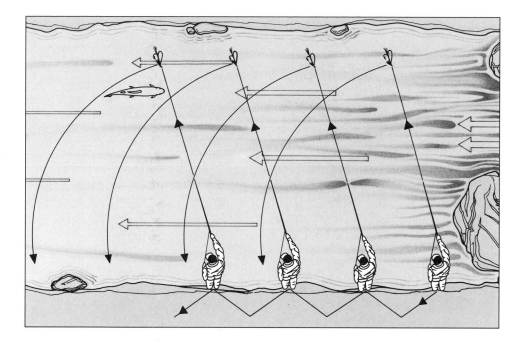

This fisher takes a couple of paces between casts – the usual interval in down-and-across presentation.

1   It can mean the number of paces the fisher takes between casts and how long he spends on a pool or run. He may cast relatively few times, covering the pool thoroughly, but over a short duration of time and then move on. He fishes fast in order to cover more and varied water in a day.

2   It can mean also how fast the fly travels, the 'fly speed.' If the fly is held in the current it has an effective 'ground speed' of the pace of the current. If the line is manipulated and stripped in, the fly adds this speed to the current's speed. If some line is paid out, the fly may travel nearly at the speed of the current, or even at that speed.

3   The third meaning of the term is the 'speed of traverse.' The fly is cast out and the speed is how long it takes for the current to swing the fly round to the fisher's bank.

How the combination of 2 and 3 affects the presentation of the fly to the fish, and also influences the retrieve; both are controllable by the fisher. This control determines how natural the fly looks to the fish, and how long it is in its potential taking zone.

How fast you work down the pool may be influenced by the likelihood of a good stock of fish and the clarity and depth of the water – in other words, you may choose to give the fish a reasonable chance of seeing the fly, and no more. The usual tactic is a couple of paces between casts, which should give the fish an inkling of the fly, a sight of the fly, and a chance of the fly, before the fly alights behind it. In areas of difficult water-flow round a lie, it may be worth making extra casts. If a fish moves to the fly, more time is spent on trying to induce it to move again.

Because speed and size have a natural relationship, fly speed is an important consideration. It makes sense to use a larger pattern in the very fast water at the head of a pool for two reasons. First, it is more natural for a larger object to have a fast water speed, and second a larger object is more visible to the fish in the rush of water. Conversely, in the calm flats at the tail of a pool the current is much weaker and a smaller fly appears more natural. Fly speed must in turn be equated with the size of the natural creature which is being imitated, or of which an illusion is being presented, and its behavior.

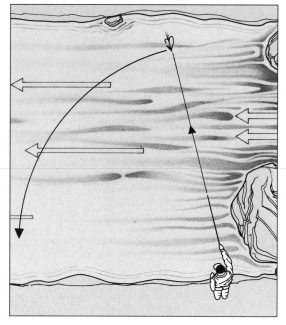

The fly swings across the current in an arc. On a short line and in a fast current the fly fishes fast.

Fishing depth

At the beginning of the year, when little food is showing at the surface, the fish focus all their attention on the larval food forms nearer the river bed. Since their metabolism is slow on account of the water being cold, they may not want to move fast even if the food supply is meager. So we need to fish slow and deep: a slow fly and a slow traverse. We know that tension on the line pulls it and the fly up toward the surface, or at least never lets them go deep. The current or our own manipulation may be putting this tension on the line and fly. We have to consider where we want our fly to have its depth, and we must calculate how long in best conditions it takes our tackle to sink to that depth, for the fly must have time to sink. Our presentation to the fish will thus start at the right level; the next task is to produce the right fly speed.

It may be necessary to use a combination of the styles shown in the diagrams below and opposite to be able to fish down a pool. As soon as combinations of weight of fly and density of line are involved, the wet fly really does search in three dimensions, although specific lies – for example, undercut banks, and eddies round projecting tree stumps and rocks – may be the most likely haunts of trout.

The wet fly may be the 'illusion' of some food item, or something so 'attractive' that the fish is convinced it should attack it. During the retrieve, the line may be manipulated to give the right twitches, wriggles, darts and swimming bursts to imitate the natural food form of which you know your fly is the representation. The rod, too, may have a role in controlling or inducing movement, or keeping in touch with the fly, either by not allowing any slack or preventing the line from being too taut.

Mending is most easily achieved with a floating line. As the current pulls a downstream belly in the line, the fisher, by lifting the rod and line upstream, puts an upstream belly into the line. This action slows the speed of traverse and may need to be repeated several times before the fly hangs below the fisher.

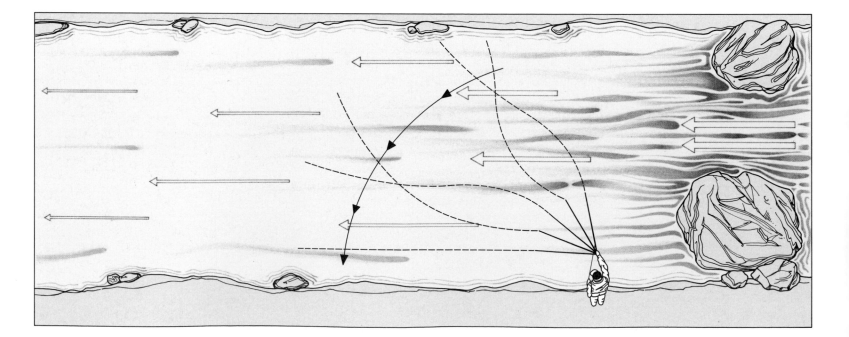

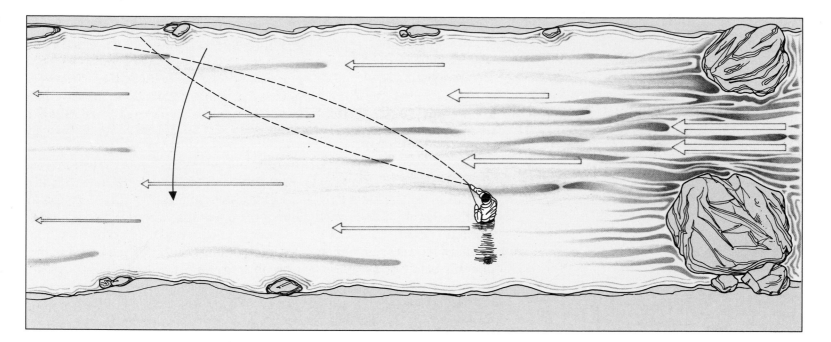

An immediate mend with a long line takes longer to swing round, and this means a slow speed of traverse. If the line is dense, medium or fast-sinking, it will find its own depth, its weight countering the upward force of the current. It is too late to mend the line when it is well sunk.

This is an alternative to casting and moving two paces downstream. Unless mended or otherwise adjusted, cast 1 traverses more quickly than cast 6.

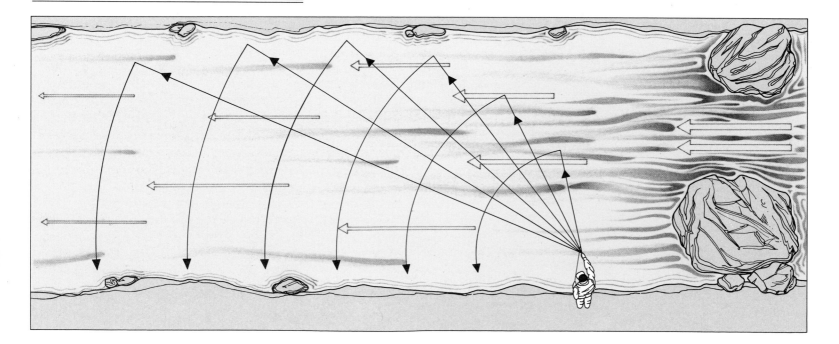

The dropper technique

It is of considerable benefit when fishing the wet fly to have more than one fly on the leader. If common patterns are being used, a dark one and a light one are advised. If all the action comes to one of the flies, then it may be worth using a variation of it to replace the other, less efficient, fly. Two flies are more enticing than one, but do not expect them to catch twice as many fish in double-headers, and an extra inducement is to have a third fly working in the surface.

There are several advantages to using droppers: each cast suggests to the fish that there is reason to be on the feed, since there seems to be a lot of food about; each fly fishes at a different level; each fly has a slightly different action; if one of the flies is not to the fish's choice, another might be. If a 'bob fly' (top dropper) is used at the surface it beckons the fish, which investigates, even though the bob may not be its choice (occasionally, however, the bob is the most effective fly and the other flies act as a stabilizing influence).

Long rods are better than short for the dropper technique with a bob fly: the best tail flies enter the water easily and sink as required, being tied with water-absorbent tying materials, while the bob fly is tied to float and to put up with the battering on the surface. Flies with a forward-pointing 'snoot' of hair drown with difficulty, and bob attractively. It is easier to fish the team downstream, although if the wind is contrary it is perfectly possible to fish across or upstream, but line control is needed to keep the flies active and to have the tackle taut enough to tighten on a fish when it strikes.

Very few winged insects are seen, with their wings, underwater. Only a few mayflies change from nymph to dun underwater and a few female imagos creep down vegetation or stones to lay their eggs – a few caddis do the same – so winged wet flies are rather inaccurate as insect representations. It does not seem to worry the fish – the semblance of life is there – whether the illusion of a small fish or an insect or recalls a memory of something seen and fed on at sea. Therefore wet flies with wings – of feather or of hair, or of man-made strands – will be used for many generations yet and have caught fish in rivers and lakes for 500 years already. A good number of wet flies are not winged in the traditional way, and are more precise imitations of recognizable food forms. These patterns may be used to search the water with the downstream casting techniques, or they may be presented upstream with particular fish or lies as targets.

Nymph fishing

Since so many of the underwater insect forms are nymphs or larvae, a branch of wet-fly fishing is generally termed 'nymph' fishing. In Europe, G.E.M. Skues was the first close observer to 'think nymph,' rather than in terms of traditional wet fly or dry fly, and in the USA Edward Ringwood Hewitt was the founding father of American nymph fishing. Modern writers like Swisher and Richards have combined their intellects to keep the field of nymphs well cultivated with inventions.

Skues observed that brown trout rose readily to food forms close to the surface; the fish even disturbed the surface as they took, but floating mayflies passed them without interesting them. For his nymphs he used natural furs for the body and a soft hackle for the legs, and drifted them just under the surface over the active fish. The range of imitations devised by Skues encompassed the nymphs of the common mayflies. They relied on 'static' movement, having a good choice of material for the body and thorax which transmitted light and was hairy, so that there was a slight

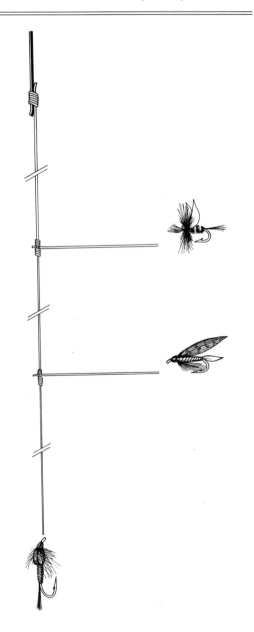

Dropper patterns have a 'bad' entry and are difficult to submerge. Point flies have a 'good' entry, sinking easily with minimal disturbance. Nymph patterns are used, as well as traditional-style wet flies.

resemblance to the gills of the naturals. Frank Sawyer was the man who saw that 'active' movement was probably more important and his addition of weight to a practical facsimile pattern (rather than using a minutely detailed imitation) and imparted movement, has produced probably the most deadly general-purpose artificial pattern yet seen in Britain.

Hewitt had not been idle: his nymph patterns were a bit flat and lifeless to begin with, but the concept of nymphs took hold and the techniques of how to use them became more closely defined, together with techniques suitable for waters bigger and stronger than the gentle rivers fished by Skues and Sawyer. The nymphs (larvae) of the stoneflies are bigger and stronger insects as well.

The skill in fishing a big nymph, deep, at a far distance in a big, strong river lies in keeping in contact with it, ensuring that it fishes the lies attractively and being able to tighten when a fish takes. Not all waters are turbulent, and a nymph carefully cast upstream and allowed to settle on the bottom can produce strikes to a careful wrist-turn figure-of-eight retrieve: a very slow retrieve right on the bottom. At times it is almost impossible to fish a nymph too slowly.

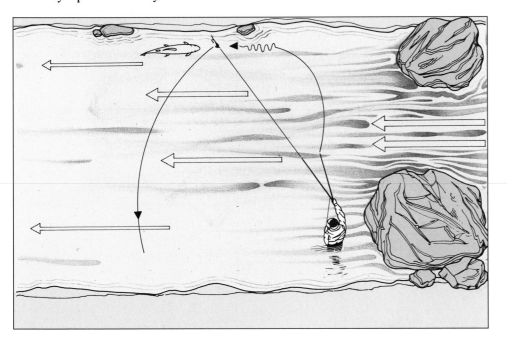

If this angler casts directly at the fish the fly has no time to achieve any depth and will start immediately to swing across the current. By casting sufficiently upstream of the fish, with a slack line, and even by paying out extra line, he gives the fly a chance to have sunk to a suitable level by the time it reaches the fish.

Whether in lake or river, many of the principles of playing a fish are the same. If the fish jumps in the air it 'weighs,' which it does not in water. The usual practice is to lessen the tension on the leader and the hookhold by lowering the rod toward the fish during the jump. However, sometimes there is so much line out that this does nothing to reduce the tension.

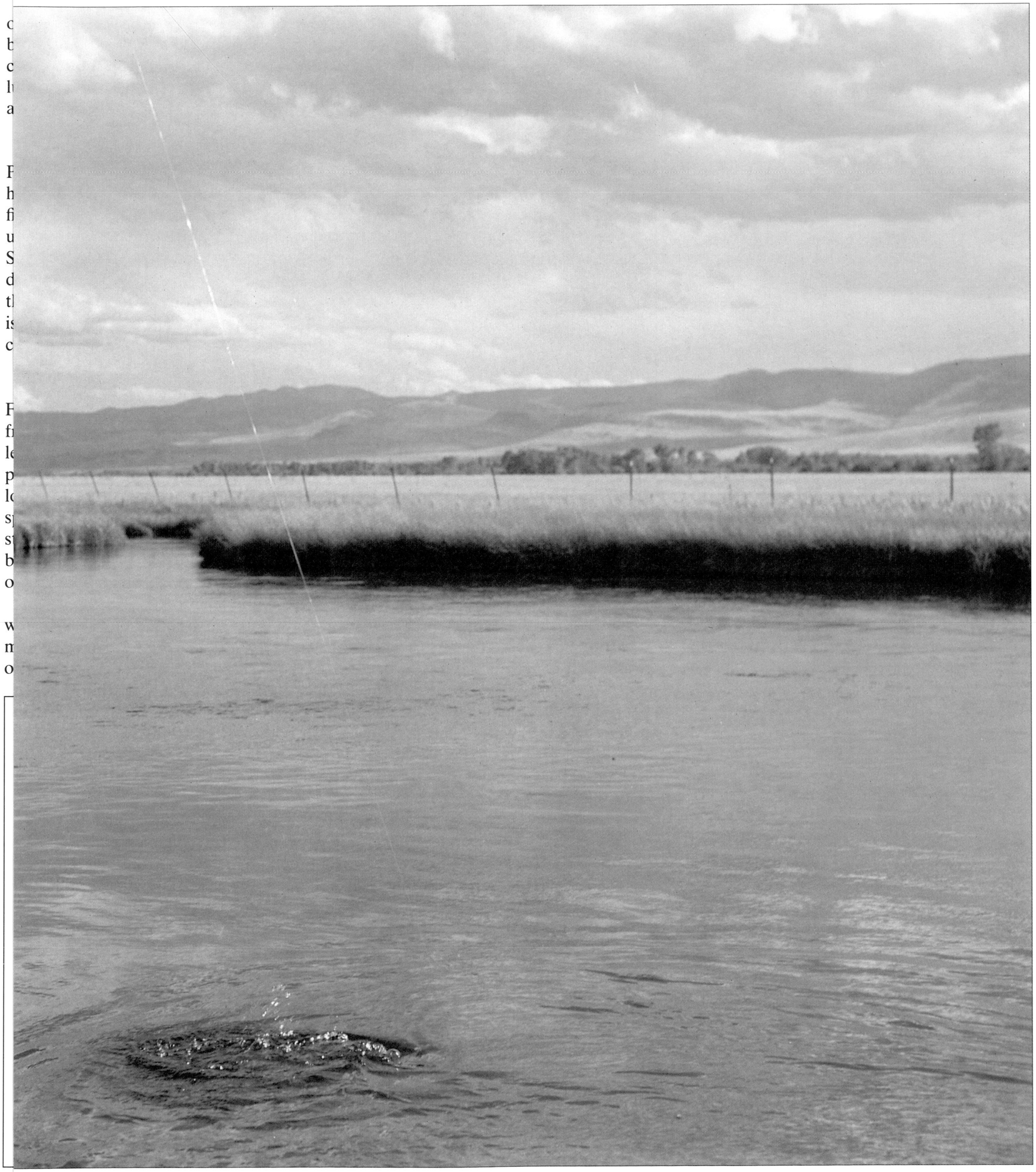

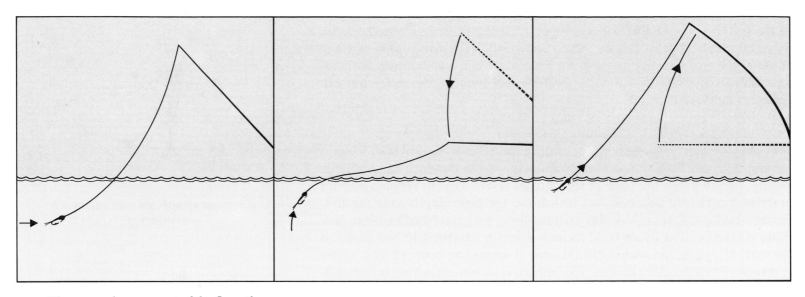

*The upward movement of the fly as the
angler starts to lift the line to cast may be
so natural that it induces the fish to take.
Make the initial movement, drop the rod
tip once more and start the pick-up again.
A take could come at any time.*

with the size of fish it catches, particularly the large 'buggy' patterns fished deep. A tactic that is occasionally effective is to increase the size dramatically .

How far a fish will follow a fly depends partly on what the temperature is, but a slow retrieve is often followed, and the fly should not be picked out for re-presentation without a few preliminary twitches. Picking out the fly requires the movement illustrated in the sequence above, which is very similar to the movement made by nymphs and larvae on their way to the surface to hatch. Be intensely alert as you start the acceleration of the fly and line off the water to start the next cast. An abrupt pick-up too close to the lie or the target fish (if visible) may cause fright, and a fish may be following, invisibly, much further from its lie than you are aware. Therefore take great care over the pick-up, rather than rushing it.

Solutions to presentation problems

Casting satisfactorily under an overhang on your own bank can be difficult. If this is the case, walk extremely carefully along the bank, having cast the wet fly or nymph to the desired level, extending the rod top over the water as little as necessary, so that you 'walk' the fly into position. If you need extra depth, coat the nymph in a mudball, which will take it down. When the mud dissolves away, the nymph is there, skulking on the bottom. These two simple tactics show that it is on occasion worth breaking out of the usual fly-casting conventions. You may devise tricks of your own in problematic situations.

PLAYING A FISH

For some, the playing of the fish – its fight and its eventual defeat – constitutes the most enjoyable part of fishing. Among such fishers the killing and taking of the fish is the consummation of the sport. Others take great pleasure in other aspects: finding the fish, by direct observation or by searching with a fly and getting it to take, may for them be 90 percent of the charm and challenge. For them, playing the fish is just another facet, capable of being isolated from the earlier take or strike, and success or failure in this area may rate as relatively unimportant. Furthermore, whether the fish is killed and kept or returned to the water and freedom may be either a matter of complete indifference to them, or it may be one of great importance.

However, many fishers are creatures of mood: on one trip they experience the philosophic calm of inducing fish to rise – the pattern is good enough and so is the presentation; another day the soul is more stirred and excited and the essence of the day is the fight, the wild rushes and the leaps as the fish seeks its freedom.

Improving efficiency

Consider how you gain the maximum enjoyment from fishing. What you will discover for sure is that incompetence is an element which detracts from that enjoyment. We all lose fish and nearly always it seems that they are the better fish, because that which is wanted most and cannot be had is always coveted the most. But losing fish through incompetence can be guarded against.

First, think of the style of the fish: what will it do when it first feels the tension of the hook and the restraint of the line? Where will it go, and how fast? How strong are the weapons at your command? At your disposal is your mobility – either on foot or by boat (or float tube) – the strength of your rod and terminal tackle, including, importantly, the strength and character of the hook. When the fish is small, the power in the rod and the reserves of breaking strain in the tackle will make its loss quite difficult to achieve if it is not subjected to rough abrupt handling with a jerking fluctuation and loss of tension. Smooth, delicate handling when bringing in small fish is invaluable practice for the time when such handling might be the only way to subdue a larger fish on proportionately much lighter tackle.

Playing a big fish

When the fish is big, the ability to decide how much to move so as to keep in touch with the fish, or stay in control of it, comes largely through experience. Hook a fish from the boat on some rivers and the guide steadily makes for the shore. Hook a fish from the bank on a salmon river as big and strong as Norway's Vosso and the guide immediately brings the boat and readies himself to follow along gorges which are impassable on foot. If the fish is not a monster and seems unwilling to leave the pool, then you must either continue to play it from the boat or step back onto land. In some situations potential problems with rocks or steep banks or overhanging vegetation make it clearly wiser to continue the fight in a more advantageous place. Deciding where the fish is fought and where it is brought for landing, netting, beaching, tailing or lifting by hand, often call for separate decisions, although there may be no choice.

Breaking strain

A fish is marginally heavier than the water in which it is swimming. It 'weighs' very little in its element, so that we can take fish which pull the scales down to far higher figures than the breaking strain of the weakest link in our tackle. Breaking strain is measured, however, by a smooth, steadily increasing pull: a sharp pull causes tackle to fail at an earlier stage, so all our playing of fish must be as smooth as possible. Even so, it should always exploit at least 90 percent of the strain the tackle can put on the fish – unless some subtle maneuvering is called for, in which case tension must be reduced. The times when this relaxation of pressure is appropriate are exceptional and are described in more detail below.

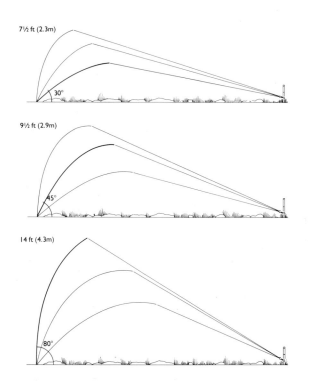

7½ ft (2.3m)

30°

9½ ft (2.9m)

45°

14 ft (4.3m)

80°

Assessing rod strain

How much strain can be put on a fish? What strain can the rod exert? In his book on salmon fishing Ernest Ringwood Hewitt produced some handsome illustrations based on the tackle of his time. For the illustrations on the left, tackle of the late 1980s and early 1990s has been chosen. Attached firmly to the fence rail is a spring balance used to weigh trout. The angle at which the rod is held is fixed and is based on the angle of the handle before tension is applied by tightening the line through the guides. My assistant read off the figures on the spring balance. This exercise may not be strictly scientific or even very accurate, but it is certainly accurate enough to demonstrate how to put pressure on the fish, but with little flexion in the rod to cushion the tension, and how to humor a fish by using the top of the rod to its maximum, but not drawing on the power from the lower tapers.

Clearly, rods do not simply lift fish from the water. What they do is apply a strength-sapping strain, and this strain is intensified by the fisher if it pulls the fish off balance into a state of instability which it seeks to remedy at cost to its energy resources.

The different fighting styles of fish

My example A is a classic fight put up by an acrobatic rainbow trout taking a surface fly. The shock of being hooked and the feeling of restraint send it off across the water in a cartwheeling burst of maximum speed and stress. If it keeps up this expenditure of effort it will burn up half its energy reserves in its muscles in a couple of minutes: the 'poison' of lactic acid accumulates in the tissues and the fish tires fast. If this fish can be pulled off balance it may be possible to turn it across the surface and straight into the net. If it were given its freedom it would sulkily regain its muscle condition perfectly healthily over a period of several hours in some deep, untroubled sanctuary in the river.

My example B is another fighter – this time a brown trout – heading steadily for its favorite snags. No energy is wasted in wild acrobatics – there is just a steady surge which has to be headed away from all dangers and deep exploration of all four (preferably sharp) corners of the pool. When eventually the strain is too much this fish will be exhausted. Then, the greatest care is needed to assist the fish's recovery in the best oxygenated water until it can swim off steadily.

Hook a fresh-run salmon (example C) and it may combine surface antics with deep resistance. Unless it is a true old stager in the pool it is unlikely to deliberately head for snags, though in its anxiety it may take a route which puts the tackle at risk. A fish like this has no sense of territory and may choose to enter the pool above, or swim down through the tail and head back toward the sea by the shortest route it knows.

Example D takes us to northern Maine, to Milt Hall's camp, where we were in pursuit of landlocks. We were catching no other species – and had ceased to expect to – when there was a solid, loggy strike on one of the rods and a fish streamed line off the reel vertically, run after run. There was little lateral movement – the fish would head for the deeps, be checked by the relentless pressure and permit itself to be pumped upward until it felt it was too close to the surface and then it would head down again. This was our first, and only, 'laker' from that camp.

The more you know about the different species and their behavior the less chance there is that you will be surprised by their style when being played. There are basic rules which the accumulated experience of generations of anglers obey when playing a fish:

1   Plan ahead. Use brain rather than brawn. As you work your way down a pool, a pace or two between casts, your mind devotes itself partly to the hope and expectation of a fish's taking and partly to a plan for playing it, then netting, beaching or otherwise landing it. There will be clear water in which it can run freely, rocks, overhanging trees, deadfalls (a tangled mass of fallen trees or branches), uncrossable tributaries, sheer cliff-faces or other such obstacles to either you or to the fish. If you can dictate the play, by having done some planning, you should not be stranded with an out-of-control fish which should have been a safe candidate for landing.

2   Keep the rod bent. We have seen in the diagrams opposite that the butt of the rod pointed at a shallow angle toward the fish can produce great strain and that neither the tip alone under strain, nor a very high rod angle, puts as much pressure on the fish. We choose to change the angle at different stages in the fight – a fish sullenly slugging along the bottom may demand a heavy pull, while acrobatics and rapid changes of direction are better met with lighter tension and the rod held higher. If the butt of the rod is held against the body it is less resilient than when held out, and your reaction time – to, say, drop the rod point – is longer. In the power phases of play the butt may be rested, or you may add an extension to a single-hander. But, if it is possible in the problematic later phases, it is worth keeping the extra sensitivity available, particularly when you are bringing the fish to the net or in to beach it.

3   Maintain constant tension in the line. This tension is sometimes the only information you can gain about what the fish is doing. You can feel the dynamic ripple or a sensation of lift – the fish may be about to jump – even if you cannot see the fish through the water. In this way you have an idea of the fish's pace, its mood and its direction, all of which remain secret if the line is slack. However, note the exceptions to this rule. Holding a fish too hard can make it 'contra-suggestive': for much of the fight the fish pulls against restraint, seeking its liberty, but if the sense of restraint is suddenly removed it might simply seek quiet water where it can puzzle out how to shed the annoying hook. In a time of crisis, therefore, giving slack line may save the day. Slack line bellying in the stream below a fish may convince it that the restraint comes from below it and that it should therefore swim upstream to escape. Such a ploy may deter a determined fish such as a salmon from running out of a pool.

A large brown trout may have a favorite snag. At last the fish has taken, been tightened on and is hooked. If you maintain no tension in the line you may be able to move to a position from which you can fight the fish from an angle which prevents it from making for the snag or weedbed. A larger fish hooked on light tackle can sometimes be surprised off balance and really hurried – by yielding line at the beginning of the fight you may well have put it off guard. The skillful use of slack line is one of the marks of the experienced angler.

4   Let the fish run. Let it run when and where it wants, and keep your hand off the reel handle. A good long run at maximum speed really takes the fight out of a fish. Also, it is both visually and aurally exciting and saves a long, boring, slugging fight. If the fish has to work against some form of braking from the fisher, it has to work even harder, and if it can be convinced to run upstream as well, the toll on its energy is greater still. 'Let a fish run if there is room' is sound advice. You can control how much braking effect you

A catch of huge salmon from the Vosso at Bolstadoyri, in Norway. The best fish weighed 47 lb (21 kg).

apply in a number of ways: how freely you let the line run through your fingers, how hard you set the brake on the reel, or how you use your fingers to slow the spool. The ideal degree of control is to about 90 percent of the breaking strain of the weakest component of the tackle. A fish which will not run will tire more quickly if strain is put on it from behind and with an inclined rod: the inclination pulls the fish off balance and the pull from behind gives it more work to maintain station against the current.

5   Keep out of the fish's sight as much as possible. You want the fish to be puzzled – both by the hookhold and by its lack of freedom. However, any panic this may induce will not be as specific as the fear it will feel if it sees you, your guide, or both, looming over it. As much discretion is needed when you are playing a fish as when you are stalking it. Some of the best fish have been cajoled on a light line over a net only seconds after being hooked simply because they have seen nothing to be frightened of. (Refer to the diagram on page 174 if you are unclear about the fish's field of vision.) If I have a guide or a gillie with me, I like him to kneel by the water's edge. In this way I can see over him and follow what the fish is doing; he can see; the line will pass over him; most of him will be hidden from the fish, and any part of him that shows will be so slight and so static that the fish will be unaware of it as a threat.

6   Establish who is giving instructions. We have all known occasions when the fisher tells the guide or gillie what he wants done and is given contradictory advice. The solution to the problem is easy: who has the greater experience? If the fisher has experience of thousands of fish, he will indicate where he will bring the fish for the guide to net it. If the guide knows all the snags and difficulties, he will suggest landing places of his own, and so on. If the fisher says, 'I think we will bring it in in this little bay,' there is time for the guide to politely suggest another tactic if he thinks this proposal unwise. If the netter has very little experience, it must be the fisher who commands the situation.

7   Drowned line adds drag which cannot be controlled by the fisher. Line dragged in a straight path through water offers friction and resistance, and if the length trailed is long enough it may even break with no load of any other sort on it. Floating fly lines, in particular, have a large diameter for their density: in the water they present considerable resistance which may be hugely increased if the fish runs deep, wide and far.

A fisher tries not to play his fish on too long a line. His rod hand may even have to be held above his head to try to keep the angle of the line's entry into the water as steep as possible, and his movements upstream or downstream will often be aimed at keeping the line from being drowned. The classic example of this situation occurs with the big migratory fish: they take, head fast downstream, then turn deep and head up the pool. The fisher is standing facing downstream, with his line screaming off the reel, yet in the corner of his vision he can see a big fish jumping hard against a relentless line-pull from downstream. If he goes downstream in order to straighten out the belly of line in the water and raises the rod as much as possible, all may turn out well.

8   A reel spool that is nearly empty has a much greater braking effect than one that is nearly full. If the spool has a resistance of 1 lb (0.5 kg) when full to the circumference, the pull will be 2 lb (1 kg) when the spool is reduced in

This fish is having a hard time since the thicker sections of the rod are working against it. The very short length of line lacks elasticity.

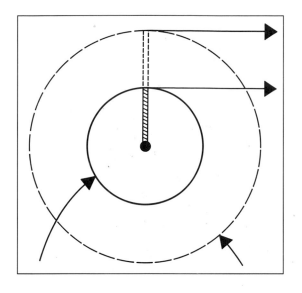

A reel spool that is nearly empty exerts a much stronger braking effect than one that is nearly full.

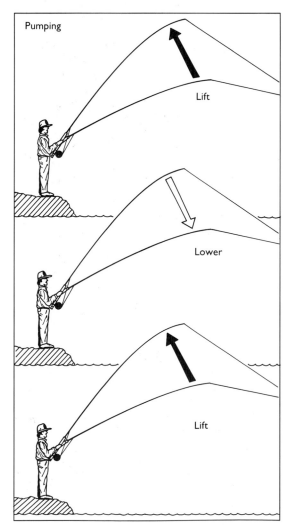

Some tension is maintained throughout the pumping of a fish, but it is vastly increased during the lifting phase.

diameter by half. When all the line and most of the backing has been stripped off, the tension is progressively even higher. Checks are normally set to prevent line spilling out when line is pulled out for casting or fishing. At this minimal check, the danger when the spool is nearly empty is largely removed. Braking effects may be produced by the spool, as described above, or by controlling the pace of the line as it passes through the fingers. If the reel's internal brake is used, it *must* be adjusted to become softer as the spool empties.

9 Change the inclination of the rod to steer the fish or to keep it off balance, as desired. The introduction to fly-casting (see pages 110-113) describes angle and inclination. The angle of the rod determines the pressure, but the dynamics of this pressure may be subtly changed if the rod is inclined to the vertical or horizontal or in between. The vertical rod is highest above the water. If the rod hand is raised above the head, the reach upward is increased. This is valuable for keeping the line out of the water. If the rod is inclined horizontally the side pressure will pull the fish off balance, making it work hard and tire more quickly than if the pull were from above. Throughout the fight a wide range of angles and inclinations can be used to advantage.

10 'Pump' the fish in. More leverage is achieved by lowering the butt of the rod to a shallow angle and then raising it, and repeating this sequence as many times as necessary, than by using the reel handle to wind in line. This pumping action maintains tension but increases it on the lift and makes it easy to wind in during the lowering stage. Pumping is standard practice in big-game fishing but is underexploited for the bigger freshwater game fish. It can be used with a fly rod as well as with a spinning or bait-casting rod. Another advantage is that it lays the line on the reel under less tension than winding in.

11 'Walk' the fish out of trouble. This is a technique suitable for the larger migratory fish which is not widely understood and is therefore woefully underused. Sometimes it is necessary to move a stubbornly entrenched fish to an area of the water which suits the fisher better. When the fish is holding station steadily against a firm pressure (though not hysterical or in panic-stricken flight) it may be possible, by clamping the line to the handle and maintaining a high rod angle, to tow it into another area. In most cases the fish will follow remarkably tamely, provided that you maintain even tension and do not attempt to wind in.

Since the tension is constant and the fish can be 'felt' down the line, there is no need to watch the fish. Indeed it is a mistake to do so for it is far better to look where you are walking, to avoid stumbling or even encountering an impassable cliff or vegetation. Such is the magnetism of the hooked fish that I have actually seen a wretched angler, eyes fixed on the line entering the water, walk right into a tree. Walking a fish is therefore very difficult for a complete novice who, despite all advice, will persist in watching the fish. Those with more experience understand that the tension in the line conveys all necessary messages between the fish and the angler, and if it signals a change in the fish from quiescence to activity, then the walking session ceases. To give one example of the use of the tactic: a big fish is far too close to the tail of a pool and there is no passageway for the fisher to follow into the pool below. Walking may take the fish up far enough to diminish the risk of losing it.

12   The shorter the line, the less the elasticity. When the fish is nearly ready to be netted (or otherwise landed) is the time when the hookhold is near its loosest. The fish is being drawn into shallower water, which gives it another stimulus of fear, and fisher and guide may suddenly become visible, increasing the fish's sense of danger. A combination of firmness and delicacy is needed in this situation. The reel check or brake should be at its minimum setting and the rod angle high, so that you have as much flexibility as possible. With a long line there is some cushioning stretch, but with a short line most of this effect is lost, so shakes and thrashes of the fish's head are relatively more severe.

Great caution is called for when the fish is ready to be netted as at this time the hookhold is least secure.

ON LOSING FISH

It is a matter for you and your conscience whether you genuinely lost a fish or merely had a take which did not hold on. But perhaps it is just a question of degree: occasionally a fish just nips, and there is no chance of establishing a good hookhold. On other occasions the fly or bait is positively engulfed and any loss cannot conceivably be blamed on a faulty hookhold. However, if you cultivate an analytical approach the following truths become apparent.

1   Some fish do not take wholeheartedly. They either close their mouths on the bait and immediately discard it, or allow the hooks so little purchase that the points do not penetrate either past the barb or, if the hooks are barbless, the points are not fully covered.

2   Some tackle is defective. Hooks have their points broken off, the metal cracks at the bend or the points become dulled. Leaders can be time-expired, acquire knots where knots should not be, and become

Playing an early-season trout.

abraded. The line itself might have been ground against sharp rock or gravel by a careless foot, or – it does happen – hot cigarette ash could have fallen into the spool, damaging the line. More commonly, it is possible for a reel to jam. Also, a rod may have a fracture that remains undetected until it is put to the strain of playing a fish, when it shows itself dramatically.

Often we hurry in tying our knots, scarcely expecting to hook a fish big enough to test them to the limits. We should realize too that poor casting will induce 'wind knots,' either simple overhands or figures-of-eight. Each such knot reduces the breaking strain to about half, or less, the rated strength of the leader material.

The spinning or bait-casting angler faces his own problems and in particular may revile himself more than most for not having oiled and maintained his swivels and mounts.

3   Some fish are lost by mischance. In such cases there is really nothing that skill or experience can do. My wife was most aggrieved when the only tree felled that month swept down the river just as she hooked a wild, early-season fish. The river bed was being raked by the branches: there was no chance that dipping the rod top in the water could pass the line under the obstruction. The angler also has little chance if a seal or an otter spots the fish in its difficulties.

What is an acceptable ratio of fish landed to fish lost seems to be as variable as how many shotgun shells should be fired for what proportion of game gathered. Different anglers after different species in different circumstances will show different figures; yet all of them may be thoroughly proficient. A trout angler who ties a good imitation and presents it well should have it taken confidently by the fish, and his losses will be few. A salmon fisher may experience almost 100 percent success for several days when the fish take readily but the remaining days of his week's vacation may be punctuated by more fish lost than landed, as conditions deteriorate in some way detected by the fish alone.

The philosophical among us will take each fish as it comes. Even so, most of us have livelier imaginations than that and, rather than accept that for each one we catch we can expect to lose one, we nurse a secret suspicion that we could do better – three taken to one lost, perhaps. However, to assume that such a ratio could be the average all the time can only lead to disappointment. Certainly, single hooks, which used to be so highly regarded, have become less favored, particularly for Atlantic salmon, and doubles are universally popular. Those who designed so many of the baits, spoons and lures found that trebles, triples, gang hooks and triangles seem to be the most effective. Where the rules allow them and where size makes them practical, trebles have taken over from doubles.

Proof of mischance is difficult with hooks. A very long shank will offer more leverage than a hook with a shorter shank, but an imitation may be inexact on a short shank or some other compromise may have to be made. Very long lures might offer exceptional leverage which could loosen a hookhold, so some anglers alter them; the action is not spoilt but the blade is not able to exert any force in the fight when a fish is hooked. Tinkering with tackle is very subjective. Even though the reputable manufacturers do their best to make their tackle items as efficient as possible, some anglers see the advantages of adaptation.

The final way in which a fish is lost is at the 'landing' stage of the fight – poor netting, gaffing, tailing and beaching techniques. However, since the use of these methods is explained on pages 105-9, it is not repeated here.

SPINNING AND BAIT-CASTING

Bait-casting and spinning have some advantages over fly-fishing. In particular, the lack of necessity for a back cast as used in fly-casting allows fishing in very restricted spaces, with the bait or lure pulling the line out behind it. Also, the line offers less water resistance, so that the bait or lure can find its depth quickly. The bait-caster or spinner nevertheless thinks of the water three-dimensionally, just as the fly-fisher does. He considers the direction of the cast, the bait or lure's movement in relation to the water-flow (in a river) and the fishing depth.

However, both the bait-casting reel and the spinning reel give a much faster rate of retrieve than the fly-fisher can manage, particularly if the reel has high gearing. Such a reel makes it possible to cast upstream in very fast water and to retrieve at an appropriate depth and speed.

There is an enviable distinction about a really first-class spinner or bait-caster: he makes the accurate judgement of distance look so effortless. It is because he has practised and gained experience. As many business executives have golf-putting kits in their office, so do many ambitious employees in tackle companies set up targets on the warehouse floor and spend their coffee-breaks (and other time no doubt) flicking out tiny sinkers until they are spot-accurate, with overhead, side or underhand casting. One of the most striking aspects of this practice is the accuracy achievable in a limited space: the very compactness makes fly-casting, however elegant, appear so wasteful of space in achieving its distance, so uneconomical of effort.

If fly-casting is throwing no weight on the end of a heavy string, bait-casting and spinning are throwing a weight on a weightless string: arm movement and rod flex and dynamics propel the weight until air resistance and friction slow it. Air resistance is the head-on force which a bait or lure faces on the forward delivery and the pressure that the wind can put on a line as the bait travels forward, pulling it off course. Gravity has to be countered, to give the forward delivery enough distance. The longer the flight the higher the bait may have to be sent, yet it may then be caught by air resistance, so speed of delivery plays a part, and this means learning to throw the bait on different trajectories to minimize the problems.

Bait-casting

This style of fishing was practised long before spinning. In the early nineteenth century anglers wanted a better casting system than swinging loose coils down the rod rings, trailing the throw of the natural minnow bait. Reels of that period had too much friction to revolve freely enough for line to spool off under the force of the cast. It was not until watchmakers looked at reels and designed freer-running spools and gears that purpose-made bait-casting reels made their appearance. The line peeled off easily and could be cranked back at multiplications of ×3 or faster. Casting was easier and retrieving could be more varied, to increase the attraction of the bait, which lately progressed to artificial baits.

The bait-casting reel

The modern bait-casting reel has the following features within the ability to free-spool:

1 tension adjustment for free-spool running
2 an internal braking system to help prevent overrunning

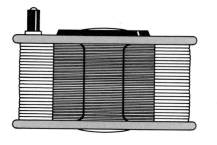
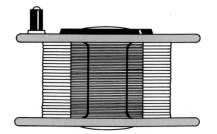

A well-filled spool offers less friction to the line as it runs out over the lip than an inadequately filled spool.

3 disengagement of gearing to the handle so that it does not rotate while the spool runs

4 some models disengage the level-wind mechanism to reduce friction within reel/on line during cast.

On retrieval of line:

1 turning the handle engages the gears: the spool takes up line at the stated rate of multiplication

2 by backwinding, we can pay out line

3 setting the ratchet returns the line against the pawl-and-ratchet, but prevents backwinding

4 the slipping-clutch can be set so that there is great or little resistance to line being pulled off the rotating spool – the fish can still pull off line against this resistance

A bait-casting outfit and a spinning outfit. Note that for bait-casting the reel sits on top of the rod, while for spinning the reel hangs below it. The silhouette's dotted lines show how the spinning reel uses the full depth of the rod rings, forming a 'cone,' when line peels off the spool.

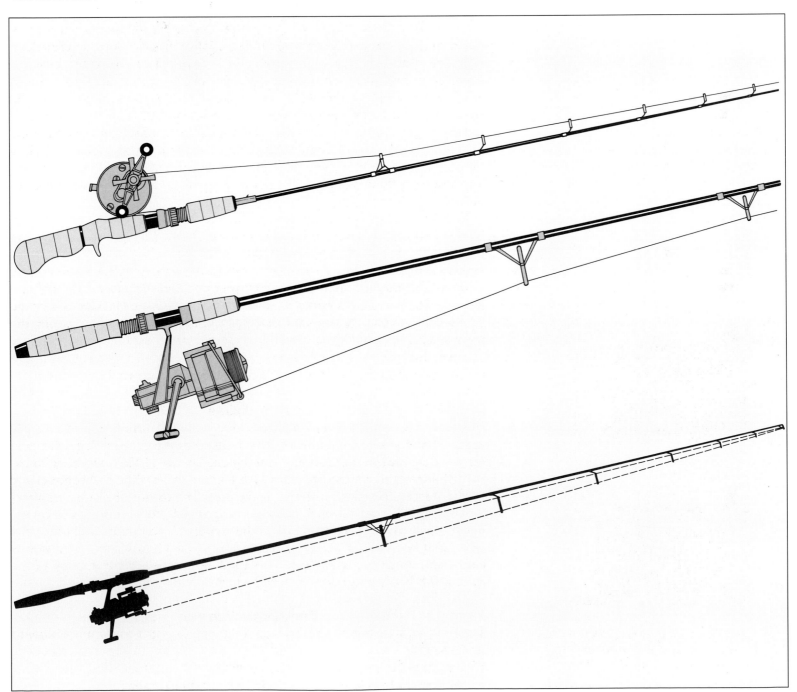

The modern bait-casting reel is a sophisticated piece of precision engineering. The multiplication ratio may be as high as 5:1 (one turn of the handle produces five of the spool) and the internal braking, to prevent over-runs, is centrifugal, magnetic or electronic. Right-hand and left-hand wind models are available.

The bait-casting reel is controlled by the thumb. Just before the cast, the thumb rests on the spooled line: it prevents rotation until it is lifted to allow the cast to extend. The thumb may apply pressure on the rotating spool to add to the internal braking system or even snub an over-cast. Normally, as the cast is projecting onward and forward, the thumb waits until the bait just about touches the water and then presses down on the spool to prevent a possible overrun. The handle is then taken up and the retrieve commences.

Mastery of the bait-casting reel comes with experience: it takes longer to learn to deliver the cast smoothly and to avoid overruns, which occur when the spool is accelerated so sharply that it rotates faster than the line can peel off it. If the most enjoyable technique is to play fish on a single-action fly reel, playing a fish on a multiplying bait-casting reel is certainly much closer to this than playing a fish on a fixed-spool. This is perhaps another reason for trading off the necessary extra skill needed against the greater pleasure of playing the fish.

The beginner with a bait-casting outfit must progress slowly. Practise short, easy casting until the operation of the reel becomes second nature and progress from there. Trying too hard is the cause of most of the troubles encountered. My own preference is for a braided line: I can see where it enters the water more easily than I see monofilament, and this helps me judge both the retrieve and where the fish I am playing is likely to be. However, it offers a little more water resistance. Whichever line is chosen, it should balance the bait's weight and the rating of the rod, for bait-casting and spinning rods are designed and rated according to the weight of bait. The guiding principle is maximum strength with minimum diameter for the rating required.

Spinning

Ths history of spinning is far shorter than that of bait-casting: the technique originated in the 1930s. Its casting principles are similar, but the reels are very different. What gave the style its impetus was the advent of nylon monofilament with its smooth, almost frictionless finish. In the fixed-spool spinning reel the spool's face points directly down the rod rings, so that the line lies on it at right angles to the rod. Instead of the spool rotating to pay off line, the line escapes over the front edge of the spool, which is fixed. The bale-arm (or flier) picks up the line and, when the handle is turned, rotates, laying the line back on the spool. The bale-arm is moved out of the way for casting and clicked back into position for retrieving line. The only friction at the reel is caused by the surface of the line brushing gently against the lip of the spool.

The spinning reel

The reel is fixed under the rod handle: it is designed to point slightly upward, to direct the line through the rings at an angle which causes least friction. As the line peels off the spool it forms a 'cone' which has a rotating brushing friction on the insides of the rings as well as a longitudinal friction as it pulls outward toward the water.

To cast, the bale-arm is disengaged and the forefinger tip crooks round the line to keep tension between the line and the spool. Monofilament is the ideal line for the system, but it is springy and must not be allowed to fall uncontrollably off the spool. At the appropriate moment the forefinger releases the line, the bait's weight pulls the line out and, soon after, the bait touches the water. The extended forefinger can add friction to the line

A spinning reel is an item of precision engineering with a line-braking mechanism. Depending on the model, this is adjusted at the front of the spool or at the rear end of the reel.

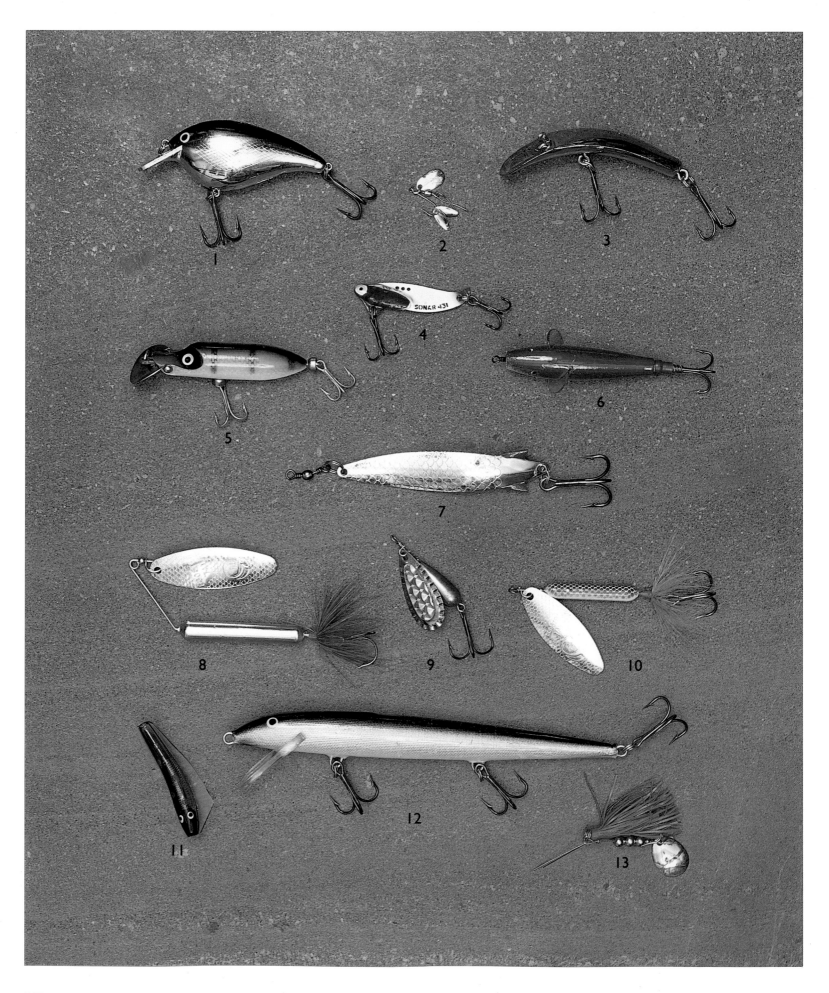

coming off the spool by slightly getting in the way, feathering the line – the equivalent (but different) of helping the internal spool brake on the bait-casting reel – and it can pinch down on the lip of the spool at any time, terminating the cast. If the retrieve is to begin immediately, the other hand turns the handle to engage the bale-arm, which starts to rotate round the spool, storing the line again for the next cast. If the retrieve is to begin only after more line has been paid out, the forefinger of the rod-holding hand is used to trap the line or let it slide out until the handle comes into operation.

Fixed-spool reels have a pawl-and-ratchet mechanism. When engaged, the winding handle clicks and backwinding becomes impossible. If the 'click' is not engaged, the handle and the bale-arm turn freely either way. If a fish takes with the reel set thus, there is no appreciable braking effect or drag but a blur of speed from the bale-arm and a flailing handle. Set the 'click' and the line pulls through the static bale-arm onto the spool itself. At this point the spool, according to the tension at which it is set on its axle, will rotate to pay off line. The drag adjustment may be on the face of the spool or at the far end of its axle. If it is too strongly set, the tackle may snap or the hook tear out; too weakly set, and the fish cannot be brought in even though winding the handle might seem to be doing something. If there is always some slight tension in the line it will not fall off the spool.

Spinning and bait-casting reels are to some extent interchangeable. The fixed-spool spinning reel is a better performer with the lightest tackle – less than ¼ oz (7 gm) – since there is no spool inertia to overcome, only friction on the spool's edge. The bait-casting reel copes better with the heavier weights because reel inertia is not a problem here, and is a better choice because the spinning reel's friction increases with larger diameter nylon and an emptying spool offers increased friction. But there are other reasons for choosing a fixed-spool reel: it is easier to use for anglers of average ability and is considerably cheaper. Nevertheless, it is a rather impersonal way to play a fish.

Baits and lures for spinning and bait-casting

The baits and lures used for spinning and bait-casting have enough weight to pull the line out behind them, or weight may be added. Movement may take the form of a straight line retrieve, or a wiggle, oscillation or rotation about the bait's own axis. The bait may also dive or rise in a vertical plane, depending on its design and buoyancy and the pressure put on it. There will be a movement, or lack of movement, or pace, or a combination which constitutes a 'good' retrieve and the fish takes.

Spoons

This type of lure has ancient origins, having been made from pieces of bone or shell by primitive hunters in the dawn of history. The modern metal spoon is said to be the outcome of a teaspoon's falling overboard and being seized by a fish on its way through the water. Here, it was Julio Buel who dropped it; in England the tale is similar and no doubt mainland Europe also has a few originators of the spoon. If a spoon is a 'wobbler' it is an oscillator: it has a fluttering action calculated to be at its most efficient and controllable at a particular speed through the water, either pace of retrieve or pressure of current, or a combination of both. Some spoons spin on their own axis but if slowed or accelerated become unstable and oscillate or flutter. But note that this action may need to be induced to improve the attraction to the fish.

The blade spoon is a 'spinner' in which a blade spins round a shank which

1. *Big S* 2. *Fly Spoon* 3. *Kwikfish*
4. *Sonar*
5. *Devon Minnow* 6. *ABU Hi-Lo*
7. *Toby*
8. *Rooster Tail* 9. *Droppen* 10. *Rooster*
11. *Vaned Minnow* 12. *Rapala* 13. *Hildebrandt.*

Because of the environmental risks of lead, alternative substances have widely replaced it to weight tackle. The traditional shapes and styles of weights and sinkers are still used.

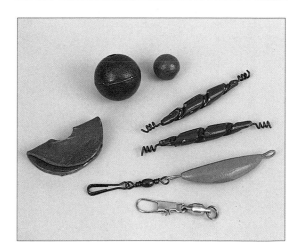

holds the hook at its extremity. The blade area and shape differ between brands and according to design: some work at their best at the slowest speed of retrieve and in the weakest current, while others do not achieve their desired action unless traveling through the water at a great pace. If a 'slow' spoon is asked to work fast, its water resistance will prevent its sinking deeply and staying sunk when tension is put on it.

Plugs

Plugs are used mainly to catch black bass. The plug imitates a food form, or the action of a food form; or it arouses curiosity by its action; or it challenges the bass in his lair. However, a good plug does all these things with game fish, and makers vie to produce patterns for brown trout, salmon and other salmonids. Some produce different models to imitate the range of swimming, wiggling, bobbing or weaving patterns, while others add weights and vanes to one basic shape. Firms like Rapala consider that their products work best at specific speeds, on the finest lines practicable and without extra weight. If weight has to be added it must be well up the trace from the lure. A further requirement of Rapala is the use of a knot which does not pull up tight against the lure: the open-loop uniknot, for example.

A plug's size is not directly related to the size of fish to be caught – though there may be species and circumstances for which this is true – so to achieve the weight you want, you may choose a denser plug rather than a larger one. The pace at which you fish it will often be determined by the temperature. High air and water temperatures call for a faster speed than lower temperatures. As for depth, the plug must work at the level where the fish feed or lie, or where their metabolism is most comfortable with the temperature.

In the illustration below right, the left-hand rig shows the use of a lightly weighted float to free-drift a natural bait just above the river bed. The right-hand rig illustrates the use of a heavier weight to anchor the bait near to the bottom. The illustrations below show three methods of weighting. In the first two the weight is prevented from twisting the reel line by the use of swivels. The third pattern is very simple and is used where little weight is required.

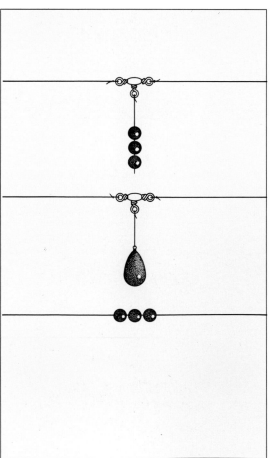

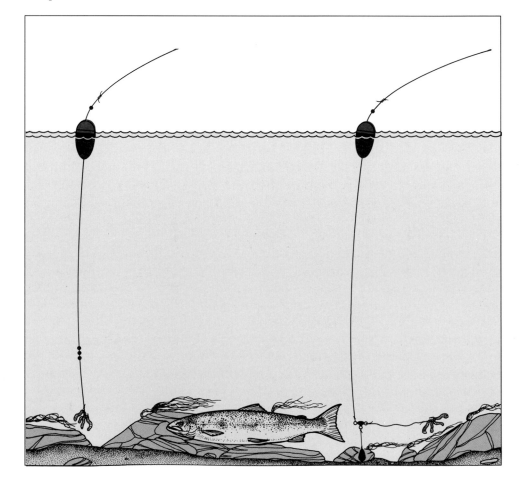

Bait action

The depth at which a bait fishes depends on its weight, the water resistance and the pull of the retrieve. Plug baits may also be designed with a diving capability: the pull of the retrieve makes them angle downward. Release the pressure and they float upward. Different combinations of diving lip and density of construction allow a wide variety of diving actions. Whereas the fly line has a capacity to control fly pace or depth by virtue of its bulk, buoyancy or degree of density, the spinner's or bait-caster's line is hardly usable in the same way as it has least possible substance and weight.

It has already been said that tackle is matched and balanced to the weight of bait. Hairlining kits which can throw ⅛ oz (4 gm) baits do not operate the medium or heavyweight baits. Rod action, reel and line are all wrong. Sometimes anglers choose to fish the combination of tackle they enjoy most, rather than present a bait or lure of a size which might be considered ideal for the conditions. However, a guide to matching tackle to bait and line may be useful:

Tackle	Bait	Line
light	⅛-½ oz (4-15 gm)	8 lb (3.5 kg) or less
medium	⅜-¾ oz (12-20 gm)	10 lb (4.5 kg)
heavy }	¾-1¼ oz (20-35 gm) much over 1¼ oz (35 gm)	12 lb (5.5 kg) stronger than 12 lb (5.5 kg)

A heavier line may be used if the water is full of snags or the fish are particularly big; a lighter one if conditions are low, bright and clear. The advantages of bait-casting and spinning are the slow speeds and acceleration necessary to lob out the bait or lure compared with the speed needed to achieve distance with a fly and a fly line. Indeed no natural bait can stay on the hook at fly-casting speeds. The aerial casts are too fast, while on-the-water casts offer too much resistance and the bait breaks off.

Natural baits

Common natural baits include earthworms, crawdaddies, frogs, hellgrammites and shiners, to name a few. Each, as Izaak Walton suggested in *The Compleat Angler,* should be treated 'as if you love him' so that it lasts as long as possible and maintains its characteristic action. Natural fish eggs are a famously good bait. Rules and regulations stipulate what natural baits may be used in the various regions and your own ethics may stop you mounting live baits. The bait's characteristic behavior is best exploited by fishing at the correct depth. Adding weight will lower or anchor the creatures. The use of a float may determine how close to the surface it can be kept; or the float can be used to indicate a strike at a bait which is sufficiently weighted to lie on the bottom.

Earthworms, described by Sosin and Clark as equal to liver as the most attractive bait for catfish, have much the same attraction for resident game fish. They are at times particularly successful with Atlantic salmon, notably when rivers are running big and colored and the fish move out of the strong main flows. Worms can be lowered into a likely hole or lie or worked along the river bed, upstream or down.

A selection of common natural baits, showing hooking technique. From top to bottom: fish eggs, shiner, earthworm, hellgrammite, crayfish.

205

CASTING

The simplicity of casting with spinning and bait-casting tackle is one of its virtues. The back cast used in fly-casting is not needed, nor is it necessary to 'load' the rod by extending the line in order to gain the weight needed for casting. The rod's properties are essentially those of lever and spring, as in fly-casting, and the power is introduced into the cast by movement of the wrist and forearm.

The rod is usually short, and shortness aids casting accuracy. The rod does not have to be longer than 5½-7 ft (1.7-2.1 m), even with heavier baits, and nearly all spinning and bait-casting are done with a single-handed rod. Where a two-hander is used, a practical length is 9-9½ ft (2.7-2.9 m); rods longer than 10 ft (3 m) are seldom used. The action is similar to that of fly rods, occurring in the tip only or progressively throughout its whole length right down into the handle.

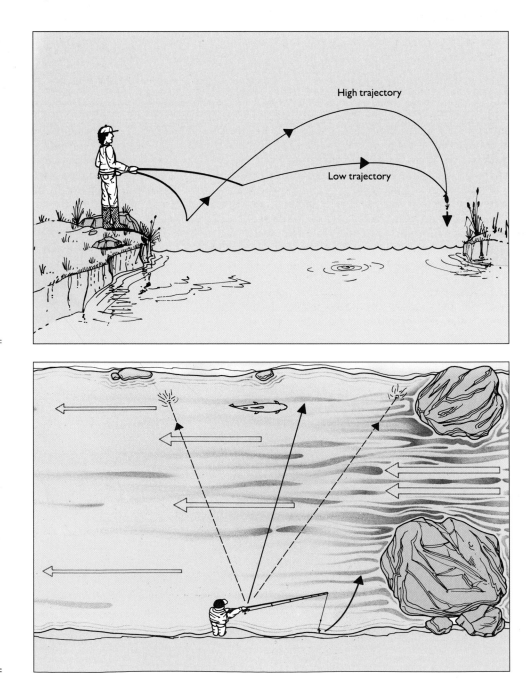

The high trajectory is achieved when the power is put in early and the line released early in the forward casting stroke. It is also a product of using a rod with a through action. The low-trajectory cast is harder and faster, and less affected by the wind. The effort and release come later in the forward cast.

The dynamics of casting at other inclinations are similar to those of the overhead cast. However, the more horizontal the inclination, the more gravity has to be overcome and the more wrist action (with minimal forearm movement) is needed. If the power and delivery are put in too soon the cast veers off to the right, while if they are too late the bait goes off target to the left. The side cast is explained on pages 210–11.

Casting for spinning has similar dynamics, but the line control differs. The forefinger maintains the tension between the bait and the line on the spool, above right, and the bale-arm is disengaged. At the moment when the thumb would release the bait-casting reel's spool, the forefinger releases the line. It is possible to check the flow of line by 'feathering,' below right, bringing the forefinger back toward the spool, so adding friction to the 'cone' of line peeling off. The line is stopped by firm pressure on the rim of the spool. The bale-arm is re-engaged, to pick up line, when the handle is turned.

Overhead cast

For casting a bait, a slightly open stance is the most comfortable, since when a single-handed rod is used there is little need for weight transfer. With the elbow bent and the hand in a vertical line with the nose at about high waist level, the caster points the rod so that its tip is at about eye level. By articulating the shoulder and bringing the forearm upward, he makes the top of the butt come up level with the eyes. No wrist movement is needed at this stage.

If the rod is stopped at the vertical position, the bait should pull the rod tip back, flexing the rod backward. The forward cast, which is where the power is needed, and provided, is begun by the forearm's forward movement and acceleration from the wrist, which snaps forward. The hand ends up at high waist level and the rod tip is centered between the eyes, much the same as in the start position. Meanwhile the thumb of the casting hand must release the bait the moment after the rod has

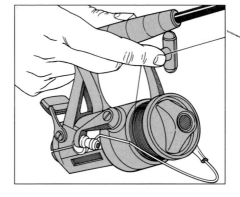

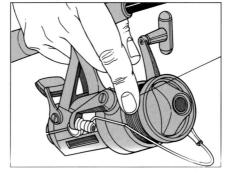

achieved maximum casting force, allow the spool to revolve until the bait has finished its flight, and then clamp down on the spool – not to *slow* but to *stop* its rotation. During the flight of the bait, it may be necessary to apply slight thumb friction to the spool, preventing it rotating faster than the line can pay off from it, before the final stop.

This is the most accurate casting method, since the rod performs along the line of sight.

1 *The rod is back, the thumb is on the spool and the 'free spool' button has been set. The bait is given a little backward impetus to 'load' the rod.*

2 *With the rod aligned with the line of sight, power is put in.*

3 *As soon as the power is delivered, the thumb is removed from the spool.*

4 *Out go the line and bait. When the bait has reached the required distance or is about to hit the water, the thumb is used to stop the spool.*

In the overhead cast it is useful to consider what happens at the rod tip during the backward movement preparatory to the forward cast. If, as in the first diagram on the right, the rod is held steady, angled over the shoulder, the bait hangs vertically. Mechanically this is inefficient because the rod's travel and the bait's travel have to be made to line up. If the bait is swung backward, as in the second diagram, there is a critical moment when it is in the rod's line of travel. Mechanically this is far better. But if, as in the third diagram, the rod is also flexed at this moment, the spring imparted to it boosts the forward cast.

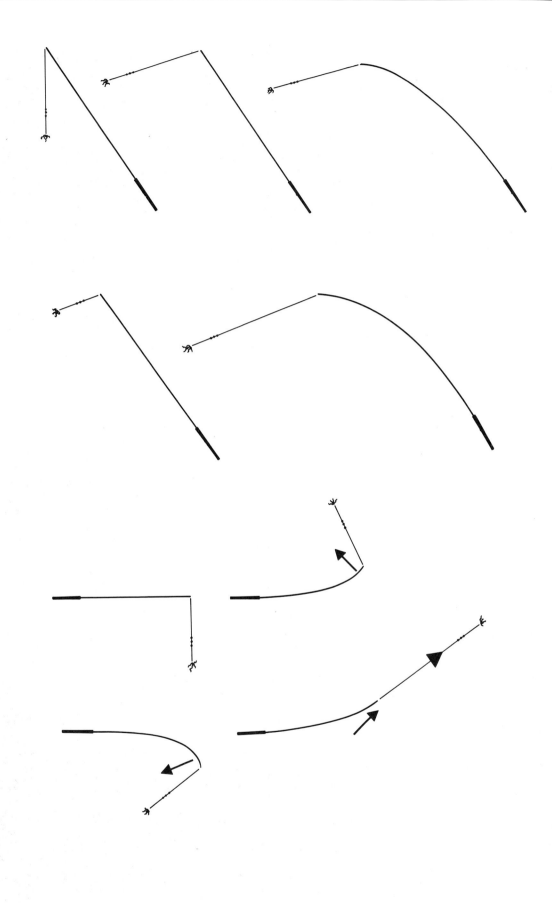

There is a further mechanical advantage in having a longer rather than a shorter length of line from the rod tip to the bait, particularly if the bait is very light. It requires practice to put sufficient effort in the backward movement to make the rod flex and the bait stand off the rod tip at the best angle. This fleeting moment must be timed accurately, because it is precisely then that the forward throw should begin.

An advantage of the short rod for bait-casting and spinning is that an 'underhand' cast can be made, although it is unlikely to achieve as much distance as the overhead or side case. The mechanical benefits of the weight's being in a suitable path of travel are necessary, in addition to as much rod flex as possible. The cast is carried out as follows:

The rod is held straight out in front, pointing in the correct direction.

On the backward movements the rod is flicked up to 10:00, when the bait should swing up from the rod tip and the rod should flex.

The rod is brought down to 4:00, forming a mirror-image of the previous curve.

The twist and return spring of the rod make it return to pointing out in front of you. The spool is now released to rotate.

If the upward, downward and upward sequence is in a vertical plane and in line with your line of sight, the bait should be placed accurately for direction. However, it takes practice to achieve the desired distance. A long pendulum length – line plus bait – beyond the rod tip can catch on the ground or against the water in front of you, so it is important to find the ideal length.

Spinning at night in North Carolina. The lack of light does not matter – feeling a take is all-important.

Bow-and-arrow cast

This cast, also known as the catapult cast, is possible with a short, flexible spinning rod, horizontally, vertically or at any other inclination. The line suspending the bait from the rod tip must be long enough for the bait to be reached by the free hand, but short enough to put the required bend in the rod when pulled taut.

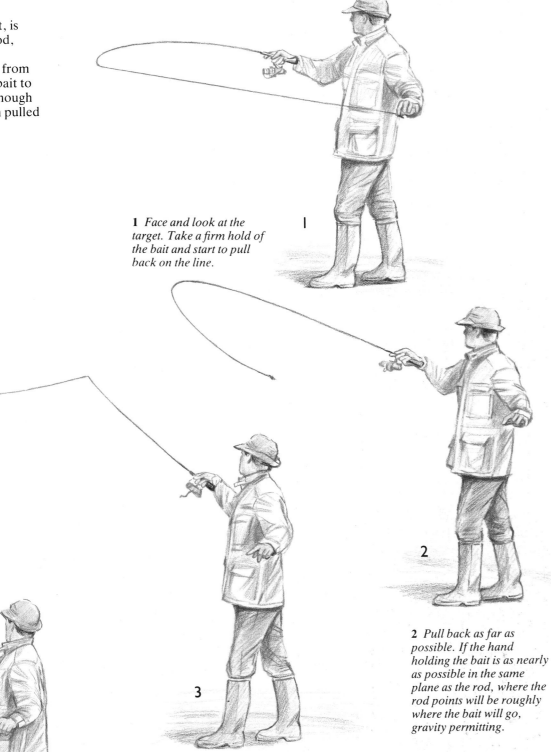

1 *Face and look at the target. Take a firm hold of the bait and start to pull back on the line.*

2 *Pull back as far as possible. If the hand holding the bait is as nearly as possible in the same plane as the rod, where the rod points will be roughly where the bait will go, gravity permitting.*

3 *Release the bait.*

4 *As the bait flies out, use the reel finger to 'feather' or check the line to achieve the required distance.*

OPPOSITE   *Spinning from a two-man boat calls for a good distance between lines.*

*The trout-rich waters of the legendary
Neversink River, New York State.*

OTHER GAME FISHING TECHNIQUES

Much of the enjoyment in game fishing comes from the casting – with the fly rod, or bait-casting or spinning rod. However, there are some presentations which do not call for all this activity. That the first to be dealt with below is now part of history seems to put it to the back of fishers' minds. If it seems sneaky, think of it as trying to outwit a quarry well equipped to look after itself.

Dibbing

This technique, also known as dibbling, does not involve casting: it may present the fly on the surface, shallowly below the surface, and deeper. The rod is extended over the water and the fly lowered on a short line and short leader, with, sometimes, a small added weight to steady the line, leader and fly (or natural bait – for example, a grasshopper). No subtlety is called for in

In dibbing a simple up-and-down movement is imparted to the fly to attract fish to the surface.

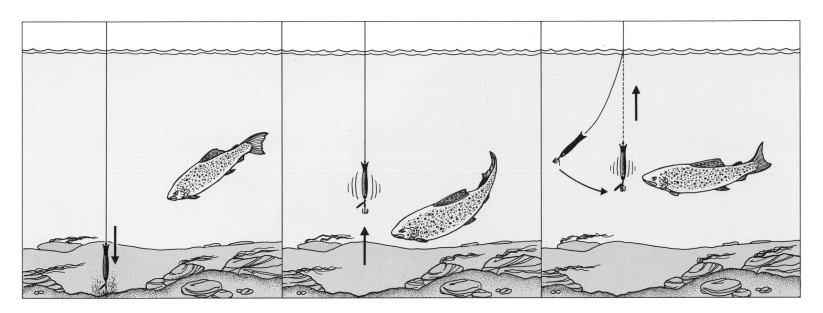

the rod or the line, and no more than adequate breaking strain in the leader. Normally dibbing takes place at the surface, for it was the earliest form of fly presentation in angling and it was difficult to get early flies to sink. The disturbance at the surface and the appearance of natural activity attract the fish.

With normally weighted nymphs and wet flies, the same presentation is possible, but when the fly is heavily bulked with lead, or is a shaped weight with hooks, the technique is called jigging. This technique, which is not far from the early gorge-fishing of our primitive ancestors, is vertical fishing with a vengeance. You find the depth of the lake or river bed, count the bait down to the bottom then reduce that length by enough to be able to give the bait an up-and-down motion. When the first fish has been taken the bait can be counted straight down to the taking zone. Dibbing and jigging can be done from anchored boats or in ice-holes. Specialized jigging rods are normally used: a bait-caster or a spinning rod is an alternative, and only under pressure of circumstances is a fly rod used.

Critical to the success of jigging is the depth at which the lure is presented, and the length and speed of the jigging movement.

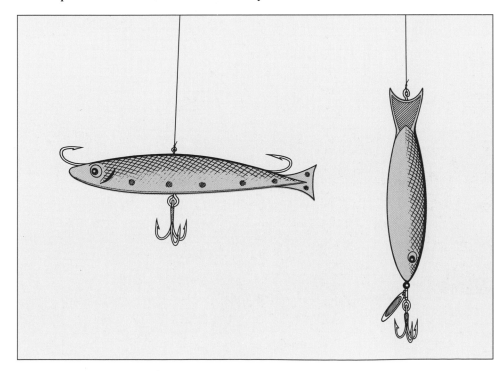

Examples of jigging lures showing different arrangements of hooks.

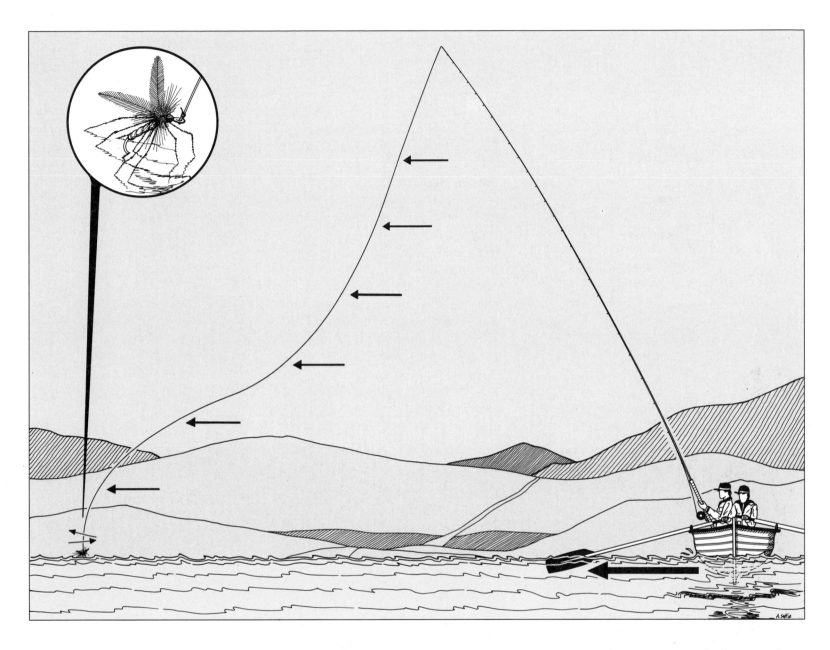

Dapping

For this technique a dapping line is needed, since this ensures a dry fly and allows the fly alone, without even any of the leader, to work on the surface. A long rod is needed – 14 ft (4 m) is not too long – and the length of dapping line, which need be at most twice the length of the rod, is tied in between the point of the fly line and the butt of the leader. The line's qualities are to offer as much surface resistance to the wind as possible and to shrug off water easily. Its alternative name is 'blow line,' indicating that its behavior is largely determined by the wind. The line is not cast: as long a length as the wind will billow out downstream of the angler is held out over the water, while the angle of the rod is continually adjusted to keep the fly, and the fly alone, on the water. In this way the fly can be static, or can be lifted to trip and walk on the surface.

Dapping has its origins in Irish lough fishing, particularly with natural mayflies and craneflies. It is not yet widely known on the American gamefishing scene, but it deserves to be. If it should prove difficult to obtain dapping lines, British suppliers would be pleased to provide it, usually in 50-metre (55 yards) spools. It is not expensive.

Dapping has a reputation for bringing the best fish up to the surface. However, if the angler does not have a blinding headache at the end of a day's dapping he has not been concentrating fully.

OPPOSITE *Considerable dexterity is required to bring the fish up safely through the ice.*

Trolling

So many fish have been caught on flies trailing behind the boat, because the angler was too lazy to reel up before he made for his next fishing spot, that trolling is a well-established method of fishing for most game fish. The classic trolled fish is the landlocked salmon in its native lakes. In spring fish hawks hover and splash down, the ice is still there in great rafts as break-up takes place, and square-stern canoes with their Evinrude 9½ hp Fisherman motors ticking over, work their way in the open water at a gentle walking pace. From each side projects a low-held fly rod, into the water dip the trolling lines, experience and conditions suggesting the big streamers 20-30 yards (18-27 m) behind. The engine man steers a wavy course, giving a little extra flutter and action to the lures. The boat is covering the area where the smelt are congregated, and any moment a rod should go, with a self-hooking strike by a regular dynamo of a fish. Brook trout also, in their paler and more silvery large-lake coloration, will strike at this time.

The time of year will determine the water temperature and the food forms likely to be available. Local guides and fishers will advise on speed and depth and, if you are lucky, their favorite hot spots. Not all local rules and regulations permit motors, but it is possible to row or paddle and still achieve excellent results. Trolling is not just a stillwater activity: it is a very effective way of encountering fish on the bigger rivers and fly rods are used as well as bait-casting and spinning rods.

The best reason not to troll a bait or a lure behind a fly rod with fly reel

and fly line is that the line offers so much water resistance. Besides, the operation is conducted more comfortably and efficiently on bait-casting tackle. The multiplying reel makes line retrieval swift, and playing a fish is more comfortable than with a fixed-spool. Since ease of casting is not the criterion, as casting is not involved, again the bait-casting outfit is the best choice. Being short, bait-casting rods are also more precise, and seem to take the strain of being held out over the water more happily than fly rods. Some fishers, though, maintain that the longer and more supple rod can produce ascertainably better action in the bait or lure, and so more strikes. There is nothing to stop you from filling a single-action fly reel with a suitable line, and putting it on the shorter rod, or trying out variations. As for line, the braided kind is preferable to monofilament. Continuous braided trolling lines are obtainable in sequences such as red, yellow, blue, green; red, yellow, blue, green; and so on, the color typically changing every 10 yards (9 m). If monofilament is used it is less easy to see it entering the water, and so it must be marked at the required intervals with an indelible pen, because there is an optimum line length with which to obtain the best action from the lure. The distance from the boat should be far enough not to deter the fish, yet there should not be so much line out that it is too springy to set the hook. The length of line out must allow the lure to work at the required depth. Lake trout, in particular, occupy a specific temperature zone, and for this reason fishing depth is an extremely critical factor in the successful pursuit of them.

Trolling is a particularly productive technique for the voracious landlocked salmon.

CARE

AND

CONSERVATION

How to look after your tackle, yourself, and our fishing heritage are the contents of this chapter. A jammed reel and even a drowned angler in the long term pale into insignificance compared with a water system polluted beyond recovery and lost to fishing for all time, or a native species of trout ousted from its environment to perish.

It may just be a matter of perspective: it could be a 'tragedy' to a fisher if the fish of a lifetime gets away because a knot was poorly tied; it would naturally be a tragedy for a loving wife and children if a fishing husband and father is lost, drowned in a boating accident; yet it may be a matter of complete insignificance to many if a polluted stream is the result of a manufacturer's drive to increase profits. But something can be done: beyond looking after his tackle to save unnecessary disappointment, and looking after himself, the game fisher should both actively and passively protect his environment by doing nothing harmful to it, and by taking the lead or at least participating in action to prevent others from damaging it.

One of the charms of the belly boat is that it brings the fisher closer to nature. Also, the low profile is less disturbing than other boats to wildlife.

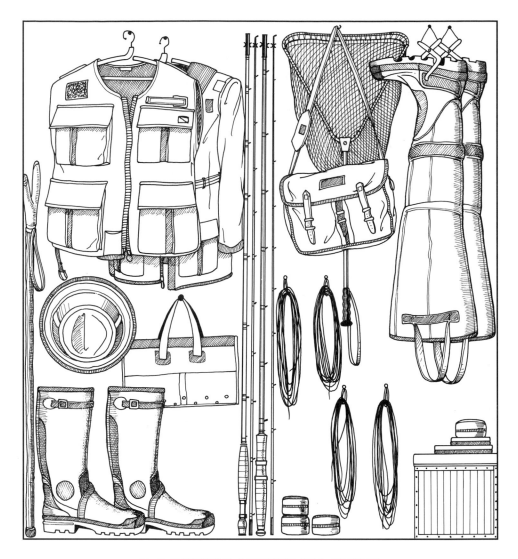

Orderly storage of fishing tackle and clothing is well worth the trouble.

LOOKING AFTER TACKLE

It is usual in the close season to run a thorough check on all tackle, discarding rusty hooks and time-expired small-diameter nylon, cleaning out the forgotten contents of vest pockets, and preparing for the coming season. Insurance of all tackle is best renewed at this time.

Care of fly lines

If fly lines are left tightly wound on reels and spools they keep a 'coil-memory' which causes kinks and tangles. There is a lot to be said for running lines off reels, giving them a good cleaning with the manufacturer's recommended cleaner (and re-plasticizer), twisting a pipe cleaner or two to hold the loose coils together, then hanging the line over a peg in the back of a cupboard away from light and heat.

If the line cannot be run off the reel and spool, before the first expedition run out the full length and put it under some tension and then clean and polish it with a soft cloth. Cleaning removes any algae or other contaminant, and gives you a chance to examine the line for wear or damage. Unwinding the line helps to remove the tiresome coil-memory. If it is a DT line, it may be time to turn it end for end. Damage may have occurred from treading on the line – easily enough done if the line is stripped in and the fish is not being played from the reel. Likewise this loose

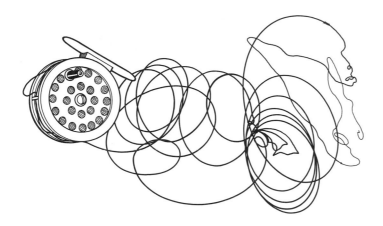

Coil-memory kinks can be infuriating. It is best to avoid them by regularly checking the line before fishing.

line may snag round vegetation. It should be disengaged rather than hauled or tugged free, and the same rule applies when, during wading, the stripped-in line snarls up on river-bed gravel or around rocks and ledges.

A crack or abrasion to the coating reduces a line's efficiency, while damage to the central core weakens it. Damage is also done to the plastic coating of fly lines by careless contamination with gas, anti-insect lotions, and chemical solvents. Some floatant greases are compatible, but not all, so check. For example, an intermediate can be made into a floater, so there is a reason for greasing a line. A number of lines are also touched against lighted cigars or cigarettes, and hot ash from them or a pipe, has often fallen onto the line on the reel with an unhappy result.

Spinning lines

The first few feet of monofilament nearest the bait or weight suffer a lot of friction at the rod top, so should be discarded regularly. They are also subjected to abrasion: from snags in the water, the fish's teeth or gill covers, and even from bankside vegetation if the line gets caught up. Since much of the strength of monofilament depends on its surface being unmarred, abraded monofilament should be discarded. It must be cut off the line, taken away and disposed of suitably – not left in the countryside, in any form – and that means burned.

Line should be run off fixed-spool reels and its length checked from time to time. Sometimes loops are trapped and subsequent casts may not be enough to clear them, so that they can prevent the free flow of line when a fish is on. The entire line may need renewing more than once a season if a lot of fishing is done. The line may be full of kinks, because baits can rotate either way by design, and so, if possible, fish right-hand and left-hand rotation baits alternately. If the kinks persist take off the bait or lure and walk through a meadow trailing the line; or trail the line in the current, or troll it from a boat. Another alternative is to set the rod up securely and, working from the tip to the end of the extended line, walk down the line gripping it with a cloth or handkerchief, applying medium pressure. In theory any kinking is removed when the reel is used: the line goes out with a twist in it, but is returned to a kink-free state by the bale-arm. In practice, swivels do not perform to perfection, and oscillating baits occasionally become unstable and rotate. A further problem is the twist put into the line by turning the handle while the clutch is allowing the spool to slip in order to pay out line under heavy pressure from a fish.

Extreme pressure on a monofilament line makes it stretch. Protracted stretching to the maximum weakens the line – another good reason to renew the entire line regularly. Do not let the line on a fixed-spool reel's spool fall too far below the ideal level, since increased friction and frustration will ensue. If necessary knot on extra line to bring the spool up to the required fullness. Monofilament can be bought in large, economy spools.

Bait-casting lines

Braided bait-casting line beds down on a bait-casting reel better than monofilament, but the choice is the angler's. Like monofilament, this line must be routinely examined for fraying, and it too can lie on the spool with loops protruding, causing undue wear, if it is wound on with any lack of even tension.

Use an indelible marker to indicate on the reel the line's breaking strain and its renewal date. The reservoir spool you will have already marked with the line's purchase date.

Leaders

All leader material should be dated when bought, and any with a breaking strain of under 12 lb (5.5 kg) should be renewed each year. Bright light, for example long exposure to sunlight, or exposure to ultraviolet, harms the material and reduces its breaking strain, so any dealer selling leader materials in ultraviolet-lit displays should expect his custom from another fisher. Any angler who leaves leader spools on the parcel shelf of his automobile is also unwise. Long-term storage should certainly be in the dark and at no extreme of temperature.

After playing a fish, check the leader for abrasion and unwanted knots (which reduce the breaking strain) and retie the fly or lure. If the material has a twist or curl, applying steady pressure by pulling it through a square of rubber from a tire's inner tube may straighten it. Check regularly for 'wind knots' and always after a poor cast. Check also for fraying if you are surrounded by vegetation, since the back cast may be catching on it. Finally, remember that in relation to the cost of a single fishing trip a few feet of tippet material costs very little, so do not skimp on this vital element.

Nylon line discarded in the water or on the bank frequently proves fatal to birds as they struggle unsuccessfully to free themselves from its tangles.

Care of rods

If you use a split-cane rod, bear in mind that natural wood of this kind has a limited life, shorter than the artificial materials like fiberglass or graphite and depends on its varnish to keep its life as long as possible. A split-cane rod should not be left damp, and should be checked regularly for cracks and defects in the varnish, since these will speed deterioration.

Whatever material the rod is made of, the ferrules must be kept clean. Metal ferrules wear less appreciably than those of fiberglass or graphite, so the makers of the latter two normally allow for wear. Rubbing the male ferrule with a very light coating of paraffin wax will increase its diameter slightly and helps prevent it from twisting loose. Badly fitting ferrules of any material may be made to fit better by the stopgap method of inserting a human hair or two, or, if very loose, a strand of finest nylon monofilament.

Rod rings may be checked by eye, or with the fingertips, for breaks or cracks. Running a silk handkerchief, or part of one, through them is a very sensitive detector of roughness. Any roughness is both abrasive, which is disastrous to the line in finish and strength, and increases friction, which is detrimental to casting. The tyings holding the rings to the rod should also be checked and replaced as necessary. Adhesive tape will do surprisingly long-lasting and durable service if wound on tightly with each turn overlapping in part the preceding, and then varnished.

Rods should be stored in cool, dark, ventilated conditions, subject to no extreme of temperature, with the ribbons on the rod sacks tied loosely, so as not to bend the sections. If it is leaned in a corner, a wooden rod will take a set. I use a wooden pole fitted with hooks to take the woven loops at the foot of each rod sack. Bugs might eat the handle if the rod is stored but never examined. Wipe the corks of the handle clean of fish slime, since this leads to rapid decay and increases the chance of insect attack.

Care of reels

The moving parts of reels should be lubricated with suitable grades of oil or grease. The thicker the lubricant, the less free-running the movement, so for ice-fishing, grease should be replaced with oil. Do not use a heavy-grade oil on a multiplier required to throw a light bait. The lubrication of fly reels is less critical, provided the works do not rust and the bearing surfaces have some lubrication on their faces. Salt is a major enemy, and even the best 'guaranteed' reels for saltwater use must be washed off in fresh water and dried after use. Ideally the line and backing should also be removed and washed down and dried.

Mud, sand and grit are further enemies, so avoid laying the rod flat on the ground with the reel touching such surfaces. Rain splashes these abrasives surprisingly high and penetratingly, so lay the reel on a hat or item of clothing to avoid this. A quick souse in the water may clear grit and a loosening of the spool latch will let the water into the works more easily: a bankside alternative to a major strip-down, thorough cleaning and relubrication. Grit can easily get in between the flange of an exposed rim and the frame. In this case it is wise to free the spool and clear the grit out. Check the screws and rivets intermittently to make sure that they are not working loose, and always check to see if the reel is fixed securely to the rod when the rod is to be carried on a roof rack.

Care of hooks, flies, baits and lures

Salt water is a major enemy of hooks, and the harm it causes is almost irremediable if not dealt with as soon as possible. Fresh water takes longer to produce a similar result. Rust and corrosion weaken the hook, blunt the point, and discolor the dressing of a fly. If the tippet/leader/trace knot is not detached from the eye, rust can form under the knot, and this forms an abrasive surface for the next knot to rub against.

It is worth establishing a discipline by which no wet, used fly, bait or lure goes back into a box or container with dry ones. Use a separate box and remove the knots and dry each fly, bait or lure before returning it to its usual container. Bad places to put flies and lures are in sheepskin patches or hats, since there they are forgotten and rust. This seems anyway to be more of an affectation than a useful fishing practice. Dry-fly hackles can look very tired after a fish has been caught. Back at home, if the fly is clean of slime, holding it in tweezers or forceps in the steam from the spout of a boiling kettle will re-radiate the fibers miraculously. When dry, the fly can be returned to its box.

Care of waders and float tubes
Strong light and high temperatures in the storage place do waders no good,

whether they are latex or PVC. Hung by the feet, so that they can air and do not crease, they are healthier to wear and last longer. If the fisher falls in, a liberal application of crumpled-up newspaper is the first stage in removing water from the waders, followed by *gentle* heat from purpose-made boot driers or a fan hairdrier. Waders which need wading brogues may abrade badly if sand or gravel enters the feet of the brogues, and therefore elasticated anklets are advisable. If gravel gets into the waders, it is best to remove it promptly.

To store float tubes, separate them from the canvas cover, wash both and keep cool and away from light. Washing gets rid of any sand or gravel, which would chafe and abrade the tubes. Inflate the tubes very slightly before storing them so that no folds or creases form which could become weak spots. Care of the valve is critical. The insert must keep out grit and must seat properly. Keep a spare and have a key to hand. Over-inflation puts the canvas cover under undue strain, and raises the center of gravity of the craft with its occupant, making it less stable. Finally, keep an air pump and a puncture-repair kit in your car.

Wading has many do's and don'ts, both for self-preservation and to help you get closer to the fish without disturbing them.

Boat fishing can be idyllic in good weather, but whenever conditions are changeable the constant need to ensure safety becomes even more important.

SELF-PRESERVATION

In fishing, unlike some other outdoor activities, the dangers are seldom from the quarry. However, water in any form must be treated with respect. Bank and wading anglers need to take as much care as if they were using a boat. Falling is the main danger when wading or bank fishing, so footwear is all-important, whether it is hip-boots or chest-high waders. Different river beds pose different problems of grip. The least satisfactory grip – almost useless everywhere – is cleated rubber, which provides minimal purchase on slime-covered rock, and if there is algal growth it offers no grip. The choice then lies between felt soles or studs. Felt has to be wriggled to cut through any algal coating on rock, but once established is secure. Studs, if blunt, can skate off rock; if sharp, and of tungsten, they can take a safe grip. The ideal is probably a tungsten-studded heel, with the rest of the sole in felt, though the choice is mostly all-stud or all-felt. The latter is my preference, but I watch out on slick grass banks.

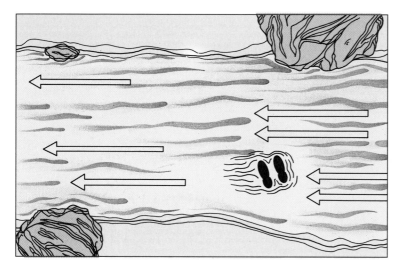

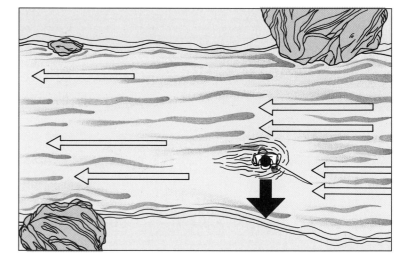

The angler may face less total water pressure by standing sideways to the current, above, than by standing more in line with it, below.

Crossing a current, above, or working upstream can be extremely hard work. To reduce effort, work downstream and toward the bank, below.

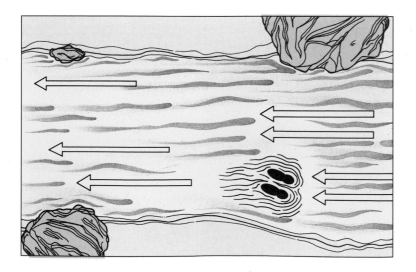

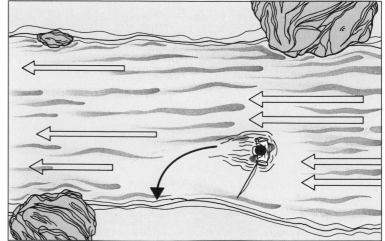

Wading

It is nothing other than wisdom to use a wading stick – as a probe, as a support, or to have to hand in an emergency. The hazards of wading come from pure negligence, engendered by lack of thought, overconfidence, or even the effects of alcohol. 'Bad luck' is usually avoidable. It is good sense to learn to wade in stages: on that account hip-boots offer an advantage to a beginner, because then learning will take place in depths not much higher than the knees. He will get an idea of the pressure that fast water can put on him even in shallow water, and how in such circumstances sand and gravel will shift under his feet. He will learn that each foot must be planted securely before the next step is attempted, and that wading upstream is harder work and encounters more water resistance than either crossing a river or edging downstream. In shallow water, a stumble may be saved from becoming a fall by going down on your knees. However, a very sharp, rocky bottom could cause an injury, and it may be better to fall and get wet.

The most common anxieties about wading are those of getting wet and cold, and the embarrassment of being seen to fall in. How dangerous a fall

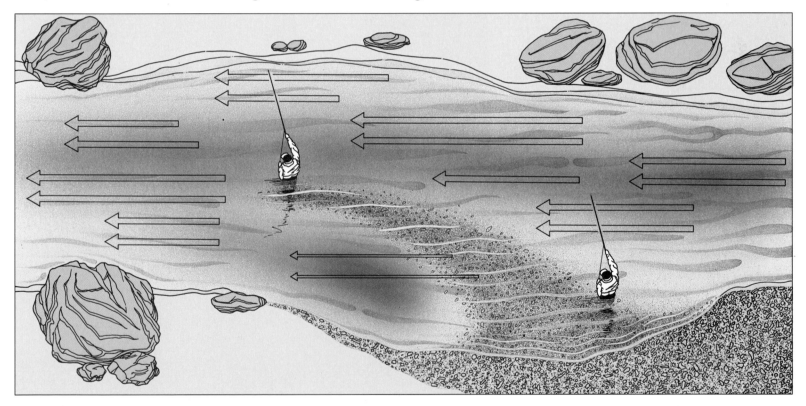

might be when wearing waders should be kept in perspective. Go to a swimming pool when the water is warm and learn to swim and move around confidently in both 'hippers' and in chest-high waders. Learn how 'heavy' they are by immersing them (not wearing them) and appreciating that it is their weight *on dry land* full of water which gives them their heaviness, not in the water, where they are just negatively buoyant. With a friend at the poolside, swim and maneuver in chest waders, so that you learn about any problems or restrictions and feel confident that you can deal with them in a crisis, in river or lake.

In nearly all falls while wading, there is no need to hurry at all. And on returning to the bank or to depths where you can recover your feet, there is time to reassure yourself that any danger is past, and to reflect that waders full of water will be heavy because of the water in them, so that a climb up a

A classic danger spot. The angler works on down a gravel spit until he reaches a point of no return, because the gravel moves under his feet when he tries to work his way back against the current. The angler on the left should not drown but he will get wet.

steep bank will be taxing. Is there an easier exit from the river or a chance of emptying some of the water? Crawl if you have to.

Monitoring the water level

The prudent wader makes a water-gauge for himself: in a noticeable place in the bank he pushes a stick in at the exact water level when he enters a pool. An occasional glance will tell him whether a dam is letting down water, or heavy rains upriver are raising the level. Guides on Atlantic salmon rivers will advise on the state of the river bed the angler is to wade. If no advice is available, take a wading stick and check for ledges, and check out gravel spits.

Before starting to fish an unfamiliar stretch of river, it is wise to wade it carefully to establish whether there are any dangerous holes.

Loss of balance in deep water may be recovered by slapping the length of the rod flat onto the water: the amount of resistance may be just enough to help you replace your feet. Likewise a very long length of line laid on the water can offer resistance when pulled against, providing a minor stabilizing influence. If no wading stick is carried, and you get into difficulties, the rod itself may prove a sort of support if you poke it butt down into the water.

When you are wading, your attention can be so concentrated on the wading and fishing that overhead power cables – which are lethal – are not noticed. (Similarly, near houses or waterside roads, there may be overhead cables, the dangers of which are easily ignored when you are assembling tackle or talking with other fishers.)

Using float tubes can easily lead to overconfidence. Learn to use them properly and practise with the foot paddles in controlled conditions.

The game fisher afloat

Being waterborne increases your fishing range and adds to the pleasure. However, a number of precautions must be taken. When using float tubes:

- Have a friend within calling distance
- Take a mini-anchor, preferably two, for stability
- Wear foot paddles or fins
- Dress as if you were going winter fishing: you will be much colder then you imagined
- Remember that tubes are for smaller waters, in good weather, and are dangerous in currents
- Tubes are unacceptably dangerous in strong currents or in bad weather
- The tube must have a safety release
- Be sure you are visible where other water activities take place, such as sailing, waterskiing or power-boating
- Use a flotation vest or collar
- Do not stay in so long that you become cramped by the cold. Come out and walk around at intervals.

When using a boat:
- Put the drainage bungs in
- Have *oars* (or paddles) in addition to the motor
- Check oarlocks have ropes or security pins
- Take a bailer
- Take an anchor with a rope at least *seven* times as long as the depth of the water
- Have fresh motor fuel: it is stale after 90 days, vital components having evaporated
- *Provide US Coast Guard approved flotation devices for each passenger and wear them in all conditions* (Inflatable cushions can double up as flotation devices)
- Listen to weather forecasts
- Plastic bottles used for domestic detergent or bleach act as fenders, or with a length of line added can make marker buoys. Filled with sand, they will make light anchors. All these devices should form part of a boat's equipment
- Take a compass, and take bearings
- Sit: don't stand in boats

When you are going onto water, make sure that you, your companions and your equipment are properly insured.

Comfort

You will only be comfortable if you can adjust your body warmth to suit the conditions. Usually you will find that you are colder than you want to be, and being wet as well increases your discomfort. All wading and boating is colder than expected, and regulations, particularly in National Parks, often forbid the lighting of camp-fires for warmth or cooking. Therefore it is very important to dress appropriately in cold weather, since being cold not only spoils the pleasure of fishing but can also be dangerous to your health.

Thick wool socks and longjohns are best for cold wading, and silk is highly recommended as the layer next to the skin: it seems to control the effects of sweating, but without becoming cold and clammy. Thereafter, wool is preferable to some artificial and natural fibers because it is not cold when wet, unlike nylon or cotton. Heat escapes upward, and so fastening a top shirt button and wearing a scarf (muffler) helps contain it. It is even more important to always wear a hat with a brim or peak when fishing. This has a number of roles. It:

- Prevents heat loss through the head
- Keeps the head dry
- Offers some protection against a low cast
- Keeps the sun off the head, preventing heatstroke or sunburn
- Saves eyestrain if it has enough brim to shade the eyes, and helps you see into the water
- Provides camouflage against some backgrounds

Loss of body temperature is increased by strong winds – the wind-chill factor – and being cold makes you clumsy or leads to cramps, which, when you are wading, can result in a fall. Cold hands lose their sensitivity, which can make fishing difficult. A variety of warming devices are available: slow-burning fuels in canisters, sachets that release heat through a chemical reaction, reheatable gel sachets and so on, some of which are designed to fit boots or gloves. More simply, a potato baked in aluminum foil can hold heat for a surprisingly long time, and can be kept in a pocket. There is no need, as at least one well-known angler has done, to go ashore, light a fire, and take the heated stones back out in the boat!

As long as a fishing hat has a wide brim or peak to help keep the sun out of your eyes, it does not matter whether it is a stetson or a baseball cap.

An Alaskan brown bear fishing at falls on Alaska's McNeil River.

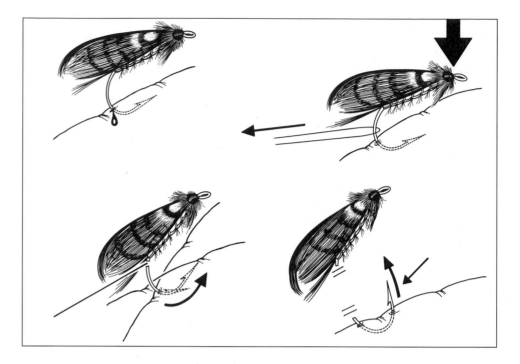

Hooked yourself? Sometimes the hook can be pulled out the way it went in. Press down on the eye and pull on the hook with a spare piece of nylon line. In difficult cases you may have to cut the hook at the bend and twist out the buried part in the direction of the point.

Avoiding being hooked

When casting a fly it is very important that it should be directed away from the angler – either clear above him or to his side. In a boat he has also to consider any companion, and his seated casting position, being lower, increases the risk of accidental hooking. An angler who does not protect his eyes is a fool in any conditions, but he and others are at even greater risk when he is fishing weighted flies of large size since correct timing of casting is more difficult and gravity exerts a strong pull.

Since a fisher concentrates on the water and the fish in front of him, he rarely turns to see what his backcast is doing. Any onlooker hooked by a backcast may have to accept most of the responsibility for being hooked. A non-angler who offers to carry a rod must be told where the fly or lure is anchored, and whether there are droppers, and if so, where. Since the fly keeper ring on most rods is exactly at the point of balance for carrying, some nasty wounds have been caused by accidental hooking.

Dangerous animals

Some areas contain dangerous wildlife. Such animals have right of way, and local advice in relation to bears, for example, will emphasize this. There are poisonous snakes, but bites are rare, since a confrontation seldom takes place. However, seek advice before entering a snake area. If you are bitten, *do not* take alcohol, because it helps in the distribution of venom through the bloodstream, and keep all movement as slow and unenergetic as possible, likewise to prevent its rapid spread.

CONSERVATION OF FISH STOCKS

The ideal water for game fishing is a wild-fish fishery which is self-supporting and capable of regular production of good-sized fish. It must be rich enough to support sufficient food, suitable in temperature, and offer sufficient available oxygen in uncontaminated water. Nevertheless lakes are destined to deteriorate over the years, and rivers change in time through erosion and deposit of silts. Management of any fishery, wild or contrived, is a struggle with all the elements.

Fishery management

Where once a river was highly productive and is now short of fish of sporting size, the fault does not lie with the fish. Stocking with further fish does not cure the problem – rather it compounds it by putting extra pressure on a habitat already under stress. In a water system with a wild strain, it is unforgivable to stock with fish of another genetic stem, or even another species, particularly if it is possible to take the natural breeding fish for hatchery work. To stock is almost a guarantee of elimination of a declining relict population, for the new introduction will challenge the wild fish for territory and try to hybridize with them, weakening and destroying a strain which has been developing and adapting itself to its own conditions for more than 15,000 years.

Some fisheries operate the catch-and-release system; others permit fish to be taken. If fish are to be taken, the lower size limit should be determined by the size at which the fish mature and spawn, so this limit should not be set below the spawning size. Successful spawning is, however, largely dependent on the water and weather; not every year is a good spawning year and fish population levels tend to fluctuate in cycles. Good management should reflect this in determining the takeable limit: the quantity of fish that can be considered a fair harvest, rather than just a determination of size.

There are fisheries which are entirely under human control, particularly in areas flooded by backwaters of dams, or where by human agency waters which were incapable of holding any game fish have now become suitable habitat – through, for example, a change of overall temperature. In such cases the management has to decide whether the fish to be stocked will establish themselves as a wild population or whether they will not be viable and so need regular replenishment. Some hybrids show satisfactory, fast growth and aggressive interest in the fly or lure. The splake, the lake trout × brook trout, may be introduced to waters colder than would suit other trouts and thrive, creating a new fishery. Rainbows may allow themselves to be caught soon after being stocked in sufficient numbers to constitute good sport and yet, by failing to overwinter, may not cause additional competition on the spawning beds.

It is not just humans who prey on fish. They form part of the food of otters, merganser sawbills and gulls, and the management of a river calls for an understanding of this demand.

Otter   Merganser sawbill   Gull

RIGHT *The ideal game-fishing river. The water is not polluted by industrial or farming chemicals or other waste matter. There is well-oxygenated water at the heads of the pools and there are depths where fish can find sanctuary from predators and avoid high water temperatures. Insect life is abundant in the stony, silted and vegetative habitats. Bankside vegetation shelters the water from the weather, offers temporary resting places for newly emerged aquatic insects, provides a habitat for terrestrial insects and protects the bank from erosion.*

Dead fish are a clear indication of pollution, but what is not seen is the massive toll on insect life.

Water abstraction and pollution

Whether a water is to be stocked or not, some form of human intervention is nearly always necessary: to counter the effects of our general use of the natural resource of land and water. Water quality – the quantity and the purity – is the key to the river's or lake's success. Abstraction, reducing the water flow, is as much to be resisted as the installation of barrages. A reduced flow is proportionately more susceptible to pollution and oxygen deprivation. A huge dam alters the quality and temperature of the water in the holding area – increasing depth particularly – and released water from the lower levels is usually of quite a different temperature and oxygen content from the water to which it is added.

Just as a small shift in chemical content can take a river from a poor to a rich category, so can a small amount of a toxic chemical, pesticide or industrial waste product cause serious pollution. Just a few parts in every million is all that is needed, and chemicals in combination are even more lethal. As soon as any part of the biomass, the food pyramid, is threatened, the effect is felt at the top of the pyramid. The game fish occupying that niche have to counter the reduction in food and the chemical effects on their own physiology. They cannot win.

Another form of pollution is not the direct input of poisons, but the input of substances which demand massive oxygen utilization to break down their constituents. This process disturbs the water balance. Enrichment by nitrates and phosphates does not enhance the whole of the food chain – just some elements; indeed water loses its clarity, particles settle and form ooze and silt beds, temperatures change. All these effects change the natural environment of game fish: insects demanding clear, well-oxygenated, fast-flowing water perish, and in their wake perish the game fish, their place sometimes taken by lesser fish forms with a lower oxygen demand and a mainly vegetarian diet.

Even if a river is not under threat from either direct or indirect pollution, improvements are often desirable. By speeding the flow, more oxygen is made available: by slowing the flow, greater depth may be created. By adding aquatic vegetation, again more oxygen may be provided, together with habitat for gamefish food forms, and sanctuary and cover for the fish themselves. Planting bankside vegetation forms a microclimate along the river which may keep the water temperature suitable to the type of fish. A further benefit is that insect life becomes richer.

A policy of restraint

The message is clear: do not cut down stream or lakeside vegetation, do not clear-fell, do not farm right up to the water's edge, encouraging erosion and silt run-off. Overgrazing can prove as disastrous as ill-conceived forestry operations.

A straight run of river with an even depth will not prove as good a fishery as one with curves and undercuts, riffles and depths. The introduction of a curve will in due course turn the straight into a series of bends as the current rebounds from side to side along the channel, and the outside of each curve will have an accelerated current and extra depth. However, fish need some protection from the force of the current, and so must have holding lies in water of suitable depth to allow them their separate territories. Good, honest rock lasts longer than timber, though timber in the form of deadfalls and stumps makes valuable cover even if it decays and is more vulnerable to floods.

Deflections of the stream can make the current scour the river bed or the

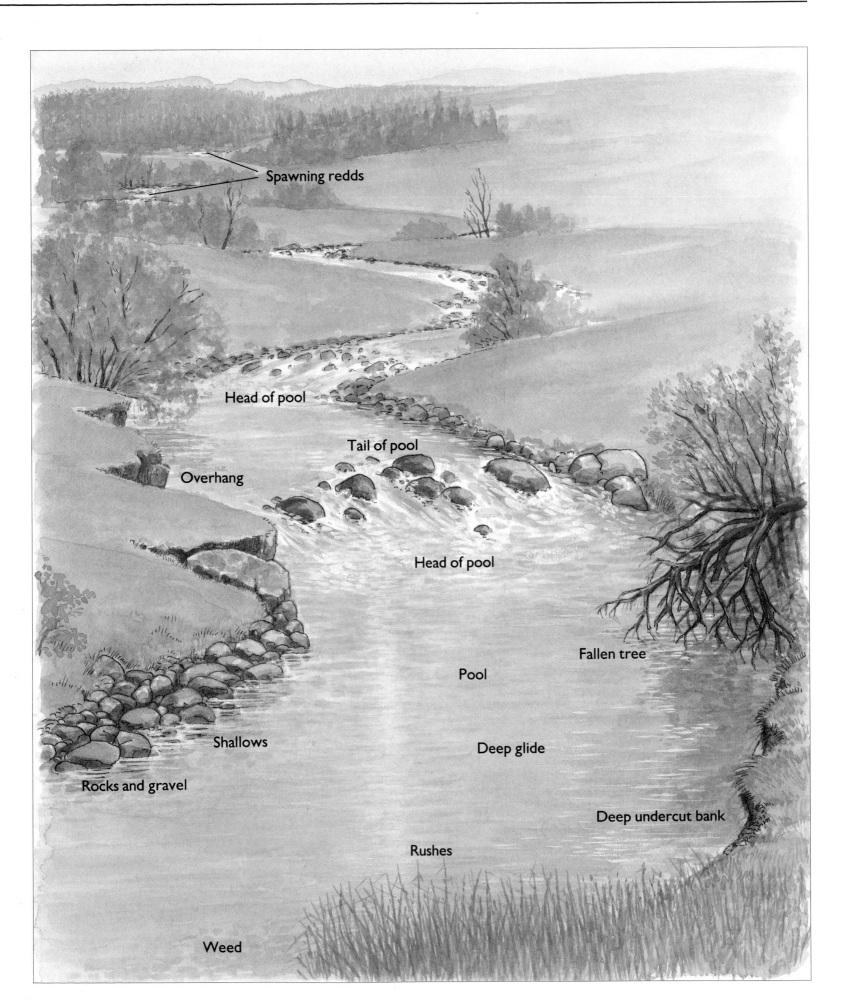

Spawning redds

Head of pool

Tail of pool

Overhang

Head of pool

Fallen tree

Pool

Shallows

Deep glide

Rocks and gravel

Deep undercut bank

Rushes

Weed

Even quite small waters can hide big fish, particularly in underhangs under the banks and in deep pockets.

opposite bank: sometimes the bank may be held together with the roots of vegetation, or trees planted in the bankside, and in some cases infilling with rock is advisable. Each stream needs a different approach, and what must not be lost is the diversity necessary for all stages of gamefish growth: good spawning grounds, good feeding and good access for the visit to the sea and no impassable barriers on the return journey for the migratory fish.

Some silt may be the key to the start of an increase in the food chain. However, too much silt may lead to flooding, which can lose stocks of fish and scour away insect life; the fish being lost by stranding when the waters subside, and the insects lost by the sweeping away of their home sand and gravel. River management may also involve some clearances.

Ecologists and thinking fishers constantly seek to improve, maintain and manage the habitat of game fish. Simply planting and stocking fish are not a viable long-term policy for the improvement of wild fisheries.

Fishery biologists and managers no longer believe that stocking is the cure for an ailing fishery. Nevertheless, introduced fish can produce good catches in regularly fished stretches of river and in stillwaters.

Caring for the environment

It is difficult not to appear patronizing or sanctimonious about the angler's obligations to the countryside. He is under a practical and moral duty to leave it as little affected by his presence as possible. This duty starts with such simple things as: sensible parking; not leaving gates open which should be closed; not disturbing agricultural stock; not running dogs at large; but it also means guarding against more complex actions like thoughtless wading, which needlessly erodes river banks or destroys aquatic microlife systems.

If there is one thing which the modern 'civilized' world can make nowadays which has the quality of durability, it is litter. *It is the duty of the angler to take away what he brought*. It is as simple as that. But if he is forward-thinking enough to remove litter left by others, so much the better.

The two substances most pernicious to wildlife are discarded lead weights of any size, and discarded monofilament, either as tippets or as spinning

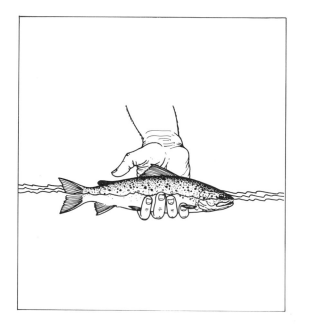

When releasing a fish, support it gently under the belly, giving it time to recuperate before removing your hand.

line. Its coils make fatal entanglements for both animals and birds, causing acute pain and distress. On the principle outlined above, whoever brings it should put in his pocket and dispose of it safely at home.

Fish handling and unhooking

Their scales and skin give fish protection against damage and disease when they are in the water. We must ensure when handling fish that we cause as little trauma as possible, preferably by not taking them from the water if they are to be released. Restraint with a net of adequate size is agreed to be the least damaging way of holding a fish. Using a net allows you to twist the hook free, particularly a barbless hook, without handling the fish at all. If the fish is to be held, it is usually supported as loosely as possible under the belly at the point of balance. The other hand then takes out the hook. Meanwhile the rod is tucked under the armpit.

Fish which are hooked deep down in the gullet (but show no bleeding) are difficult to unhook. In such cases it may be possible with care to reach through the gill-flaps to dislodge the hook, or it may be better to leave the fly in the fish, snipping through the leader. A fish hard-hooked and bleeding is unlikely to survive: it is better to put an end to it and reclaim the hook.

If you are fishing with natural baits and wish to return fish, the interval between the fish's taking the bait and your tightening on it should only be long enough to permit a hookhold, not long enough to allow the fish to swallow the bait. If this happens, snip the leader. The acids in the fish's digestive system will quickly dissolve the hook.

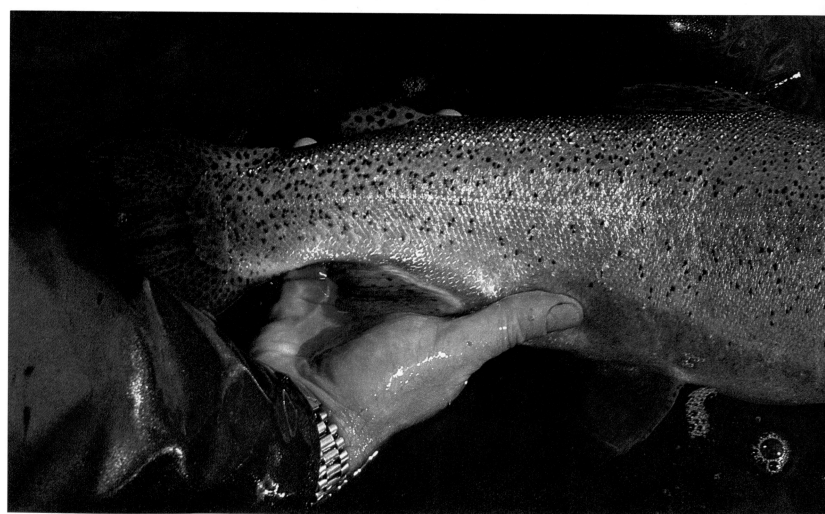

Barbless hooks are widely available or the barb on an ordinary hook may be pinched down with a pair of flat-nosed pliers. Comparison of records seems to indicate that barbless hooks are just as effective as barbed hooks, because they penetrate more easily, and a barbed hook sometimes does not penetrate in over the barb. Certainly the flesh in a fish's mouth suffers less obvious tearing and damage from barbless patterns.

Returning the fish

On being released, some fish are so full of energy that the playing and netting of them seems not to have affected them at all. Others need nursing back to vigor: a gentle grasp holding them pointed into well-oxygenated water normally proves a suitable restorative, and they attempt to escape as soon as they regain some strength. Restoring them sufficiently so that they swim away healthily may take several minutes, and a fish unable to remain stable in a swimming position must be nursed until it is in full control. A fish left on the river bed on its side will not live.

There are several ways to justify not killing fish, but we cannot overlook the fact that a game fish in peak condition is an excellent and nutritious foodstuff. It is not necessarily a crime to eat it. But to catch, kill and waste fish is dishonorable. It is quite as dishonorable to practise catch-and-release yet not take the slightest care in handling the fish while removing the hook, subjecting it to such damage that it cannot recover.

Lee Wulff propounded an admirable concept: a trout is too valuable to be caught only once. All game fish are far too valuable to be wasted.

Possibly the greatest thrill in fishing is seeing a fairly outwitted and caught fish swim away unharmed.

INDEX

Page numbers in italic indicate illustrations

streamer, 47, 149, *149*, 151, 176, 184
striking, 152–3, *152*
subimago, 13
submersant, *102*, 103
sunglasses, 103
swim bladder, 21

T

tackle, 61–109
  care of, 226–31
tailer, 109, *109*
tailing, 107–9
terrestrials, 18, *18*
through action, 81, *81*
tiger trout, 54
tip action, 81, *81*
tippet, 92, 93, 94, 95
treble hook, 151, *151*
triangle taper line, 65
Tricorythodes, 14
trolling, 50, 222–3
trout, 6, 9, 11, 14, 29
  brook, 46, 47, 50, 54, *54*
  brown, *25*, 28, 44–7, *45*, 47
  rainbow, 46, 48, *48*, 50, 55
  sea, 42–3, 156
two-handed casting, 128–9, *128–9*
tube fly, 150, 151, 167, *167*

U

ultra-light fishing, 49
unhooking, 250–51
uniknot (or Duncan or grinner) 97, 99

V

Vosso River, 187, 191

W

waders, 101, 104, 234
  care of, 230–31
wading, 155, *155*, *230–31*, 231, 234–7, *234*, *235*, *236–7*
water,
  abstraction of, 244
  oxygenation of, 10–11, 16, 18, 27, 244, 251
  pollution of, 244
  quality, 9–11, 18, 20
  refraction in, 22–3
  temperature, 26, 54, 140, 167–8, 178, 244
  types of, 18
weight-forward (WF) line, 64, 65, 65,

weighting patterns, 204, *204*
wet-fly fishing, 176–86, *176–81*, *184–6*
  patterns for, 147, *147*, 151, 152–3
whitefish, 55, 58, *58*
Wulff, Joan, 71
Wulff, Lee, 18, 71, 76, 151, 251

X

Xink, *102*, 102

Z

Zinger, *102*, 102

BIBLIOGRAPHY

The Art of Trolling	K. Schultz, Viking Penguin, 1987
The Atlantic Salmon	Lee Wulff, Lyons and Burford, 1988
American Nymph Fly Tying Manual	Randall Kaufmann, F. Amato Publications, 1975
Caddisflies	Gary LaFontaine, Lyons and Burford, 1981
Complete Book of Western Hatches	D. Hughes and R. Hafele, F. Amato Publications, 1981
Fishing the Thunder Creek	K. Fulsher, Freshet Pr., 1973
Fly Fishing for Pacific Salmon	Ferguson, Johnson & Trotter, F. Amato Publications, 1985
Fly Tying Methods	Darrel Martin, Lyons and Burford, 1987
Guide to Aquatic Trout Foods	Dave Whitlock, Lyons and Burford, 1982
Hairwing Atlantic Salmon Flies	K. Fulsher & C. Krom, Saco River Pub., 2nd edn., 1982
Hatches	Al Caucci & Bob Nastasi, Lyons and Burford, 1986, reprinted 1990
Lee Wulff on Flies	Lee Wulff, Stackpole, 1985
Matching the Hatch	E. G. Schwiebert, Jr., Stoeger Publishing Co. no date available
A Modern Dry-Fly Code	V. Marinaro, Lyons and Burford, 1988
Native Trout of North America	R. H. Smith, F. Amato Publications, 1984
Naturals	Gary A. Borger, Stackpole, 1980
Nymphs	E. Schwiebert, Winchester Press, 1983
Reading Trout Streams	Tom Rosenbauer, Lyons and Burford, 1988
Salmon Flies	Poul Jorgensen, Stackpole, 1978
Sea-Run Cutthroat Trout	L. Johnson, F. Amato Publications, 1979
Selective Trout	D. Swisher and C. Richards, Lyons and Burford, 1983
Spinner Fishing for Steelhead, Salmon & Trout	J. Davis, F. Amato Publications, 1985
Steelhead	M. Marshall, Winchester Press, 1973
Steelhead Fly Fishing and Flies	Trey Combs, F. Amato Publications, 1976
Steelhead Fly Tying Manual	T. Light & N. Humphrey, F. Amato Publications, 1979
Streamers and Bucktails	J. D. Bates, Jr., Knopf, 1980
Trout	R. Bergman & E. C. Jones, Knopf, 1976
Trout	E. Schwiebert, NAL-Dutton (2 vols), 1984
Trout on a Fly	Lee Wulff, Lyons and Burford, 1988
Ultra-lite Steelhead Fishing	Ralph F. Quinn, ICS Books, 1988

The above titles were in print at the beginning of 1991. Those recommended below may be available secondhand.

Atlantic Salmon & the Fly Fisherman	Gary Anderson
The Dry Fly and Fast Waters	G.M. LaBranche
Fishing with McClane	Al McClane
Nymphing	Gary A. Borger
Salmon & the Dry Fly	G.M. LaBranche
Swimming Flies	G. Odier
Through the Fish's Eye	M. Sosin & J. Clark
Trout Fishing	Joe Brooks